'FULL OF ALL KNOWLEDG'
GEORGE HERBERT'S *COUNTRY PARSON* AND
EARLY MODERN SOCIAL DISCOURSE

THE MENTAL AND CULTURAL WORLD OF TUDOR AND STUART ENGLAND

Editors

Paul Christianson
Camille Slights
D.R. Woolf

'FULL OF ALL KNOWLEDG'

George Herbert's *Country Parson* and Early Modern Social Discourse

Ronald W. Cooley

UNIVERSITY OF TORONTO PRESS
Toronto Buffalo London

© University of Toronto Press Incorporated 2004
Toronto Buffalo London
Printed in Canada

ISBN 0-8020-3723-2

∞

Printed on acid-free paper

PR
3508
. C66
2004

National Library of Canada Cataloguing in Publication

Cooley, Ronald Wayne
    'Full of all knowledg' : George Herbert's Country parson and early
modern social discourse / Ronald W. Cooley.

(The mental and cultural world of Tudor and Stuart England)
Includes bibliographical references and index.
ISBN 0-8020-3723-2

1. Pastoral theology – Anglican Communion – Early works to 1900.
2. Rural clergy – England – Early works to 1800.   I. Title.   II. Series.

PR3507.P7C66 2003   253   C2003-903714-2

University of Toronto Press acknowledges the financial assistance to its
publishing program of the Canada Council for the Arts and the Ontario
Arts Council.

This book has been published with the help of a grant from the Humanities
and Social Sciences Federation of Canada, using funds provided by the Social
Sciences and Humanities Research Council of Canada.

University of Toronto Press acknowledges the financial support for its
publishing activities of the Government of Canada through the Book
Publishing Industry Development Program (BPIDP).

Contents

Acknowledgments

I am grateful to the many colleagues and friends who have provided encouragement, research assistance, and advice on difficult questions and awkward preliminary drafts. I am especially grateful to my editor, Barb Porter of the University of Toronto Press, who diplomatically pointed out many errors and infelicities, and to Micky Wilkinson and Carrie-Ann Runstedler for their painstaking work indexing, proofreading, and checking quotations. The faults that remain are entirely my own. Thanks are also due to Cynthia Clark, Janet Drysdale, Sidney Gottlieb, Peter Hynes, Greg McKee, David Parkinson, Jeffrey Powers-Beck, Florence Sandler, Bill Slights, Camille Wells Slights, Andrew Taylor, Lisa Vargo, Chauncey Wood, and others too numerous to mention, who have helped me throughout the slow process of research and composition. I thank you all. Portions of the study were presented at successive annual meetings of the Pacific Northwest Renaissance Society; all who attended those sessions earned my gratitude with their patience, probing questions, and generous suggestions. Preliminary research for the book was supported by the Social Sciences and Humanities Research Council of Canada through the President's Fund at the University of Saskatchewan. Portions of this work have appeared, in different form, in *English Studies in Canada* and the *George Herbert Journal*, and are reprinted with the permission of the editors.

Finally, and especially, thanks to my wife, Paula, and our children, Alison, Stephen, and Hannah, for constant love and support.

'FULL OF ALL KNOWLEDG'

Introduction

A Pastor is the Deputy of Christ for the reducing of Man to the Obedience of God. This definition is evident, and containes the direct steps of Pastorall Duty and Auctority. For first, Man fell from God by disobedience. Secondly, Christ is the glorious instrument of God for the revoking of Man. Thirdly, Christ being not to continue on earth, but after hee had fulfilled the work of Reconciliation, to be received up into heaven, he constituted Deputies in his place, and these are Priests. And therefore St. *Paul* in the beginning of his Epistles, professeth this: and in the first to the *Colossians* plainly avoucheth, that he *fils up that which is behinde of the afflictions of Christ in his flesh, for his Bodie's sake, which is the Church.* Wherein is contained the complete definition of a Minister. Out of this Chartre of the Priesthood may be plainly gathered both the Dignity thereof, and the Duty: The Dignity, in that a Priest may do that which Christ did, and by his auctority, and as his Vicegerent. The Duty, in that a Priest is to do that which Christ did, and after his manner, both for Doctrine and Life.

> *A Priest to the Temple, or The Country Parson*
> *His Character and Rule of Holy Life,*
> Chapter I, 'Of a Pastor'[1]

This study is an attempt to situate a single text, George Herbert's 1632 pastoral manual, *A Priest to the Temple, or The Country Parson His Character and Rule of Holy Life*, in the network of discourses through which people in early seventeenth-century England understood their social world. While *The Country Parson* has received more serious scholarly attention in the last ten or fifteen years than ever before, most Herbert scholars have continued to find Herbert's 'Chartre of the Priesthood' less engaging than his playful and enigmatic sacred verse.[2] Nevertheless, in the wake of the 'new historicism' in literary studies, and the 'revisionist' and 'counter-revisionist' movements in historical studies of early modern England, Herbert's pastoral handbook is an apt focus for a sustained analysis blending literary criticism with the insights of social, cultural, and intellectual history.

Composed of thirty-seven brief chapters written in the subtle, plain style of a former Cambridge University Orator, *The Country Parson* is not a taxing book, by seventeenth-century standards. In its terse, aphoristic prose and tight syntactical parallelism, it resembles Bacon's *Essays*: 'His children he first makes Christians, and then Common-wealths-men; the one he owes to his heavenly Countrey, the other to his earthly, having no title to either, except he do good to both' (239). Nevertheless it occasionally indulges the metaphysical poet's impulse to 'torture one poor word ten thousand wayes.'[3] Its chapter titles, for instance, are often figurative, elliptical, or gently ironic: 'The Parson in mirth' begins with the playful assertion that 'The Countrey Parson is generally sad' (267); 'The Parson's Library' deals not with books, but with the elements of 'a holy Life' (as reading was treated earlier under 'The Parsons Accessory Knowledges'); and 'The Parson's Dexterity in applying of Remedies' considers the balm for spiritual hurts, while medical practice is discussed extensively under the innocuous heading of 'The Parson's Completenesse.' In short, *The Country Parson* is an exemplary instance of the proverbial 'art that hides art,' gently inviting and amply rewarding the close reading lavished more often on literary texts than on historical documents. Yet it also addresses, with a compelling directness, the questions of social order, daily life, religion, politics, and economy that are of pressing interest to social historians. In 'The Parson's Surveys' Herbert tackles 'the great and nationall sin of this Land ... Idlenesse,' outlining the social obligations of all ranks and degrees, and declaring, aphoristically, that 'None fouls his hands in his own businesse' (274, 275). On ecclesiastical matters, he is exquisitely sensitive to the pressures of Laudian and Caroline policy, and to the possibility of censorship, employing terms like 'Priest' and 'Priesthood' liberally in his opening and closing chapters and substituting 'Parson' and 'Pastor' throughout. Finally, despite its tendency to idealize, *The Country Parson* offers the fullest, general contemporary account of the social role of the early modern English clergy.[4]

The clergy had constituted one of the traditional 'estates' or orders of medieval society, and though the scheme of estates had lost much of its currency and explanatory force in early modern England, the clergy were the one group that fit most clearly into the old model.[5] But this too was changing. Herbert's handbook for rural clergymen is both a record of, and a contribution to, the professionalization of the English clergy, its transformation from estate to occupation, as early modern England gradually and haltingly embraced what Max Weber terms 'legal-rational' structures of authority. Hence, in his opening account, 'Of a Pastor,' Herbert renders Paul's assertion that the apostolic pastor '*fils up that which is behinde of the afflictions of Christ* [Col. 1:24]' in distinctly legalistic and bureaucratic terms: as a process by which Christ 'constituted Deputies in his place.' This process of clerical professionalization coincides with the dissolution of a residual system of estates, and ironically, with the marginalization of the clergy, as the other 'learned professions' (law and medicine) begin to assume their modern roles in the formation of social policy. *The Country Parson* records, responds to, and promotes the emergence of the modern in early modern England, as modernity is expressed in worship, social regulation, agricultural technology and land use, and domestic relations. Each of these subjects has become increasingly important in the study of early modern English history, literature, and culture in recent years, but since each constitutes a distinct and demanding field of specialist investigation, the connections between them have sometimes been neglected.

By exploring how the competing claims of tradition and innovation in these realms ebb and flow in a single text, I hope to suggest something of the density, the complexity, and the contradictory character of early modern social discourse. The thrust of my thesis is strikingly encapsulated in historian Kevin Sharpe's brief account of the emergence of 'the Whig view of history,' in his recent book, *Remapping Early Modern England.* Sharpe observes that

> The Whigs who forcibly removed James II to bring in William of Orange [in 1688] needed to make that violent fracture into a natural succession of government. They needed to marginalize the Jacobites and appropriate from them the languages of scripture, law and history through which all authority in seventeenth-century England was validated.[6]

This ideological, cultural, and rhetorical strategy is hardly unique to the Whigs of the late seventeenth century; it is characteristic of both the Reformation and the Renaissance humanist enterprise. In Herbert's words from 'The Church Porch,' a scholar's task is to 'copie fair, what time hath blurr'd; / Redeem truth from his jawes' (ll. 86–7). There is, at once, a reverence for ancient 'truth' and an urgent impulse to 'redeem' it from the ravages of time by making a fair copy, to make the old new without sacrificing the dignity accorded to age. The same ambivalent impulse is to be found in the advice and conduct literature so popular in Herbert's England. As Jeffrey Powers-Beck writes of the early modern family 'advices' which underpin Herbert's didactic 'Church Porch' and his 'Outlandish Proverbs,' as well as *The Country Parson*, their 'traditional elements ... made them conservative in nature, but seldom reactionary, as they aggressively promoted Protestant and humanistic ideals of marriage, education, labour, domestic life.'[7] Common to this literature, and to much early modern legal, medical, and agricultural writing, is a strategy of defending innovation by appropriating and transforming the language of custom and tradition, a strategy that is the governing principle of Herbert's *Country Parson*.

The Debate over Herbert's Theology

In exploring the interplay of tradition and innovation in *The Country Parson* I take the emerging consensus about Herbert's Protestant theology as a starting point and move on from there. I should pause, therefore, to suggest that what Gene Edward Veith has aptly termed 'the religious wars in George Herbert criticism' are more or less over.[8] What has decided the matter is the inevitable, if somewhat belated, process of literary history catching up with ecclesiastical history. One of the major barriers to general acceptance of the 'Protestant Poetics' argument introduced by William Halewood in *The Poetry of Grace*, and subsequently refined and extended by Ilona Bell, Barbara K. Lewalski, and Richard Strier, among others, has been the lingering association of pre–Civil War English Protestantism, at least in the minds of many literary critics, with Puritanism, Presbyterianism, separatism, iconoclasm, the closing of the theatres, nonconformity, regicide, the Protectorate, and the radical sects of the interregnum period.[9] To emphasize Herbert's Protestant theology was, for many years, to risk placing a patron saint of the Church of England in a line of supposed book-haters and cranks that runs from Philip Stubbes and Stephen Gosson to the Ranters. As long as 'Protestant' was understood a synonym for 'radical' (and that understanding could suggest either approval or scorn) there was strong motivation to place a devoted conformist like George Herbert in the conservative 'Anglican' camp as an enemy of Puritanism and all it stood for.[10] But as a number of Herbert scholars, most notably Daniel Doerksen, have been pointing out for some years now, the various caricatures of early Stuart Protestants, as cultural philistines or proto-revolutionaries, retain little currency among ecclesiastical historians.[11] Rather, the prevailing view of the Church of England in the early seventeenth century, articulated most forcefully by Anthony Milton, Kenneth Fincham, Nicholas Tyacke, and Patrick Collinson, is of a Jacobean Church working to consolidate, rather than attenuate, the achievements of the English Reformation, of a Church of England predominantly Calvinist in its official theology, though unashamedly episcopal in its organization.[12] In the most emphatic version of this view the disruption instigated by an ideologically committed minority is not associated with Calvinism, but with the Laudian 'reforms' of the 1630s. But even in more cautious accounts, 'Calvinist' and 'conformist,' far from being mutually exclusive, turn out to be at least potentially complementary categories, and Herbert's emphatically Protestant soteriology, evident in poems like 'The Holdfast' and 'The Water-course,' slips rather easily into place alongside his avowed dedication to the established church.[13]

While the essential points of this case have been presented in Doerksen's articles over the last decade or so, and in his book *Conforming to the Word*, the study that best exemplifies the emerging consensus about Herbert's Protestantism is Christopher Hodgkins's *Authority, Church and Society in George Herbert*. Hodgkins presents *The Temple* as a defence of the Elizabethan *via media*, which he defines in terms of 'constitutionally limited monarchy and episcopacy ... a "godly" parish ministry like that of the moderate Puritans ... passing important spiritual responsibility on to laymen; and ... simple, scriptural intelligibility in liturgy, in church architecture, and in poetry.' In a style both forceful and graceful, he places Herbert firmly in the Calvinist episcopal mainstream, arguing that Herbert's vision is nostalgic, not so much in its theology as in its politics. 'As the old Elizabethan social edifice creaked and crumbled around him in the larger world [writes Hodgkins], he would seek to rebuild it to exact scale in a rural hamlet.'[14] In this account, the threat to Herbert's Church of England comes not from Calvinist enthusiasm but from modernity and Stuart royal absolutism, and Herbert becomes a sort of proto-anti-Laudian. Hodgkins's view has much to recommend it, though I take issue with his adoption of the language of nostalgic retreat applied to Herbert by so many commentators, and with the characterization of Herbert's religious, social, and political vision as distinctly Elizabethan. Just ten years old when Queen Elizabeth died, George Herbert must be seen as a Jacobean writer and churchman. The Church of England in which he embraced a religious vocation was the one James and his bishops were striving to build, not the one Elizabeth had left behind. The particular character of this church, and the contribution Herbert strove to make by writing a handbook for its clergy, will be the subject of my second chapter. But I should say at the outset that the Jacobean Church of England, however much it disappointed 'the hotter sort' of Protestants, was more evangelical and socially activist than its Elizabethan predecessor. James and his bishops sought not merely to suppress Puritanism, as Elizabeth had done, but also to capture and diffuse its energy by accommodating some of its key features into the established practice of the Church of England. These aspirations help to give *The Country Parson* its distinct note of zeal and idealism.

Historicism and Historiography

Methodologically, this study is an attempt to respond to a challenge and an invitation offered by historian David Cressy in an article that appeared in *English Literary Renaissance* in 1991. Cressy's 'Foucault, Stone, Shakespeare and Social History' is an indictment of literary new historicism for its selective engagement with historical scholarship, manifested in what Cressy sees as an uncritical dependance on the theoretical paradigms of Michel Foucault, and on the idiosyncratic and controversial historical scholarship of Lawrence Stone. The substance of Cressy's critique of literary-historical Foucaultianism is that Foucault is 'ahistorical,' drawing sweeping conclusions from slender evidence, and that even if Foucault's French Enlightenment illustrations do substantiate his theories, 'to argue from France to England, and from the 1780s to the 1610s is an exercise in anachronism and dislocation.' This is in part because early modern England lacked the administrative machinery to implement the sort of panoptic system of social control Foucault describes in *Discipline and Punish*. As Cressy writes in a different article, 'from a practical point of view ... it was impossible to get the English population to behave in the same way, to believe in the same things, or to march in the same direction. There was no standing army, no organized police force, no professional bureaucracy.'[15] Yet if historians have concluded that early seventeenth-century England had not yet developed efficient instruments of social control, they have also shown that it was beginning to do so, and as I argue in chapter 3, *The Country Parson* seeks to construct the parish clergy as one such instrument.

Long before Foucault, Max Weber addressed methods of social control, in distinguishing between traditional and legal-rational systems of authority. A traditional social order, as Weber defined it, rests 'on an established belief in the sanctity of immemorial traditions and the legitimacy of the status of those exercising authority under them.' In a legal-rational order, authority depends 'on a belief in the "legality" of patterns of normative rules and the right of those elevated to authority under such rules to issue commands.'[16] The analytical distinction is, of course, slightly forced, particularly when applied to seventeenth-century England, where the legal authority of the crown and its officers rested on the fiction of an 'immemorial' common law.[17] As Herbert writes in *The Country Parson*, 'our Law is Practice' (277). Nevertheless, in each of the spheres on which this study touches, religion, legal and medical professionalization, agriculture, and domestic relations, there are clear traces of Weber's rationalization. Writers on all these subjects, in the seventeenth century, seek to consolidate, codify, and evaluate traditional knowledge and practice. And on balance, the characteristically English fusion of traditionalist and rationalist discourses functions, rhetorically, to disarm traditionalist critique by appropriating its terms.

Cressy's second charge is that the historicist literary critics of the 1980s tended to ignore the 'delightful ... full-flung debate about evidence and its interpretation' that had become so central to the work of historians in this area. Related to this is the charge that literary historicists often engaged in 'uncritical borrowing' from a narrow sampling of the work of social historians, most notably from Lawrence Stone's *The Family, Sex and Marriage in England, 1500–1800*, a book Cressy characterizes as incautious and unreliable. For Cressy, as for many historians, Stone's body of work represents 'a stage in historical analysis which ... peaked in the early 1970s, but which has been in retreat' since then.[18] There is, as Cressy insists, simply too little consensus among historians of early modern England to allow us merely to repeat familiar truisms about the 'pre-revolutionary' character of the period, about the 'rise of the gentry' and the 'winning of initiative' by Parliament. These phrases exemplify an account of early modern English history that Cressy describes as being 'in retreat,' an account informed theoretically by Marx and Weber, and articulated, with variations, by both Marxists and liberal historians (or 'Whigs' if we prefer the derogatory term) like R.H. Tawney, C.B. McPherson, and Christopher Hill, as well as Lawrence

Stone. This account, which sees English society in terms of class, notably an emerging middle class, and English politics in terms of mounting tensions between an absolutist Stuart monarchy and a parliamentary opposition, seeks to identify long-term and large-scale conflicts and social transformations.

Increasingly this 'Whiggish' account has been undermined by revisionist studies stressing ideological consensus and hierarchical bonds of loyalty, studies that attribute conflict to divergent local interests and factional struggles.[19] In the revisionist view, the England of the 1630s was 'a stable polity,' and 'it took some spectacular miscalculation on ... [King Charles's] part to create the circumstances in which resistance became feasible.'[20] Critics of revisionism have responded by acknowledging that 'the moves to [civil] war were complex, hesitant and contradictory,' while continuing to explore 'long-term ideological and social tensions,' often employing the very methods championed by revisionists.[21] Cressy is surely right to insist that literary scholars practice 'wider reading and sharper skepticism,' and in the decade since his article appeared many have taken up the challenge, though often they have done so by reading deeply in the historical literature on narrowly defined subjects: sex and marriage, medicine and physiology, religion and worship, land and property.[22] Such analytical movements demand corresponding attempts at synthesis, and it is such a synthesis that I seek to offer here, within the limited scope of a study dedicated to a single author. In the interests of this synthesis I have often elected, quite deliberately, to 'stand on the shoulders of giants,' relying heavily on the insights of specialist historians rather than attempting to revisit the archive and recast their analyses of the primary evidence.

Theory

This is not in any sense a theoretical study. Indeed, just as many historians will be annoyed by my unwillingness to jettison Foucault, many theoretically inclined literary critics will probably be distressed by my adoption of theoretically implicated terms that might seem incompatible. The most obvious tension (some will say contradiction) is between, on the one hand, a conception of power that owes more than a little to Foucault's *Discipline and Punish* and *The History of Sexuality*, and on the other, notions of ideology borrowed from the materialist tradition of history and historical sociology. As Foucault himself has argued, the key Marxist concept of ideology as false consciousness, and the related notions of originating subjectivity and economic determination, are incompatible with Foucault's account of power as immanent in all social relations, as productive rather than repressive, as somehow calculating and yet nonsubjective.[23] To arbitrate or mediate between these positions would demand a theoretical discussion entirely outside the scope of a book on George Herbert (not to mention beyond the capacity of its author). To simply strive for consistency, operating within the theoretical vocabulary of either a Marxist or a Foucaultian tradition, might seem more responsible, but given the richness and complexity of those traditions the problem of appearing to stand on both sides of an important debate would continually reappear. For example, the cultural materialism of Raymond Williams, so appealing to a literary critic because of the prominent role it assigns to literary and cultural production, is dismissed as a denial of the fundamental tenets of materialism by Marxist historian R.S. Neale.[24] And Marxist historians are divided among themselves over such central questions as the function of the absolutist state in the transition to capitalism, and the relative importance of forces of production and relations of production in determining economic and historical change.[25] In the end, the process of choosing sides threatens to displace the game itself, unless one is willing to live with a measure of eclecticism that might be hard to defend systematically.

The defence I do offer is implicit, rather than explicit, in the body of my discussion of Herbert's *Country Parson* and that book's situation in early modern social discourse. Herbert's book is characterized by a calculated deployment of contradictions that I am inclined to describe in Foucaultian terms as discursively constructed and nonsubjective. While I would insist, with the materialists, that those contradictions enable the political, social, and material advantage of some, to the disadvantage of others, it is not clear that they originate in the collective consciousness of a class.[26] In exploring these contradictions I draw also on Marc Angenot's definition of social discourse as a set of expressions about the world that 'is never ... made out of a set of statically dominant ideas, representations, systems of belief, 'ideologies.' Rather, it is made out of regulated antagonisms between conflicting images, concepts, cognitive discrepancies and incompatibilities that are relatively stabilized without ever reaching a state of equilibrium.'[27] As Ann Hughes has recently argued, 'a genuinely "post revisionist" position would reject a simple choice between, for example, conflict and consensus, but explore the contradictory potentials within English political culture.'[28] This is my aim. Beginning with a single text, I seek to describe the 'contradictory potentials' and 'regulated antagonisms' of the social practices, political forces, and literary and quasi-literary forms in which Herbert's text is embedded, and which are embedded in it.

The Country Parson and Its Genres

The most basic question to ask, in an investigation such as the one laid out above, is the question of genre. What kind of text are we dealing with? As Alastair Fowler suggests, literary genres function 'not merely as systems of coding rules ... [but also] quasi-pragmatically, as a literary surrogate for real-life situations of utterance. Acting as substitutes for context in this way, the genres supply shared guides to relevance.'[29] To say what *kind* of book *The Country Parson* is would be to assign it a social as well as a literary context, to say something about its audience and about that audience's understanding of its function. This is at once an easy and a difficult task: easy because *The Country Parson* is, superficially, an instance of a venerable literary type, the pastoral manual, and difficult because on closer examination it appears an elaborate hybrid of generic models, fused and adapted into a rather haphazard and open-ended form.[30]

The most important generic precedent is surely Pope Gregory I's sixth-century *Regula Pastoralis* (commonly translated *Pastoral Care*), of which more than a dozen Latin printed editions had appeared by Herbert's time (though only one printed in England, in 1629). Alfred the Great's ninth-century preface and West Saxon translation of *Pastoral Care* was even more widely known, in large part because of the particular interest Archbishop Matthew Parker and other sixteenth-century reformers and antiquarians had taken in it. Parker translated and published the preface, as well as Asser's *Life* of Alfred, and echoed the former in his own preface to the 1568 Bishop's Bible, 'to provide a venerable precedent for the ... biblical translation project.'[31] Alfred's lament for the state of the English clergy anticipated the perpetual refrain of sixteenth- and seventeenth-century English reformers, helping to render their cause ancient and respectable. Structurally, Herbert's book is remarkably similar to Gregory's. Both contain a series of brief chapters, some only a paragraph in length, some a few pages, with each chapter elaborating on a topic, proposition, or maxim. Many of Gregory's topics would fit quite easily into *The Country Parson*: Gregory's 'How to admonish subjects and superiors' and 'How to admonish the slothful and the hasty' are not so far, in tone and content, from Herbert's 'The Parson in Reference' and 'The Parson's Consideration of Providence.' Other chapters of Gregory's express sentiments entirely consistent with Herbert's, even as they mark a crucial difference between *Pastoral Care* and *The Country Parson*: 'Men who flee from the burden of ruling out of humility, are then truly humble, when they do not resist the divine decrees'; 'The ruler should realize well that vices often masquerade as virtues.'[32] Gregory composed his treatise on the occasion of his election to the papacy in 590, and its implied reader is a prince of the church, an ecclesiastical ruler like a bishop or archbishop. In its chapters and chapter headings Gregory shifts between the terms 'ruler' and 'pastor' with an ease that renders those terms virtually synonymous. Herbert's concern to explore 'the Dignity ... and the Duty' of the priesthood arises out of circumstances almost diametrically opposite: his improbable decision, as a well-educated son of an important family, to accept ordination as a humble parish priest, with no immediate prospect of advancement. His audience, as I will argue in the next chapter, included many like himself, university men entering the priesthood ill prepared to assume pastoral duties in a rural parish. To be sure, the loftiness of Gregory's ecclesiastical state and the humility of Herbert's lead both writers to explore the inversions of decorum implicit in the theology of Christ's incarnation and passion, and central to Christian literature from Augustine onwards.[33] Nevertheless the difference in the audiences of the two books, as well as in their authors' situations, suggests that we must look beyond Gregory for generic models of *The Country Parson*.

When we look for English Protestant pastoral literature composed before *The Country Parson*, however, we find very little.[34] Mostly it consists of the published texts of pastoral sermons, like Donne's first two sermons as Vicar of St Dunstan's, delivered in April 1624.[35] Many such sermons, like Samuel Hieron's *The spirituall fishing* and Samuel Crooke's *The ministeriall husbandry and building*, were delivered in the universities or at clerical assemblies. In terms of subject matter, these are predominantly sermons on homiletics, though a few, like Crooke's *The ministeriall husbandry and building*, touch on the social role of the clergy beyond the pulpit. Of more ambitious and wide-ranging treatments of the pastoral function, only a couple of credible examples predate *The Country Parson*. One is George Gifford's *Country Divinity*, a plea for godly ministry, composed 'after the order of a dialogue.' Though Gifford's book concentrates on the social role of the clergy it is primarily a controversial work, denouncing clerical misconduct and urging a broad social reformation.

Another, slightly closer to *The Country Parson* in its prescriptive mode, is Richard Bernard's *Faithful Shepherd*. Revised and reissued in 1609 after its initial appearance in 1607, and 'Wholy ... transposed and made anew, and very much inlarged' for a third edition in 1621, Bernard's book is the leading vernacular resource for the seventeenth-century English clergyman. Yet it serves more to illustrate the need for a book like *The Country Parson* than as a generic model. *The Faithful Shepherd* is typical of reformed polemics and homiletics in its laborious argumentation and exhaustive citation of scriptural evidence. Bernard's introductory chapter addresses '*encouragements to the Ministrie, from the antiquity, necessity and excellencie thereof, and from the dignitie and authority of Ministers in that Calling,*' essentially the same subject Herbert treats in his opening chapter, quoted in full in the epigraph above. But whereas Herbert's pithy introduction consists of barely two hundred words and relies on a single quotation from scripture, Bernard's runs to nearly two thousand words, and includes twenty-seven citations, some referring to multiple verses. Moreover its hortatory tone clearly marks Bernard's book as an instance of pulpit rhetoric adapted to the printed page. Particularly bracing is his 'Exhortation to the Gentry' on the subject of clerical calling:

> A Minister and Pastor therefore in his place (though out of the pulpit) is no contemptible person, but worthy of honour. Why then should any of you disdaine (o ye sons of the gentry) to take this calling upon you, though you cannot climbe up in your thoughts to Episcopall jurisdiction? Heare mee, I pray you, may it possibly seeme unto you a base place, to be the Heralds of the living God? to be set apart to be God's voice to the people, and againe, the people's unto God? To be the stewards of the King of Heaven's household? To be the Guardian and Watch-men over men's soules? To have power to binde and loose, to open and shut Heaven, and to be the sweet savour of life to all that are saved, and to them that perish? S. Paul saith ... who is sufficient for these things? And can you suppose your selves to bee too good? Is the corrupt birth, which you so boast of, and many falsely too, stained by this dignity, and not by a loose and licentious liberty, which too many of you follow after?[36]

Apparently, by 1630, George Herbert had resolved that his own gentle birth would not be 'stained by this dignity,' but he also seems to have resolved that a pastoral very different from Bernard's, in both style and content, was required by his new colleagues.

Homiletics dominate the content of Bernard's *Faithful Shepherd*, just as they set the rhetorical tone. The work consists of four books, the first two dealing largely with questions of vocation and vocational preparation, and the last two dedicated to aspects of preaching and doctrine: 'Of the dividing of a text'; 'Of the interpretation of scripture'; 'Of collecting doctrines'; 'Of the use of doctrine.' In Bernard's second chapter, however, there is a glimmer of the approach Herbert would take throughout *The Country Parson*. There, Bernard remarks that a minister must

> weigh well in what state ... [his parishioners] stand, and of what sort of people they bee. For as they be, so must he deal with them. Husband men sow their seed after the nature of the ground; the Physician workes upon the patient, according to the bodies constitution; the Lawyer giveth advice to his Client, when hee understands the case, and thus wisely must ministers proceed, and know how to speak seasonably.

We perhaps anticipate here some account of the material and social conditions under which each 'sort of people' lives and worships, and some attempt to tie the life of the soul to the life of the body, the better to attend to the former. What we get, however, is a sixfold schema defining the 'several sorts of people,' without reference to rank or occupation, entirely in terms of abstract mental and spiritual categories: those who are '*ignorant and indocible*,' those who are '*ignorant, but willing to be taught*,' those who are '*taught but unsanctified*,' and so on.[37] Parishioners, for Bernard, are to be understood entirely as the audience for a sermon. If the agrarian figures of speech were not so thoroughly commonplace, we might almost think Herbert has in mind Bernard's aphorism that 'Husband men sow their seed after the nature of the ground,' when he writes, in chapter V of *The Country Parson*, 'if a shepherd know not which grass will bane, or which will not, how is he fit to be a shepherd?' But despite the common metaphorical ground, Herbert continues in a manner that marks a significant departure: 'wherefore the parson hath thoroughly canvassed all the particulars of human actions, at least those which he observeth are most incident to his parish' (230). Herbert's ideal parson is to understand his parishioners not in terms of general sorts but particulars, not in terms of their patterns of thought, but of their actions.

Herbert's long title, *A Priest to the Temple, or, The Country Parson His Character and Rule of Holy Life*, points toward one important contemporary genre that does grapple with 'the particulars of human actions,' the

Theophrastan 'character' essay made popular in the early seventeenth century by Joseph Hall, Sir Thomas Overbury (and the other authors of the 'Overburian Characters'), and John Earle. This, readers have usually felt, is Herbert's most important generic precedent. His biographer, Amy Charles, describes *The Country Parson* as 'an expanded and somewhat idealized "character," perhaps the lengthiest of this type.'[38] In the character essays, as in the essays of Herbert's friend Francis Bacon, and in Gregory's *Pastoral Care*, there are precedents for *The Country Parson's* brief chapters and crisp aphoristic prose. Moreover the extraordinary popularity of the characters, especially those of Overbury and Earle, might have appealed to Herbert's desire to emulate Christ by making 'Doctrine slip the more easily into the hearts even of the meanest' (261), though in this case 'the meanest' might be understood as the meanest among the clergy. The chief relevance of the 'characters,' however, is in the important psychological and ideological common ground between Herbert and the character writers, ancient and contemporary. As Cristina Malcolmson observes,

> The characters of Theophrastus, the Greek originator of the genre, are built on Aristotle's assumption that people are essentially social creatures and that they create and express themselves through their acts. English character writers, like Joseph Hall, modified this Aristotelian notion because, for them, inner disposition determined action; an individual's words and deeds were clues to the motives of the heart.[39]

Like the character writers, Herbert insists on the correspondence between the inner and the outer person: he advocates 'lifting up ... heart and hands, and eyes, and using all other gestures which may expresse a hearty, and unfeyned devotion' (231). In Malcolmson's words, 'Herbert's parson inscribes his holy character into the flux of experience, making his inner quality legible to his parishioners through his habitual words and deeds.' In writing an extended character of the godly pastor, therefore, Herbert engages in an act of exemplary self-fashioning, repudiating his earlier courtly ambitions and embracing a synthesis of feudal social order and 'a modern emphasis on vocation and labour as the source of the individual's social significance.'[40]

Malcolmson's suggestive account can be extended and amplified by considering the trajectory of English character writing in the genre's brief seventeenth-century vogue. Given the shift described by Malcolmson from an Aristotelian emphasis on social action as constitutive of character to a more Platonic early modern view of social action as expressive of an essential nature, one might expect, in the English characters, a progressive move inward, the qualities of the soul being dissected ever more finely and anatomized according to ever subtler distinctions. In fact, however, the evolution of the English character essay up to Herbert's time follows precisely the opposite course. Joseph Hall's 1608 *Characters of Virtues and Vices* consists almost entirely of moral types: 'The Faithful Man,' 'The Humble Man,' 'The Flatterer,' 'The Ambitious.'[41] Only one character, 'The Good Magistrate,' describes what might be called a vocational or occupational type. Hall's characters may reflect the belief that inner disposition determines social action, but they tend not to describe that social action extensively, at least not in vocational terms. Overbury's nearly contemporary characters not only shift from Hall's focus on moral instruction to witty satire, they also rely much more heavily on occupational types: 'A Courtier,' 'A Country Gentleman,' 'A Sailor,' 'A Tailor.' Overbury, and the 'other learned gentlemen' who contributed to the posthumous collection published under his name, superimpose on Hall's inventory of general moral types a social inventory resembling the catalogue of the 'Degrees of People in the Commonwealth of England' found in Harrison's *Description of England*, and the descriptions of regional characteristics contained in Elizabethan and Jacobean cartographic and chorographic works.[42] The effect is not to move inward, in the direction of greater psychological refinement, but rather outward, to emphasize increasingly the importance of rank, occupation, and locality in determining conduct and temperament.

This movement is consolidated in John Earle's *Micro-Cosmographie*, nearly contemporary with Herbert's *Country Parson*. Of the fifty-four characters contained in the 1628 first edition, over half might be called vocational or occupational types: 'A young rawe Preacher,' 'A Grave Divine,' 'An Upstart Knight,' 'A Constable,' 'A Shop keeper.' Two of these characters, the 'young rawe Preacher' and the 'Grave Divine,' obviously have special relevance to *The Country Parson*, particularly since Earle was a recipient of Herbert family patronage, and much later, Bishop of Salisbury.[43] The former is a satirical portrait, mocking the cleric who 'preaches but once a yeare, though twice on Sund[a]y: for the stuffe is still the same, onely the dressing a little altered. He has more tricks with a sermon, then a Tailer with an old cloak, to turne it and piece it, and at last quite disguise it with a new preface.' In contrast, Earle's 'Grave divine' 'Preaches at fit times, and his conversation is the every dayes exercise.' Earle pursues the 'Grave Divine' beyond the pulpit and into the world: 'he is no base Grater of his Tythes, and will not wrangle for the odd egge. The Lawyer is the onely man he hinders, he is spited for taking up quarrels.'[44] Virtually all of Earle's observations about clerical foibles and virtues turn up in *The Country Parson*, and it is not implausible to suppose that the two men may have exchanged thoughts about the state of the English clergy across the Earl of Pembroke's dinner table.

The turn toward vocational characters may, in part, be a simple function of the literary marketplace: in their search for novelty and variety, the Overburians, and especially Earle, may merely have required a wider range of examples than the customary virtues and vices offered. But the increasing prominence of vocational characters may also be seen as part (albeit a comparatively small and playful part) of a larger cultural exercise in mapping and surveying not only English territory, but the English populace and national character. It is no accident that Herbert entitles his chapter on secular vocations 'The Parson's Surveys' (274). As Richard Helgerson observes, those who set out to describe 'the "facts" of England's history and geography had an inescapable part in creating the cultural entity they pretended only to represent.'[45] Or to put the point in Herbertian terms, the project of copying out a 'sweetnesse readie penn'd' constantly encounters the tendency of new thoughts to 'burnish, sprout and swell.' ('Jordan' [II], ll. 18, 4).

This mapping or copying of England and of the English, their characteristics and occupations, is evident not merely in the ambitious and rather specialized publications considered by Helgerson, but throughout the seventeenth-century English book trade. There, a proliferation of occupational handbooks and how-to manuals expanded the subjects of the vocational characters, and balanced their witty and satirical tone with earnest prescription and description. As H.S. Bennett points out, the book market of the later sixteenth and early seventeenth century saw the emergence not only of 'literary' books (verse collections, play texts, and prose romances) and the much-discussed pamphlets, sermons, ballads, and broadsheets, but also educational and informational publications on a significant scale. There were medical books and herbals, both learned and vernacular, legal textbooks, abridgements of the statutes and handbooks for magistrates, and perhaps most important, a flood of general and specialized manuals on husbandry and related topics, from surveying to domestic economy.[46] Such texts clearly owe something to Tudor humanist works like Elyot's

Governour, Castiglione's *Courtier,* and Ascham's *Scholemaster,* but they address, and attest to, a much broader audience of ambitious, literate country folk, with few courtly pretensions.[47] This market grew steadily, prompting the seventeenth-century hack writer Gervase Markham to produce over twenty such books, on topics ranging from husbandry and horsemanship to housewifery.[48] If Herbert's *Country Parson* is a character book, it is equally a part of this flowering of early modern vocational literature.

We can gather something of the cultural meaning of this publishing enterprise from the controversy surrounding early vernacular medical books. According to Bennett, many opponents of translation and vernacular publication 'felt that the mysteries of the medical art were mysteries and should remain so.'[49] Such opposition, emphasizing esoteric secrecy and mystery, links early modern medicine, albeit residually, to the systems of magic and ritual that had helped sustain a traditional social order. As William Eamon has argued, early modern science and medicine only gradually were divested 'of the tradition of esotericism in natural philosophy.'[50] Vernacular publication is part of the secularization and rationalization of scientific and medical knowledge that we associate with modernity. Of course, no straightforward distinction can be made between a closed traditional order of knowledge and an open rational order. After all, the Royal College of Physicians had as one of its main objectives the maintenance of a 'closed shop' of physicians. But increasingly the justification for closure was legal and rationalistic, grounded in statute, and bolstered by an insistence on the technical complexity, rather than the secrecy, of medical knowledge. If the proliferation of vernacular medical books is linked to the rationalization of medical knowledge, there is some reason to draw similar conclusions about the larger body of vocational literature in which Herbert's *Country Parson* has a place. What we see in early modern occupational handbooks and manuals is part of an uneven but discernible trend toward the rationalization and systematization of a culture's collective knowledge and self-knowledge (or to put the matter more sceptically, its self-representation). If *The Country Parson*'s genres function 'quasi-pragmatically,' to use Fowler's term, they do so by linking Herbert's text to a loose body of generic antecedents that share a common preoccupation with rational and national self-fashioning. But the 'self' so fashioned remains primarily a corporate one, defined by nationality, rank, local affiliation, and vocation, with comparatively little regard to unique individual subjectivity.

Re-Reading *The Country Parson*

If we understand *The Country Parson* as an exercise in professional, rather than personal, self-fashioning, we need to reconsider the way we read it. Until fairly recently, Herbert's critics have tended to appeal to *The Country Parson* for solutions to the interpretative problems posed by the poems, implicitly asserting that the prose treatise is the univocal discourse of the 'real' George Herbert, who stands behind the competing voices and sensibilities we find in *The Temple.*[51] Ironically, the text so privileged is impoverished in the process, stripped of its own complex and contradictory agendas. Conversely, if we read *The Country Parson* as one thread in an intricate web of social discourses, we find it as variously textured and as changeable as 'The Collar' or 'Miserie' or 'Jordan' (II). Biography (or rather hagiography) tended, for too long, to inhibit this kind of reading. One of the central scholarly concerns of the late Amy Charles was to debunk what she called the 'Waltonian heresy,' the version of Herbert's life based on the Pauline and Augustinian pattern of conversion, and on the example of Donne:

> the young man of high birth, fond of fine clothes and knowing the ways of the world, after a brief and unrewarding fling at secular life, manages to submit his will and high spirits and to become as saintly as Walton's Donne ... an anticipation of gentle Jesus meek and mild.[52]

According to this paradigm the *Temple* poems are, in the words Izaak Walton attributes to Herbert, 'a picture of the many spiritual Conflicts that have passed betwixt God and my Soul, before I could subject mine to the will of *Jesus my Master*: in whose service I have now found perfect freedom,' and *The Country Parson* is proof of the resolution of those struggles and of Herbert's final submission.[53] Critics and biographers before Charles largely followed and elaborated Walton's model of the poet's development. George Herbert Palmer divided Herbert's literary life into an intense period of artistic productivity and personal crisis (1627–30), followed by the period of 'consecration' (1630–3), and rearranged the poems of *The Temple* to suit this narrative.[54] Charles places the beginnings of this crisis considerably earlier, perhaps as early as 1613–14, and suggests a process considerably longer and less dramatic than the archetypal conversions of Herbert's illustrious predecessors.[55] Her successors have further undermined the Waltonian position by suggesting a more sustained and consistent worldliness on Herbert's part than hagiography would have been inclined to admit.[56]

Yet despite Charles's attacks on the 'Waltonian heresy,' a residually Waltonian view of *The Country Parson* persists. Charles herself sees the prose treatise as an expressive text that communicates the distinctive experiences and values of Parson Herbert; she admires its author's 'working knowledge of human nature ... good sense, forthright diction, and economical phrasing.'[57] Ironically, these are precisely the terms in which nineteenth-century readers and editors praised the poems of *The Temple*.[58] Missing from such a view is a sense of *The Country Parson* as, on the one hand, the deliberate, artful construction of an accomplished poet, orator, and rhetorician, and on the other, a manifestation of ideology, an articulation of views held not so much consciously and individually as collectively and unconsciously. At the opposite extreme is the 'frankly ... ideological and political' reading offered by Douglas J. Swartz. In Swartz's view, '*The Country Parson* establishes as its ideal objective the almost absolute control, through the priest and his mastery of religious discourse, of parishioners' spiritual, moral, political and material lives.' This view may be thought of as the mirror image of earlier hagiography, substituting an entirely impersonal monologic 'official discourse' of the autocratic state and church for the personal holiness of the saintly author/pastor. But *The Country Parson* is no monologic expression of the parson's 'absolute authority within the parish.'[59] Rather, it is hesitant, ambivalent, and inconstant, struggling always to construct an elusive *via media* out of intractable cultural materials. Subsequent chapters will examine the substance of these ambivalences, but here I briefly consider their formal manifestations, in the book's overall structure and in its handling of authorial voice.

Curiously, *The Country Parson* bears a structural resemblance to 'The Altar,' the very first poem in the central section of *The Temple*, a poem built around an emblematic dialogue of the Christian's inner and outer life. 'The Altar' moves from the realm of external action (albeit figuratively conceived) into the life of the heart, and then re-emerges into the world, a movement reflected again in *The Temple*'s tripartite structure of 'The Church-Porch,' 'The Church,' and 'The Church Militant.' The outer surfaces of 'The Altar,' its first two and last two lines, are predominantly expressions of vocation, in which the speaker describes the gift he has made for God – 'A broken ALTAR, Lord, thy servant reares, / Made of a heart, and cemented with teares' (ll. 1–2) – and pleads for its acceptance – 'O let thy blessed SACRIFICE be mine / And sanctifie this ALTAR to be thine' (ll. 15–16). Reading just these lines creates a strong impression of the speaker as an active agent, raising an admittedly flawed ('broken') altar to God. The brokenness of the altar and the plea for its sanctification emphasize its status as a product of fallen human artifice, but they in no way repudiate that artifice. The inner part of the poem, the central pedestal, presents a different picture of the altar's construction:

> A   HEART   alone
> Is   such   a   stone,
> As   nothing   but
> Thy pow'r doth cut.
> Wherefore each part
> Of my hard heart
> Meets in this frame,
> To praise thy Name.   (ll. 5–12)

Here the emphasis is on God's unique power: people cannot transform their own hearts. Only a divine maker can turn stony hearts into altars. Of course dividing the poem in this way is as absurd as dividing the inner and outer person. In Protestant terms, the speaker is only a good worker or maker in the world because God is already working and remaking from within. It is the fusion of these two conditions – the outer condition of acting and the inner condition of being acted upon – that constitutes regeneracy. The sanctified life is a manifestation of the transformed heart.

A similar dialectic of inner and outer structural elements operates in *The Country Parson*, but in an inverted version. The inner man, the authorial voice who speaks in the first person and appeals to God for personal salvation, appears most clearly in the outer portions of the text, or in what we might call the frame of the portrait: the preface headed 'The Authour to the Reader,' and the closing prayers. These sections are marked by formulaic expressions of inadequacy, expressions that render the most personal parts of the text simultaneously the most conventional: 'The Lord prosper the intention to my selfe, and others, who may not despise my poor labours, but add to those points, which I have observed, untill the Book grow to a compleat Pastorall' (224); 'O Almighty and ever-living Lord God! ... How shall we dare to appear before thy face, who are contrary to thee, in all we call thee?' (288). In contrast, the ideal parson depicted in the chapters is a fabric of precepts for external behaviour. The outer portions of the text seem most concerned with the speaker's relationship with God, while the inner portions emphasize worldly obligations, 'the benefit of our neighbor'

(246).[60] And it is with the discharge of those worldly obligations that the book is primarily concerned.

On closer examination, however, complications proliferate. It becomes clear that the apparently flat and didactic chapters also deploy the rhetoric of insufficiency that characterizes the framing portions of the book, that the first-person authorial voice alternately identifies with and diverges from the model parson throughout the text, and that Herbert employs a range of techniques for registering identification and differentiation. Sometimes the speaker will shift abruptly into the first person plural as in chapter VII, 'The Parson preaching,' where he proclaims that the character of holiness is gained 'by dipping, and seasoning all our words and sentences in our hearts' (233). Such shifts, echoing the modesty *topoi* of the preface and closing prayers, tend to coincide with an emphasis on the parson's deficiencies, or at least on the qualities he shares with all humanity. Like the opening and closing sections, they are at once personal and, of necessity, generic. At other times there is a somewhat heavy-handed use of the third person, as in chapter XXXVI: 'The Countrey Parson wonders, that Blessing the people is in so little use with his brethren' (285). Here the tone is not merely didactic but chastening, emphasizing the distinction between those who subscribe to the views of the speaker, as projected onto his ideal parson, and those who do not. The first form of identification is conventionally self-effacing, as the speaker and the parson merge with the reader, the parson's congregation, and the rest of humanity. The second form is more confident, giving axiomatic force to a particular view on a debatable question.[61] Yet even here, the slightly elegiac note registers the gap between the real and the ideal, and undermines the text's authoritative pretensions. 'Thou shalt ... ' shades into 'if only ...'

A slightly different effect occurs in chapter XX, 'The Parson in Gods stead,' where the authorial voice asserts the godlike role of the pastor. Here the phrasing carries definite connotations of presumption and usurpation, and the resulting conception of God is rather mundane and legalistic. The ways in which '*the Parson endeavoureth to be in Gods stead*' largely involve '*rewarding vertue, and ... punishing vice*' (254):

> therefore as God, although we should love him onely for his own sake, yet ... hath set forth heaven for a reward to draw men to Piety, and is content, if at least so, they will become good: So the Countrey Parson ... sets up as many encouragements to goodnesse as he can ... that he may, if not the best way, yet any way, make his Parish good. (243–4)

Only by collapsing the divine to fit the constraints of human understanding can the claim that the parson is 'in Gods stead' be sustained.
The characterization of heaven as an incentive to virtue, the suggestion
that God is content with a mercenary devotion, the claim that the parson is licensed to use any means to 'make his Parish good': all this is
reminiscent of the misguided and self-serving legalism of the persona in
Herbert's poem 'The Thanksgiving.' The emphasis on virtue at almost
any price disrupts the pious idealism of the text and raises the question
of how far zeal for moral reformation can go before it becomes self-
aggrandizement.[62] In a Herbert poem we might say with some confidence that this excess is ironic, that it is advanced in order to be
retracted or corrected. In the prose treatise it is harder to judge. The
self-effacing gestures employed in *The Country Parson* are not evidently
more 'genuine' than the didactic and authoritarian ones, but the interplay between them is undeniably purposeful, serving to destabilize the
pastoral ideal by acknowledging competing visions. As in many of Herbert's poems, the apparently fixed values embodied in the ideal parson
are actually in motion, and we need to be wary of saying either 'this is
what Herbert believed,' or 'this is the orthodoxy Herbert transmits'
about any given fragment of the text. Rather, in offering multiple views
of the pastoral character, *The Country Parson* creates a collage effect in
which elements necessary to the whole may nevertheless, taken individually, clash with the overall design. In *The Country Parson*, as in *The
Temple*, we have 'a picture of ... many ... Conflicts,' or, perhaps more
accurately, a composite of many conflicting pictures, embodying what
Angenot would call the 'regulated antagonisms' of Herbert's culture.[63]

chapter two

The Country Parson and the Early Stuart Church

The Countrey Parson hath a speciall care of his Church, that all things there be decent, and befitting his Name by which it is called. Therefore first he takes order, that all things be in good repair; as walls plaistered, windows glazed, floore paved, seats whole, firm, and uniform, especially that the Pulpit, and Desk, and Communion Table, and Font be as they ought, for those great duties that are performed in them. Secondly, that the Church be swept, and kept cleane without dust, or Cobwebs, and at great festivalls strawed, and stuck with boughs, and perfumed with incense. Thirdly, That there be fit, and proper texts of Scripture every where painted, and that all the painting be grave, and reverend, not with light colours, or foolish anticks. Fourthly, That all the books appointed by Authority be there, and those not torne, or fouled, but whole and clean, and well bound; and that there be a fitting, and sightly Communion Cloth *of fine linnen, with an handsome, and seemly Carpet of good and costly Stuffe, or Cloth, and all kept sweet and clean, in a strong and decent chest, with a Chalice, and Cover, and a Stoop, or Flagon; and a Bason for Almes and offerings; besides which, he hath a Poor-mans Box conveniently seated, to receive the charity of well minded people, and to lay up treasure for the sick and needy.* And all this he doth, not as out of necessity, or as putting a holiness in the things, but as desiring to keep the middle way between superstition, and slovenlinesse.

A Priest to the Temple, or The Country Parson
His Character and Rule of Holy Life,
Chapter XIII, 'The Parson's Church'

As Christopher Hodgkins and Daniel Doerksen have demonstrated, a careful reading of *The Country Parson* can contribute a great deal to an

understanding of George Herbert's theology and ecclesiastical politics.
Yet such an approach also presents difficulties. *The Country Parson* is not
a theological treatise, so any attempt to draw conclusions about Herbert's theology from it involves '[c]atching the sense at two removes.'
Moreover, the book was composed, presumably with an eye to publication, during a period of considerable uncertainty in the Church of
England, the early years of the Arminian ascendancy.[1] Herbert's comments on ecclesiastical matters must be read not merely as expressions
of his personal convictions, nor as straightforward elaborations of the
settled policies of his church, but as calculated interventions, and
potentially risky ones, in a highly charged struggle. The result is a subtle
but continual modulation of position. Hence, in the opening paragraph
of chapter XIII, 'The Parson's Church,' he refers to a communion table
rather than an altar, apparently declaring allegiance to a waning, pre-
Laudian orthodoxy in the Church of England. Yet he goes on to make
an apparent concession to Laudian ceremonialism, in admitting festive
decoration and painting within the church, a concession immediately
attenuated by the insistence 'that all the painting be grave, and reverend, not with light colours, or foolish anticks.'[2] With the reference to
'books appointed by Authority,' he balances in a phrase the traditional
Protestant insistence on independent reading of Scripture and the
interpretive 'Authority' of church and state, rendering that authority as
an enabling force rather than as an impediment to devotion. Such deft
touches are paradigmatic instances of the ideological and rhetorical
strategy that animates *The Country Parson*, a strategy of almost simultaneous advance and retreat, of putting forward positions, sometimes
innovative or controversial ones, in the terms most appealing to opponents of those very positions.

Matters of discipline and ceremony, on which *The Country Parson*
touches repeatedly, were considered *adiaphora*, or matters indifferent to
salvation, by the post-Reformation Church of England. Too often, however, modern commentators take indifferent to mean inconsequential,
or assume that because Herbert's Church of England held ceremony to
be indifferent to salvation, it took a latitudinarian attitude to these questions. In fact, the opposite was often the case. The theory that ceremony
and church discipline were indifferent to salvation permitted the state
church to enforce conformity without trampling on matters of conscience. In his *Determinationes*, Herbert's bishop, John Davenant, insists
that 'The English Church is fully Competent to bind to the observance
of Ceremonies.'[3] The unity of the church and of the state demanded

conformity, but the standards of conformity were certainly in flux in the delicate situation of 1630–2. Careers were being made and broken over the question of what constituted the orthodox doctrine and practice of the Church of England. What would have prompted George Herbert to write a book of advice for the parish clergy at such an awkward time? What sort of advice was needed at this moment, and what sort of advice would have been safe to give? What kind of intervention into ecclesiastical politics would *The Country Parson* have been, had it appeared with *The Temple* in 1633, a year after its completion, and, coincidentally, the year of Laud's elevation to the archbishopric of Canterbury?[4] Furthermore, since Herbert's decision to write the book must have followed hard upon his ordination as priest in 1630, or even, perhaps, preceded it, the historical issues raise biographical ones. What would prompt a man who had been procrastinating about taking orders for some years to do so at this time, and what does the writing of one of the first English Protestant pastoral manuals suggest about Herbert's faith, his clerical ambitions, and his conception of the church whose service he was entering?[5]

The most important and comprehensive studies placing Herbert in a Protestant tradition share an insistence on Herbert's commitment to a common core of ideas and emphases captured in Gene Edward Veith's phrase 'Reformation Spirituality.'[6] They de-emphasize the local variations, nuances, and transformations of Reformation theology, a strategy that is perhaps necessary in arguing against a body of criticism that seeks to situate Herbert's faith in the context of medieval and Counter-Reformation spirituality.[7] A secondary effect of this emphasis on a common core of Protestant doctrine is a tendency to neglect, sometimes even to deny, the historical specificity of Herbert's theology and churchmanship, making Herbert into a Protestant Everyman, rather than a Protestant Englishman of the 1620s. Hence, for instance, Richard Strier's insistence on Herbert's deliberate rejection of the 'subversively rationalistic' and moralistic thrust of the 'covenant divinity' associated with some of the most important English divines of Herbert's age, such as William Perkins, William Ames, Richard Sibbes, and John Preston.[8] Taking a slightly different approach, Christopher Hodgkins sees Herbert's Protestantism as specifically and anachronistically Elizabethan in character, backward-looking in a positive sense that Hodgkins captures in the phrase 'regenerative nostalgia.' In this view, Herbert, an Elizabethan in spirit, 'could coexist with the Jacobeans, whose neglect he was probably able to call benign because they maintained the old Calvinist orthodoxy of God's sovereign grace, which sanctified the church's forms and covered a multitude of other evils.' Hodgkins argues that 'if James's and Charles's country clergy had practiced Herbertian 'thorough' with half the energy recommended by Herbert himself, the leaven of established Protestant doctrine would very likely have permeated the kingdom, probably reducing the Puritan pressure that led in part to the civil war.'[9] These formulations underestimate the degree to which Protestant doctrine and the ideals of godly ministry had permeated, transformed, and been transformed by the Jacobean church. As the recent work of ecclesiastical historians has shown, James and his bishops fostered a deliberate program, though ultimately an unsuccessful one, for the improvement of ministry and church administration and the cultivation of lay piety and religious unity.[10] Indeed James displayed much greater concern for these matters than Elizabeth, who tended to subordinate all the others to unity and obedience. Such formulations also underestimate Herbert's commitment, especially evident in *The Country Parson*, but also in many of his poems, to the emerging social dimension of Reformation spirituality: the emphasis on the creation of a godly community, and the connections between this emphasis and the acknowledged centrality of soteriology.[11]

I argue that *The Country Parson* displays a characteristically Jacobean ambition for godliness, diligence, and obedience among clergy and parishioners alike. Far from expressing Herbert's personal 'regenerative nostalgia,' it expresses a collective spirit of reformation, reorganization, and clerical and social discipline, which sought to transform the parish clergy of the state church into an effective instrument of social control. Such a project must, I think, be understood as ideological rather than cynical. The notion that the church should serve the state in the maintenance of public order and public morality would seem entirely natural and unremarkable to Herbert and his contemporaries. After all, the state and the King were, along with the church, God's instruments for governing his creation, and if theologians occasionally debated the limits of state authority in matters of faith and conscience, it was precisely because they also acknowledged the considerable extent of that authority. As James himself put it in *The True Lawe of Free Monarchies*, 'Kings are called *Gods* by the propheticall King DAVID, because they sit upon God his throne in the earth, and have the count of their administration to give unto him.'[12] Of course by the time Herbert wrote *The Country Parson* James was no longer King, and a very different ecclesiastical program was underway, one that borrowed some aspects of the Jacobean plan and abandoned others. But many of the Jacobean bishops still held office, and it was perhaps becoming clear that men like Herbert, adherents to the Calvinist-episcopal mainstream of the Jacobean church, had to take advantage of the opportunities for advancement open to them while they still could.

John Davenant and the Jacobean Ecclesiastical Program

To present Herbert's *Country Parson* as a contribution, admittedly a slightly belated one, to the Jacobean ecclesiastical and social program, it is necessary to sketch that program in some detail. One way of drawing together the two main threads of this analysis, one biographical and the other institutional, is to examine the early Stuart church through the career of Herbert's bishop, John Davenant.[13] Though we have no evidence about the relationship between the two men, Davenant's career and his writings illustrate the delicate theological and political balancing act performed by many Jacobean clerics, and the dynamics of the transition to a new regime in the late 1620s and early 1630s. This, in turn, may help to clarify what sort of intervention into ecclesiastical politics *The Country Parson* would have been in 1633. Herbert, who was 'setting foot into Divinity,' by 1617 or 1618 at the latest, would almost certainly have encountered Davenant at Cambridge, where the latter served as Lady Margaret Professor of Divinity until he became Bishop of Salisbury in 1621.[14] Furthermore, Herbert must have known of Davenant's participation as one of the English delegates to the Synod of Dort in 1618–19. Davenant was a key spokesman for the Jacobean ecclesiastical and theological mainstream, a Calvinist theologian who could affirm, in the mode of English Protestant nationalism, that 'The Church of Rome is an Apostate Church,' while insisting, against the 'hotter sort of Protestants,' that 'Civil jurisdiction is rightly conceded to Ecclesiastical persons' and that 'Diversity of Degrees in the Ministers of the Gospel is not repugnant to the Word of God.'[15] Given the blend of conformist churchmanship and reformed soteriology evident in Herbert's poetry, it seems likely that the two men would have agreed on many of the central questions that increasingly came to divide members of the Church of England after the death of King James.

The Jacobean program for the Church of England had received its definitive formulation early in the reign, at the Hampton Court conference of 1604. In terms of church government and ceremonial, the Jacobean religious settlement differed very little from the Elizabethan

compromise, and in this it frustrated the Puritan authors of the Mille-
nary Petition who had hoped, by a moderate and conciliatory approach,
to secure some encouragement about further reform in these areas
from the new King. But as Patrick Collinson points out, if James dashed
Puritan hopes for structural change at Hampton Court, he also demonstrated a conception of the ministry that differed sharply from that of
his royal predecessor:

> Unlike the more conservative bishops, and very much unlike Queen Eliza-
> beth ... [James's] Calvinism led him to believe that the ministry of the
> church ought, as a matter of course, to be a learned preaching ministry. So
> on the final day of the conference he committed to the bishops as a
> weighty matter the provision of sufficient resources to provide for 'the
> planting of a learned and painful minister in every parish.'[16]

In this James was indeed responding to one of the central concerns of
Puritans, seeking to reform the parish ministry through improvements
in education, personal conduct, and economic status. He was also, of
course, pursuing a political agenda. Kenneth Fincham and Peter Lake
have suggested that James sought, perhaps rather naively, to 'settle the
issue of Puritanism once and for all by driving a wedge between the
moderate and radical wings of Puritan opinion.' The King made an
.implicit bargain with some of the self-consciously godly when he
'embraced the godly imperative of a preaching ministry in every parish,
and offered favor and preferment in return for a formal renunciation of
Puritan scruples.'[17] To those who would do so within the episcopal hierarchy, James offered opportunities to pursue the evangelical Protestant
imperative, opportunities that had been denied under Elizabeth.

If a vigorous preaching ministry was to be created, the most obvious
need was for adequate compensation for parish clergy, 'to remove the
twin evils of pluralism and nonresidence.'[18] Following the conference,
Archbishop Bancroft attempted, without success, to have impropriated
tithes restored to the clergy by statute. Not surprisingly, the economic
interests of lay impropriators carried greater weight in Parliament than
arguments about the need for adequate clerical income.[19] This circum-
stance, combined with Herbert's strained financial situation, may have
been one of the more mundane factors that led the poet to postpone
his decision to take orders.[20] Even in the absence of these reforms, however, godly Jacobeans found means to ensure the preaching of the Gospel. They instituted salaried or stipendiary lectureships as a means of

securing preachers for communities that had none, and sometimes, as an expression of the piety of a godly minority among the laity, in communities already supplied with a preacher.[21] As Collinson has shown, lectureships are rooted in the Elizabethan Puritan tradition of prophesying, a tradition proscribed and vigorously suppressed under Elizabeth.[22] Under James, on the other hand, 'meetings for sermons, commonly termed by some prophecies or exercises, in market-towns, or other places' were permitted, subject to episcopal regulation.[23] Of the three bishops with whom Herbert had personal connections (Williams, Andrewes, and Davenant), two, Williams and Davenant, are known to have sponsored lectureships, and Davenant seems to have been instrumental in establishing a lectureship in Laud's home town of Reading in 1629, an action which could not have earned him any favour with the future archbishop.[24]

The lectures highlight what some have seen as the central tension of the Jacobean church, a tension not between 'Anglicans' and 'Puritans,' or even between Laudian Arminians and Episcopal Calvinists (though the various formulations of the divide sometimes overlap), but between two visions of the true church, one inclusive and the other exclusive.[25] As Collinson puts it, 'the doctrine that God is English foundered on the contradictions between the ... claims of the all-inclusive National church, and the religious self-awareness of the godly people, the virtuoso minority whose practice of religion was prodigious.'[26] James's strategy, and I would argue, Herbert's agenda in *The Country Parson*, involved a precarious fusion of these two visions, an attempt to create an inclusive national church in which the zeal of the 'virtuoso minority' would be harnessed and institutionalized. But lectures were established in the service of both visions, and the Jacobean church, in sharp contrast to the Elizabethan church of the 1590s, tacitly sustained many who adhered to a narrower definition of godliness. Both these conceptions of the church had their theological roots in Calvinism, and the distinction between them has often come to be expressed, in theological terms, as a distinction between 'experimental' and 'credal' predestinarianism.[27] Credal predestinarians emphasized the unknowability of God's decrees and the necessity for an inclusive national church. Experimental predestinarians, in contrast, stressed the visible signs of election:

[they] wanted to place their view of predestination, election and assurance at the centre of their practical divinity, to erect a style of piety on the foundations provided by a Calvinist doctrine of predestination, and to define

the Godly community (and in some cases the visible church) in terms of those who both understood those doctrines and acted upon them.[28]

Such a view transforms the 'inwardness' of reformed spirituality into a social program. The concept was potentially divisive, underwriting attempts at systematic social control by the godly minority in communities like Terling (Essex), Dorchester (Dorset), and Herbert's cathedral town of Salisbury.[29] Nevertheless, when accommodated to ideas of national election and to the claims of a national church, it could have a much broader appeal. The experimental tradition, despite its strenuous emphasis on election, was, paradoxically, more casuistical, voluntaristic, and moralistic: more concerned with practical divinity and social order. A fusion of these two strains of Protestant tradition had tremendous appeal to a King who fancied himself '*rex pacificus*, a new Constantine, a truly Godly prince.'[30]

Along with Samuel Ward and the other English delegates to the Synod of Dort in 1618–19, John Davenant was one of the theological architects of the necessary accommodation. At Dort, the distinction between broad and narrow visions of the church emerged through the debates about the nature of the atonement. This was the most contentious of the issues to be resolved among the counter-remonstrants (that is, the Calvinist opponents of the Arminian Remonstrance). Indeed, the English theologians were divided among themselves, and sought advice from royal and ecclesiastical authorities in England. In the words of one member,

> the issue amongst us is whether the words of the Scripture, which are likewise the words of our confession, (*Christus oblatus est aut mortuus pro toto humano genere, seu pro peccatis totuis mundi*) [Christ died for the whole human race, even for the sins of all the world] be to be understood of all particular men, or only of the elect who consist of all sorts of men. Dr. Davenant and Dr. Ward ... [claim] that it is to be understood of all particular men.[31]

The position taken by Davenant and Ward represented a slight softening of the prevailing Calvinist orthodoxy. Appealing on Ward's behalf to James's desire for unity, not merely among his own subjects but among European Protestants generally, Dean Young of Winchester was able to persuade the King to support the position taken by Ward and Davenant. Their 'hypothetical universalism' is reflected in the *Judgement* (or

Canons) of the Synod which affirm that the 'death of the sonne of God is the onely, and most perfit sacrifice, and satisfaction for sinnes, of infinite price, and value, abundantly sufficient to expiate the sinnes of the whole world,' and further, that

> the promise of the Gospel [is] that whosoever beleeves in Christ crucified, should not perish, but have life everlasting: Which promise together with the injunction of repentance and faith, ought promiscuously, and without distinction, to bee declared and published to all men and people, to whom God in his good pleasure sends the Gospel.[32]

Though few are actually saved, and those few are known to God from all eternity, Christ's grace is 'sufficient to expiate the sinness of the whole world,' so, hypothetically speaking, universal salvation is possible. In other words, not all are saved, but any may be.

The *Judgement* of Dort, had, of course, no formal authority in the Church of England. Nevertheless, it embodies a formulation of Calvinist theology strongly influenced by English divines, and influential in their own practice, a formulation that seeks to reconcile inclusive and exclusive conceptions of the church. In the words of Peter Lake,

> in ... modifying both the presentation and the content of English Calvinism, Ward and Davenant were drawing on ... that strain of ... practical divinity [experimentalism] which ... set out to inculcate an active piety in the laity ... In the modified or moderated Calvinism produced by Ward and Davenant at Dort, this experimental tradition can be seen operating on and subtly changing the doctrinal core of credal Calvinism ... [T]he logic of an inclusive, national church can be discerned imposing itself on a style of divinity which, at times, came uncomfortably close to providing a rationale for semi-separatism.[33]

In Davenant's 1631 *Treatise on Justification*, this desire to 'inculcate an active piety in the laity' is evident in his laborious examination of the themes of inherent or habitual righteousness and actual righteousness, or, good works. One of Davenant's chief concerns is to 'clear away the calumnies of the Jesuits, who are repeatedly exclaiming, that the Protestants do not acknowledge any internal renovation, any habitual righteousness in the justified.'[34] While conceding nothing to Rome on the political front, he seeks to appropriate the moralist strain of a theology of good works. This is precisely the sort of theological rapprochement we see Herbert pursuing in *The Country Parson*. Concerned almost exclusively with practical piety and the day-to-day conduct of an exemplary preaching minister, it is nevertheless deeply committed to the vision of an English national church, and to the universalist implications of that vision. The sins with which the parson must be concerned are both the particular 'faults of his own Parish' and the 'diseases of the time' including especially the 'nationall sin of ... Idlenesse' (274). Herbert also insists that preaching must accommodate doctrine to the understanding of the audience, 'especially with Countrey people; which are thick, and heavy, and hard to raise to a point of Zeal' (233), so that the gospel may, in Davenant's words, 'promiscuously, and without distinction ... bee declared and published to all.' In the 'Prayer Before Sermon' appended to *The Country Parson*, Herbert explicitly embraces Davenant's 'hypothetical universalism' when he asserts that Christ died 'for his enemies ... even for those that derided him then and still despise him' (289).

The Country Parson and the Jacobean Clerical Profession

The Jacobean synthesis of exclusive and inclusive church ideals required a significant reformation of the English clergy. As Rosemary O'Day has shown, the English clergy underwent an 'immense transformation ... in the post-Reformation period,' brought about in part by systematic attempts at reform. The pace of this transformation accelerated considerably in the seventeenth century so that by the 1620s 'recruitment into the church at the parish level was overwhelmingly graduate,' and the ministry was becoming a profession in something approaching the modern sense of the term, adding more uniform educational standards and occupational duties, and the beginning of a class identity to an existing mechanism of professional closure (that is, ordination).[35] The establishment of a resident, learned, preaching ministry had been a Reformation ideal from the beginning, though ecclesiastical patronage, a shortage of qualified candidates, and the Queen's priorities for the church combined to inhibit progress in the sixteenth century. The early Elizabethan bishops, many of them former Marian exiles and zealous Protestants, had little control over recruitment, and had to be content with efforts to re-educate beneficed clergy, efforts which encountered official resistance. This sort of 'extra-mural education' for clergy was one of the main functions of the 'prophesying' meetings that Elizabeth suppressed.[36] 'The Queen ... wanted conformity above all in her clergy,' and in the years following the suspension of Grindal for his defence of prophesying, 'the progressive bishops gave way by death to a new, conservative bench.'[37] The character of the Jacobean episcopate, as Kenneth Fincham has shown, was quite different. James I and his bishops strove, with some success, to establish a model of '"apostolic" episcopacy,' in which bishops were 'better prepared for office than their Elizabethan predecessors,' and 'tackled their pastoral responsibilities with vigour and flair.' James 'ended the rustication ... imposed on Elizabethan bishops, so that after 1603 the episcopate resumed a traditional role of ecclesiastical statesmen and privy councillors.' At the same time the ideal of apostolic episcopacy demanded continued involvement in diocesan affairs. According to Fincham, 'most bishops conducted their visitations in person, supervised their consistory courts and preached fairly frequently.' Both the bishops and the parish clergy were instrumental in James's project to exercise his authority through a 'unified and broadly based national church.'[38] In attempting to extend this apostolic ideal to the parish level, the Jacobean bishops, unlike their Elizabethan predecessors, had demographics on their side. Only when 'the choice of clients before patrons ... was limited initially to educated ordinands' could the preferment of learned men be ensured, and this gradually came to pass as the universities turned out increasing numbers of candidates for ordination in the early decades of the seventeenth century.[39]

Another dimension to the campaign for a godly ministry is the more subjective matter of personal suitability. If, as Christopher Hodgkins has argued, Herbert hesitated over his ordination largely out of reverence for the ministry and anxiety about his personal vocation, he was probably part of a select minority. The seventeenth-century biographer Samuel Clarke attributes similar feelings to John Winter, who was 'unwilling to enter upon that great and dreadful work of the ministry' upon completion of his MA.[40] But Winter and Herbert might have been distressed by the lack of such scruples among some of their contemporaries. Paradoxically, one result of the increasing stress on clerical education was a 'decreasing emphasis ... upon pastoral suitability,' the very deficiency that the Reformation had sought to address through clerical education.[41] John Earle's stereotypical 'young rawe preacher' may be university trained, but he is nevertheless 'a Bird not yet fledg'd, that hath hopt out of his nest to bee Chirping on a hedge, and will be stragling abroad at what perill soever.'[42] The success of the church hierarchy in recruiting graduates into the ministry was not matched by programs to 'improve the vocational performance of ministers.'[43]

Lectureships and curacies did serve as a kind of informal clerical apprenticeship, though it has been argued that meager rewards and bleak prospects for advancement may sometimes have made these situations into nurseries of nonconformity and resentment.[44] A number of godly ministers established household seminaries to fill this void, taking in university graduates who sought 'a period of vocational training' before seeking ordination. But such enterprises 'depended heavily upon the central charismatic figure, and rarely survived the death or departure of the central light'; they served only a minority of the new graduates and probably had a rather slight impact on the clergy as a whole.[45] This lack of adequate preparation for the duties of ministry is a void that *The Country Parson* also seems designed to fill, by giving a detailed account of the parson's 'character and rule of holy life.' As a textual instance of what is now called 'in-service' education, Herbert's book seeks to address the deficiencies of both the old and the new clergy, using the method of criticism and exhortation through hyperbolic flattery that was a standard device of courtly literature.[46] Just as Herbert the University Orator had idealized Prince Charles as a peacemaker on his return from Spain in 1623, in an effort to make his pacifist argument more palatable, Herbert the clergyman describes his ideal colleague as 'exceeding exact in his Life, being holy, just, prudent, temperate, bold, grave in all his wayes' (227).[47]

While such a deferential approach might have some slight appeal to the remnants of a complacent older generation, jealous of the dignity of their position, *The Country Parson*'s chief audience must surely have been the 'young rawe preacher[s]': less experienced, but more literate, more self-consciously urbane, and more impressionable. In his second chapter Herbert singles out those who live in universities 'in a preparatory way,' and urges them 'to subdue and mortifie all lusts and affections: and not to think, that when they have read the Fathers, or Schoolmen, a Minister is made' (226). Moreover, throughout the book he offers descriptions of 'country people' that strongly suggest a readership unfamiliar with rural life and manners. Such an audience only comes into being once the centres of clerical recruitment have shifted from the local communities to the universities.

In addressing this audience Herbert seems to be attacking one of the side effects of clerical professionalization, the increasing sense of distance between the pastor and his flock, and the resulting anticlericalism.[48] The new educated clergy were often, in financial terms, no better off than their most humble parishioners. Nevertheless,

As a group they appeared ... caste-like and self-perpetuating, with a strong element of dynasticism and a conviction that in university education lay the key to professional advancement. Natural common interests stemming from this educated background and from professional duties bound the clergy together yet more firmly. The remoteness of which the clergy were accused stemmed less from their physical rather than psychological distance from the community.[49]

Here, it seems, the Reformation's emphasis on the ministry as a calling like other Christian occupations gives way (or perhaps gives rise) to a renewed sense of clerical prestige and superiority. This process was reinforced by the stabilization of the state church in the 1590s and by the work of apologists such as Richard Hooker, but it was also accentuated by the Puritan and Jacobean emphasis on godly ministry, and continued (with important differences) by the emerging Laudian establishment. All of the main branches of seventeenth-century churchmanship, as Patrick Collinson argues, 'breathed a neo-clerical ideology.'[50] Among the clergy the main distinction was between the traditionalist who 'identified with the community of which he was a part, shared its round of work and leisure, talked its language, and made little attempt to impose ... an exacting and alien moral code' and 'the professional and godly minister ... a strongly contrasted type. In dress, speech and domestic lifestyle he drew apart from his flock, castigated their sins, and denounced them to the bawdy court.'[51]

Herbert appeals, in *The Country Parson,* to elements of both visions, a fact that may suggest that the contrast was not always so stark. Chapters such as 'The Parson in Circuit' emphasize the pastor's involvement with the daily 'round of work and leisure,' and 'The Parson in Mirth' and 'The Parson Condescending' warn against too-distant relations between clergy and laity. Nevertheless, these chapters attenuate, rather than displace, a prevailing tone of moral severity. If the Parson 'intermingles some mirth in his discourses occasionally' (268) it is to temper the 'generally sad' demeanour of one who 'knows nothing but the Crosse of Christ' and who 'meets continually with two most sad spectacles, Sin, and Misery; God dishonoured every day, and man afflicted' (267). Moreover, as Herbert's poems suggest, sin and misery afflict the priest himself as deeply as they do his parishioners. Even as Herbert's book shares the contemporary emphasis on the special dignity of the parson's position, it turns repeatedly to insist on the spiritual experience shared by the parson and his congregation. Herbert's rhetoric in *The Country Parson* is alternately exclusive and inclusive, uncompromising and conciliatory, identifying and differentiating. To rephrase this point, *The Country Parson* works to defend, consolidate, and advance the new clericalism of the 1620s and 1630s by reconciling it with the older Reformation ideal of the 'priesthood of all believers.'[52]

Davenant's Dilemma: Calvinist Conformity after 1625

The episcopal experience of John Davenant after James's death illustrates the fragility of the Jacobean synthesis. Apart from his participation in the Synod of Dort, Davenant is known to historians mainly for two incidents. The first is a court sermon on predestination, which was delivered in 1630 in the face of royal prohibition of controversial preaching. Davenant was summoned before the Privy Council to be disciplined, and he was subsequently rebuked by King Charles.[53] Writing of the matter to Archbishop Ussher, Davenant's friend and long-time correspondent, Samuel Ward expressed himself 'right sorry, the established doctrine of our Church should be thus questioned.'[54] Though Davenant submitted to correction and sought official reconciliation, he seems to have held fast to his views. He continued to write on the subject, declaring in his 1634 *Determinationes* 'that men were predestined to be accepted and rejected, as soon as fallen and sunk into a condition of misery by their own fault; so that this state of corruption is the foreseen condition of the subject, for either delivering any man through the good will of election, or abandoning him by the decree of reprobation.'[55] Nevertheless, Davenant is typical of the Jacobean Calvinists who continued in their posts into Charles's reign, and who seem to have been willing to endure a great deal of restraint in order to retain their positions of influence. Perhaps they recalled the unhappy outcome of Grindal's confrontation with Queen Elizabeth. As Margo Todd has argued, '[d]isobedience which could result in the loss of a pulpit was called for only by an order which clearly so undermined the evangelical message as to destroy it.'[56] The Jacobean bishops and dons like Davenant and Ward seem to have been attempting to preserve under Charles the tacit bargain they had made with King James at Hampton Court.

Their reasons for doing so are suggested by the other important incident in which Davenant was involved, the case of Henry Sherfield, prominent common lawyer, Recorder of Salisbury, and 'the most eminent member of a small, but temporarily dominant, puritan oligarchy' in the Cathedral town.[57] This group was responsible for a sustained program of godly social reform in Salisbury, a program Davenant opposed.[58] In 1630 the select vestry of St Edmund's parish authorized the removal of an allegedly idolatrous painted window from the parish church. Bishop Davenant countermanded the order, but Sherfield took it upon himself to destroy the window, an offense for which he was prosecuted in Star Chamber and fined £500. According to historian Paul Slack, Sherfield's parliamentary career as 'a fierce antagonist of Buckingham, an opponent of Montague and Arminianism, and a critic of the raising of tonnage and poundage' helps explain 'why this banal, somewhat ludicrous case should come before so illustrious a court.'[59] But Davenant's position in the case requires further explication. After all, he too was, at least theologically, an opponent of Arminianism. Why, in this case, do we find him on the side of Arminians like Laud and Neile, who sought to make an example of Sherfield? Slack points out that both Sherfield and Davenant were caught between competing pressures; it seems likely that, in some measure, Davenant shared the resentment expressed by Laud at Sherfield's trial over lay encroachment on episcopal authority, a resentment that would also help explain Davenant's opposition to the innovative schemes of poor relief instigated by Sherfield's faction in Salisbury. In his condemnation of Sherfield, a common lawyer by profession, Laud 'treated the reasonings of the lawyers [i.e., the lawyers *in* the chamber, who had dared to argue for leniency] as an assault upon the episcopal order.'[60] As J. Sears McGee has argued, 'a deep conviction that the reformation had deprived clergymen of authority and influence that was essential to the health of religion, monarchy, and society' was central to Laud's position.[61] Conforming Calvinist bishops like Davenant, and the famous defender of episcopacy Joseph Hall, might have differed from Laud on the question of whether the Reformation was responsible for the erosion of clerical dignity and influence, but on the central question they were united. Whatever their theological differences, both Laud and Davenant considered the church's dignity and the authority of its officials as paramount, and saw some manifestations of lay religious zeal as threats.

If increased clerical prestige had been James's reward for Calvinist conformity, the Sherfield incident demonstrates both the failure of James's strategy entirely to dissipate Puritan ambitions, and the jealousy with which those who had accepted the King's offer guarded their reward. As Peter Lake points out, the 'apparent latitudinarian stability of the church under James owed a great deal to its protean capacity to ...

sustain a variety of mutually exclusive views.'[62] Even James had difficulty with his own scheme, and he issued directions to preachers in 1622 to curb public preaching on inflammatory and doctrinally sensitive subjects. As such restrictions increased steadily with the growing Arminian ascendancy of the late 1620s and early 1630s, dissenting voices emerged. Sherfield himself was no radical nonconformist. He had 'been accustomed to kneel at the reception of the Communion, and had been active in punishing separatists,'[63] but as a 'Puritan magistrate' he seems to have felt the need to both 'cleanse his parish from idolatry and superstition and demonstrate the town's independence of the Cathedral Close ... to assert his local authority.'[64] A Calvinist bishop like Davenant, who had pursued the Jacobean program and made a place for himself in the church hierarchy, carried on James's struggle to eliminate such lay challenges to episcopal authority, even as his episcopal brethren increasingly denounced Jacobean orthodoxy as Puritanism. Men like Davenant had staked everything on getting and holding a position of influence in the church and now found themselves struggling to keep it.

George Herbert and Calvinist Conformity

Given the extremely controversial nature of any public pronouncement on matters of faith and worship in the late 1620s and early 1630s, it seems remarkable that anyone would be inclined to undertake such a risky venture as composing and publishing a pastoral manual. And yet to have finished *The Country Parson* in 1632, Herbert must have settled on the project very early in his pastoral career, perhaps even before his ordination as priest in 1630. This suggests a sense of urgency and purpose entirely at odds with the persistent image of Herbert 'ebbing out his days in vanishingly obscure Bemerton.'[65] Cristina Malcolmson is perhaps closer to the mark in suggesting that Herbert 'may have understood his transition from urban gentleman to country parson as ... a shift from a social to an ecclesiastical elite' and that his escape from 'the pressurized competition of an urban and courtly career' nevertheless indicates 'a modern emphasis on employment and labour as the source of an individual's social significance.'[66] There is little reason to assume that George Herbert expected to end his days as a humble parish priest, though a period of exemplary service in that capacity might have seemed a prerequisite to further advancement. As Ian Green has argued, many seventeenth-century university men now had to 'serve an ecclesiastical apprenticeship on the lower rungs of the ladder' and try to 'work their way up.'[67] Moreover, Bemerton should not be seen as a particularly obscure first parish, either geographically or politically, situated as it was between the cathedral town of Salisbury and Wilton House, the seat of Herbert's kinsmen, the Earls of Pembroke, who were among the most powerful men in England.[68] With the assassination of Buckingham in 1628 the monopoly on royal patronage was broken, and Herbert probably had more reason to hope for assistance from his kinsmen than in the early years of Charles's reign.[69] Furthermore, Herbert's predecessor at Bemerton, Walter Curll (admittedly a Laudian), had succeeded Laud as Bishop of Bath and Wells in 1629.[70] Given what we know of the episcopal appointments of the 1630s and Herbert's attachment to Pembroke's anti-Laudian faction, we may well conclude, in hindsight, that Herbert had no *real* prospects, but in 1630 or 1631 this would probably not have been apparent to him.[71]

The man who wrote *The Country Parson*, then, was a man embarking on a career, not a man who despaired of having one. Still, this picture cannot entirely account for the *kind* of book Herbert wrote. In the atmosphere of the early 1630s a book written primarily to gain ecclesiastical preferment, or even merely to avoid provoking the authorities, would have been an emphatically Arminian book: one that emphasized the sacramental and ceremonial aspects of worship and de-emphasized the public godliness that had become associated with Puritanism. But this is not at all the sort of book Herbert wrote. If, as Stanley Stewart insists, Herbert 'lays on no demand for a priestly "life unreprovable,"' he nevertheless sets the standard very high in imagining a man 'exceeding exact in his Life, being holy, just, prudent, temperate, bold, grave in all his wayes' (227).[72] By far, the bulk of the book concerns the parson's pastoral rather than liturgical duties, an emphasis inconsistent with Laudian imperatives. When Herbert's relatives did try to publish *The Country Parson*, some time between 1638 and 1640, the Laudian censors rejected it.[73] Whether the censors would have accepted it in 1633 is difficult to say; certainly Herbert was sailing very close to the wind in an effort to steer a course between a retreating conformist Calvinism and an advancing Arminian authority.

Herbert's effort at mediation is perhaps most clearly evident in his comments on the highly charged subject of kneeling to receive the sacrament, a point on which the *Canons* of 1604 were clear and the Laudians especially adamant:

> For the manner of receiving, as the Parson useth all reverence himself, so
> he administers to none but to the reverent. The Feast indeed requires sit-
> ting, because it is a Feast; but man's unpreparednesse asks kneeling. Hee
> that comes to the Sacrament, hath the confidence of a Guest, and hee that
> kneels, confesseth himself an unworthy one, and therefore differs from
> other Feasters: but hee that sits, or lies, puts up to an Apostle: Contentious-
> nesse in a feast of Charity is more scandall then any posture. (259)

As a defence of kneeling the passage clearly has formalist overtones, so
it is perhaps not surprising that Horton Davies presents it as a classic
exposition of the 'Anglican viewpoint,'[74] and yet it is far from an
unequivocal assertion of Laudian ceremonialism. On the contrary, it
appears that Herbert is attempting to square conformity with Calvinist
consciences and, in doing so, softening the Laudian emphasis on obedience. By beginning with the proposition that 'the Feast ... requires sit-
ting,' Herbert foregrounds the Protestant conception of the Eucharist
as a feast rather than a sacrifice, a conception that, to many, seemed
threatened by the Laudian practice of placing railed-in communion
tables 'altar-wise' at the east end of the nave.[75] Only after establishing an
emphatically Protestant context does Herbert proceed to argue that the
special nature of this feast demands a posture of greater reverence than
might be expected on other occasions.[76] At least two audiences are in
view here: an audience of censors who would not have countenanced a
book of this sort that did not promote uniformity, and an audience of
readers who, judging from Herbert's persuasive tone, must be assumed
to have scruples. Clearly Herbert wants to persuade the scrupulous of
the wisdom and safety of conformity. Nevertheless the last line of the
passage, 'Contentiousnesse in a feast of Charity is more scandall then
any posture,' is a triumph of strategic ambiguity, building on the canonical stipulation that 'no minister ... shall *wittingly* administer ... [the
Communion] but to such as kneele.'[77] Even the *Canons* seem to contem-
plate a situation in which a minister may be unwittingly compelled to
administer the sacrament to a parishioner who surprises him by refusing
to kneel. If Herbert's sentence condemns those parishioners contentious enough to disrupt the order and solemnity of divine services over
an 'indifferent matter,' it also seems to suggest that a minister wishing to
avoid contentiousness himself might sometimes have to tolerate nonconformity.[78] To disrupt the sacrament by insisting on a recipient's
kneeling might be worse than to permit seated participation. After all,
as Herbert makes clear elsewhere, it is the pastor who must take the

greatest pains to avoid scandal (227). Herbert is justly described as a defender of the *via media*, but on the basis of passages like this, a different view of the middle way begins to emerge. What Herbert says about kneeling for communion is neither a simple statement of his own beliefs, nor a slavish formalism, but a complex negotiation among a range of possible formulations: what he thinks he must say, what he might like to say, and what different sorts of readers might need or want to hear.[79]

This is equally true in 'The Parson Arguing,' where handling scruples and problems of conformity, while avoiding scandal, is the specific subject. Here, after insisting on the importance of 'loving, and sweet usage' in winning converts, Herbert rehearses a Socratic approach to reducing both the 'Papist' and the 'Schismatick' (that is, the Puritan nonconformist) to conformity (262–3). But the underlying assumptions and the strategies appropriate to each situation are as different as the bases of disagreement. As Daniel Doerksen points out, 'Herbert implies that attempts to persuade a Papist are likely to involve "fundamental things" whereas in the case of the "Schismatick" it is "things once indifferent being made by the precept of Authority more then indifferent."'[80] The central point is clear, and appealing to Laudian sensibilities: authority makes obedience in 'indifferent' matters essential. Yet Herbert's recommended strategy displays an implicit respect for the motives of the 'Schismatick,' a respect lacking in the treatment of the 'Papist.' Identifying the church as the 'pillar' of the Catholic recusant's cause, he suggests a line of questioning designed to undermine that pillar by insinuating the authority of Scripture: 'whether ... [the church] hath a rule, whether having a rule, it ought not to be guided by it' (263). His recommended approach to the Protestant nonconformist is quite different. Here, despite the 'indifferent' points in dispute, Herbert implicitly acknowledges that the fear of scandal is central to the cause of the 'Schismaticks.'[81] Rather than supply an alternative to the fear of scandal, he suggests endorsing and capitalizing on that motive, arguing that 'in disobeying there is scandall also' (263). Paradoxically, Herbert assumes that the nonconformist with the 'fundamental' disagreement has the least credible basis for that disagreement and that the nonconformist who disagrees over an 'indifferent' matter does so for laudable, if misguided, reasons. Whereas the Roman Catholic's loyalty to the church is a barrier to be overcome, the scrupulous Puritan conscience is an asset to be harnessed and exploited. By avoiding the word 'authority' in referring to the Roman Catholic Church, Herbert avoids the obvious charge of undermining and reinforcing authority simultaneously. Obe-dience to a 'foreign' church is a danger to the English social order; obedience to the national state church, to legitimate 'authority,' is a virtue. Herbert's insistence on gentle persuasion, 'voyd of all conten-tiousnesse,' reveals both the traces of the virulent anti-Roman rhetoric that had been a mainstay of English Protestant discourse for more then fifty years, and the care he has taken to attenuate that rhetoric in the face of Laudian disapproval.[82]

'An Humblenesse Very Sutable'

Herbert's conformity, then, is far from static. Rather, it is constructed through a process of assertion and qualification, advance and retreat, a process very much like the self-correction we encounter repeatedly in his poetry.[83] This strategy, moreover, involves multiple axes of debate, not merely between puritan and formalist stances, but also between cler-icalist and populist ones. Herbert's movement along this second axis is particularly evident in the moral theology of *The Country Parson*, which modulates between the emerging Protestant casuistry of the seven-teenth century and the older Protestant insistence on the absolute suffi-ciency of Scripture as a moral and spiritual guide. On the one hand, Herbert's ideal parson 'greatly esteemes ... cases of conscience, wherein he is much versed' (230). On the other hand, Scripture remains 'the chief and top of his knowledge ... the book of books, the storehouse and magazene of life and comfort ... In the Scriptures hee findes four things; Precepts for life, Doctrines for knowledge, Examples for illustration, and Promises for comfort' (228). As Camille Wells Slights has noted, the formation of an English Protestant casuistry both by Puritans like William Perkins and William Ames and by formalists like Robert Sanderson and Jeremy Taylor demanded a 'move away from biblical literalism,' a move connected to the increasing 'concentration on prac-tical divinity during this period.'[84] At times, Herbert is willing to make such a move – witness the figurative re-invention of the creation story in 'The Pulley' – but he also voices anxiety, even outrage, at any 'who deny the Scripture to be perfect' (247).

Several of *The Country Parson*'s later chapters are strongly legalistic and casuistical, emphasizing the specialized knowledge necessary to adjudicate cases of conscience.[85] In 'The Parson's Eye,' for example, Herbert suggests that a man storing up mony for his necessary provisions, both in present for his family, and in future for his children, hardly perceives when his storing becomes unlawfull: yet is there a period for his storing, and a point, or center, when his storing, which was even now good, passeth from good to bad. Wherefore the Parson being true to his businesse, hath exactly sifted the definitions of all vertues, and vices; especially canvasing those, whose natures are most stealing, and beginnings uncertaine. (264–5)

It is the clergyman's special skill, or in Herbert's telling phrase, his 'businesse,' to help the parishioner ascertain the boundaries of virtue. Like his superior education, the parson's professional expertise in matters of conscience sets him apart from his congregation. This stance is neither distinctively Puritan nor formalist; it is a manifestation of the 'neo-clerical ideology' common to the competing orthodoxies of Herbert's day.

Other gestures in the text attenuate the emphasis on clerical expertise. Reinforcing the traditionally Protestant insistence on the authority of Scripture, Herbert repeatedly resorts to the use of self-effacing first-person pronouns in the casuistical chapters. Thus the discussion of covetousness in 'The Parson's Eye' shifts from the detached third-person perspective to an involved first-person stance: 'if ... I either do nothing, or pinch, and scrape, and squeeze blood undecently ... I am Covetous' (265). When he finds himself on the clericalist ground shared by Puritans, formalists, and churchmen in between, Herbert turns to answer or disarm anticlerical objections. Though it is a clergyman's unique 'businesse' to sift the definitions of virtue and vice, he is nevertheless susceptible to the same frailties and temptations as anyone else. In fact his qualification to pronounce on matters of conscience depends precisely on this shared experience of temptation, and on his evident godliness: 'the Parson having studied, and mastered all his lusts and affections within, and the whole Army of Temptations without, hath ever so many sermons ready penn'd, as he hath victories' (278). The parson may stand above his parishioners, but that stature, Herbert repeatedly insists, must be earned through the spiritual trials common to all Christians. For Patrick Collinson these are the pious idealizations that make it impossible to read *The Country Parson* as a genuine practical handbook. Yet they serve the distinctly practical purpose of negotiating among the competing contemporary visions of the parish clergy, not all of which were flattering.

The same sort of modulation takes place in many of *The Temple*'s poems of pastoral vocation. In 'Aaron,' for instance, the opposition is between the ideal exemplified in the dress of 'true Aarons' (l. 5) as described in Exodus 28, and the 'Defects and darkness' (l. 7) of the 'Poore priest' (l. 10) who is the poem's speaker. For a reconciliation to take place, for the 'Poore priest' to become a true Aaron, he must undergo precisely the same conversion that every believer undergoes. He must relinquish priestly distinction, as he does in stanzas three and four, before he can re-emerge 'new drest' in Christ (l. 20) and call to his people in the final stanza. Clerical vestments, those controversial symbols of priestly dignity, signify the experience of having 'put on Christ,' an experience that, according to the Apostle, erases social distinctions (Gal. 3:25–9). 'The Priesthood' and 'The Windows' contain a similar dialectic between the excellence and power of God's 'Blest Order' ('Priesthood' l. 1) and the human deficiencies of the 'foul and brittle' speaker (l. 11). In 'The Windows,' man is 'a brittle crazie glasse' (l. 2), scarcely capable of conveying the divine word, until Christ makes his own life 'shine within / The holy Preachers' (ll. 7–8). Like these poems, *The Country Parson* is a texture of oppositions. Its opening pages offer a catalogue of dualistic formulations: the parson's 'Desires and Performances,' his duty 'to please [God]' and 'to feed my Flocke,' 'the Form and Character of a true Pastour,' and his 'Dignity ... and ... Duty' (224, 225). Even as Herbert praises the *via media* in chapter XIII, the authorial voice draws on the scripturally based dualities so prevalent in Protestant literature, whether Puritan or formalist: 'For these two rules [order and edification] comprize and include the double object of our duty, God, and our neighbour; the first being for the honour of God; the second for the benefit of our neighbor' (246).[86] This emphasis on a 'double object' is, in effect, an assertion of the treatise's task as well as the parson's, and the success of one is bound up with the success of the other.

Herbert's formulation of the double object commonplace echoes that of Richard Hooker, the great apologist for the *via media*, in Book 5 of his *Lawes of Ecclesiasticall Politie*: 'the object of ... [public ministry] is both God and Men ... So that the summe of our whole labour in this kinde is to honour God and to save men.'[87] But if there are surface similarities here, there are also important differences. Herbert draws support for his account of order and edification in the church from 1 Cor. 14, a central text for the doctrine of the 'priesthood of all believers,' and for the Protestant insistence on a preaching ministry: 'he who prophesies edifies the church' (1 Cor. 14:4).[88] Moreover, Herbert's first-person plural pronoun, 'our duty,' seems much more inclusive than Hooker's 'our whole labour,' which functions as part of an us versus them construction. The parson's duty to honour God and serve his neighbour is one he shares with all Christians. Hooker, anticipating the Laudians, emphasizes the distinction between the clergy and the laity: 'Ministeriall power is a marke of separation, because it severeth them that have it from other men and maketh them a speciall *order* consecrated unto the service of the most high in thinges wherewith others may not meddle.'[89] Hooker's elevated conception of clerical vocation does find repeated expression in *The Country Parson*, but as in this instance, there is almost always a gentle counterpoint serving to soften that emphasis and reduce the distance between the parson and his flock.

The chapters of *The Country Parson* are also punctuated with their own shifts and modulations in emphasis, which work to sustain the balance between humility and elevation by emphasizing the heavenly part of the parson's double object. Chapter IIII, 'The Parsons Knowledg,' is a fine example, employing the technique of re-invention that Helen Vendler finds characteristic of many poems in *The Temple*. In its opening lines the chapter offers an elevated conception of the ideal parson, who is 'full of all knowledg.' As a teacher of his parishioners he 'condescends even to the knowledge of tillage, and pastorage, and makes great use of them in teaching, because people by what they understand, are best led to what they understand not' (228). These are lines to which it will be necessary to return in chapter 4 of this study. For now it suffices to observe that Herbert's chapter follows a similar course, from an emphasis on what the parson understands to what he understands not. Almost immediately, the authorial voice begins limiting and refining this expansive model: the chapter's subject becomes not the parson's entire knowledge, but only the 'chief and top ... the book of books, the storehouse and magazene of life and comfort, the holy Scriptures' (228). With this narrower focus and renewed scripturalism comes a diminution in the parson's stature, from the paternalistic teacher to the dependent child who 'sucks, and lives' (228) nourished by God's Word. When Herbert turns to the pastor's means 'for the understanding of [the Scriptures]' he repeats the process. 'The means he useth are first, a holy Life ... The second means is prayer, which if it be necessary even in temporall things, how much more in things of another world, where the well is deep, and we have nothing of our selves to draw with?' (228–9). The emphasis on prayer and 'things of another world' triggers a shift in focus from the parson's capacities to his incapacities, and, through the

use of the first-person plural pronoun, a corresponding identification of
the speaker and the parson with the rest of fallen humanity. At the same
time, the coldness and detachment of the predominant third-person
mode noticeably abates. The penultimate sentence of the chapter
clinches the point, qualifying the initial assertion that 'The Countrey
Parson is full of all knowledg': 'as one Countrey doth not bear all things,
that there may be a Commerce; so neither hath God opened, or will
open all to one, that there may be a traffick in knowledg between the
servants of God, for the planting both of love, and humility' (229). Like
the adult-child analogy, the agricultural image from the beginning
of the chapter has been inverted. The parson is transformed from the
metaphorical farmer, planting the seed of knowledge in his parishioners, to the soil in which seeds of 'love and humility' are planted.[90]

Again in chapter VI, 'The Parson Praying,' a subtle modulation
occurs from assurance to doubt to assurance again, and from an outward to an inward to an outward focus:

> The Countrey Parson, when he is to read divine services, composeth him-
> selfe to all possible reverence; lifting up his heart and hands, and eyes, and
> using all other gestures which may expresse a hearty, and unfeyned devo-
> tion. This he doth, first, as being truly touched and amazed with the Maj-
> esty of God, before whom he then presents himself; yet not as himself
> alone, but as presenting with himself the whole Congregation, whose sins
> he then beares, and brings with his own to the heavenly altar to be bathed,
> and washed in the sacred Laver of Christs blood. Secondly, as this is the
> true reason of his inward feare, so he is content to expresse this outwardly
> to the utmost of his power; that being first affected himself, hee may affect
> also his people, knowing that no Sermon moves them so much to a rever-
> ence, which they forget againe, when they come to pray, as a devout behav-
> iour in the very act of praying. (231)

Here the overdetermined character of Herbert's prescriptions, his
simultaneous participation in a series of interconnected debates, is
clearly evident. In describing the parson praying, Herbert must negotiate not only between the Puritan ideal of impassioned extemporaneous
prayer and formalist love of orderly ceremonial, but also between clericalist and populist conceptions of pastoral conduct. The image of the
priest 'presenting with himself the whole Congregation, whose sins he
then beares, and brings with his own to the heavenly altar to be bathed,
and washed in the sacred Laver of Christs blood' has some of the sacer-

dotal quality associated with Laudian formalism. And yet it is important to remember that this is a chapter about prayer, not about the Eucharist. Even as Herbert adopts the ceremonialist rhetoric of the Laudian avant-garde, he aligns that rhetoric with the sacrament of the word. As Terry Sherwood has noted, Herbert follows Calvin and Cranmer in seeking to resolve the Protestant dilemma of a Eucharist that is theologically central but no longer uniquely propitiatory by mingling 'Eucharist and prayer ... treating them as inextricable expressions of the same truth.'[91] Here, as in Herbert's poem 'Prayer' [I], prayer is 'the Churches banquet.' It is to the heavenly altar, not to the earthly communion table, that the pastor brings his own sins and those of his congregation.[92] In the insistence on gestures designed to 'expresse a hearty, and unfeyned devotion' there is an attempt, arguably rather forced, to achieve, within the confines of a set liturgy, the qualities of 'assurance, simplicity, naturalness, intimacy, and a moving directness in the approach to God' that Puritans associated with extemporaneous prayer.[93] There is also a clear effort to diminish the distance between pastor and congregation. As he stands in God's stead before the congregation, Herbert's pastor also stands before God as an ordinary sinner. In the passage's close, a complementary inversion takes place of the earlier authorial observation that 'the way to please ... [God] is to feed my Flocke diligently and faithfully' (224). Herbert's ideal parson feeds the flock – 'moves them to a reverence' – by performing his own reverence, directing his attention not toward them, as in a sermon, but toward God, through 'devout behaviour in the very act of praying.'

'Sermons are dangerous things'

To fully appreciate the complexity of the ecclesiastical, theological, and personal pressures and opportunities to which Herbert responds in *The Country Parson*, we need to examine his treatment not only of particular theological and liturgical issues, but also of the relationship between issues like prayer, preaching, and personal conduct. The debates among Puritans, conforming Calvinists, and formalists, though they often crystalized around crucial symbolic issues, usually involved matters of degree, balance, and proportion. Where was the boundary between decent order and idolatrous ostentation in ritual, church furnishings, or clerical apparel? What was the most effective means to preach the divine word? A godly, learned, preaching ministry had been a central objective of the Reformation from the outset, and neglect of preaching, ignorance, and moral laxity were the most frequent charges brought against the clergy by advocates of continuing reform. Conversely, some of the highest authorities in church and state came increasingly, in the 1620s and 1630s, to view controversial preaching as socially and politically disruptive.[94] In 1622, James issued his 'Directions Concerning Preachers,' severely restricting the subjects on which the lower clergy could preach, forbidding those 'under the degree ... of a bishop, or a dean' to explore 'the deep points of predestination, election, reprobation, or of the universality, efficacy, resistibility or irresistibillity of God's grace.'[95] The 'Directions' were prepared not by any member of the Durham House group, but by John Williams, the Calvinist Bishop of Lincoln, who was soon to be George Herbert's first ecclesiastical patron, and later, the 'most famous opponent'of Laud's altar policy.[96] Even John Donne, who preached in support of the restrictive 'Directions' in 1622, echoes (elsewhere) some elements of the 'Puritan' position when he insists on the minister's 'actuall preaching' as the cornerstone of clerical calling, but unlike his Puritan contemporaries, he plays down the importance of education and personal godliness, arguing that 'learning, and other good parts, and an exemplar life fall into second places,' at least insofar as the congregation is concerned.[97] Richard Hooker, conversely, anticipates the Laudian position in asserting that the minister's role in public prayer is paramount, and that the duty to preach is satisfied, in part, by the 'interminglinge of lessons with prayers.' In fact for Hooker, 'The ministers greatnes or meanesse of knowledg to doe other thinges, his aptnes or insufficiencie *otherwise then by reading* to instruct the flock standeth in this place as a straunger with whome our forme of common prayer hath nothing to doe.'[98] As Peter Lake has argued, Hooker's central place in the 'Anglican' mainstream was granted only retroactively. In his own day he 'was breaking new ground among English Protestants' in constructing 'an image of the minister as an intercessor, or mediator, through prayer, between God and the people.'[99] What we see in Davenant, Williams, Hooker, and Donne is not an achieved *via media* with an identifiable character, but four distinct and rather strained attempts to construct one. In *The Country Parson* we see much the same thing.

Herbert's position on prayer, preaching, and personal holiness seems, at first glance, confused; certainly it is a composite of many elements. But given the range of stances available, and the potential costs of a misstep, a mixed position might represent a strategic advantage. 'Sermons,' Herbert writes in his chapter on 'The Parson Preaching,' 'are dangerous things.' In the immediate context he clearly means dangerous to the spiritually complacent parishioner, since 'none goes out of Church as he came in, but either better, or worse' (233). This witty formulation may suggest a 'Puritan' faith in the redemptive power of preaching the Gospel. It may also contain a veiled acknowledgment of the political danger involved in embracing such a position too openly. Given this, it is not surprising to find, in *The Country Parson*, some sceptical remarks about the efficacy of sermons that seem remarkably close to Hooker's formalism: 'no Sermon moves [the congregation] so much to a reverence, which they forget againe, when they come to pray, as a devout behaviour in the very act of praying' (231). This is a sentiment Herbert repeats in his praise of catechizing, the pastoral activity prescribed as a substitute for Sunday afternoon sermons in the 'Directions Concerning Preachers':[100] 'whereas in Sermons there is a kinde of state, in Catechizing there is an humblenesse very sutable to Christian regeneration, which exceedingly delights him as by way of exercise upon himself, and by way of preaching to himself, for the advancing of his own mortification' (255). Yet the rationale Herbert offers for the policy, that the catechist is humbler than the homilist, is one calculated to appeal not to a formalist mentality preoccupied with ecclesiastical authority, but to populist and Puritan conceptions of pastoral duty. Fewer sermons, Herbert insists, do not mean a diminished commitment to preaching because catechizing is also preaching, albeit a more individualized, engaged, and diffuse form.[101] Herbert's solution to the tension between the Reformation's traditional demand for more preaching and the pressure from church and state for less is to oscillate not merely between those two positions, but also between broad and narrow definitions of preaching. In effect he distinguishes between preaching and sermons, allowing for more preaching and yet fewer (or shorter) sermons. This distinction allows him to assert at the beginning of his chapter 'The Parson Preaching' that 'The Countrey Parson preacheth constantly, the pulpit is his joy and his throne' and at the end of the same chapter that he 'exceeds not an hour in preaching' (232, 235). Constant preaching means, in this context, not protracted preaching, but uninterrupted preaching, preaching that manifests itself in all aspects of the godly life: 'the purity of his mind breaking out, and dilating it selfe even to his body, cloaths and habitation' (228). As any chapter in *The Country Parson* will testify, Herbert differs from both Donne and Hooker in stressing the importance of 'an exemplar life,' an emphasis that places him closer to the Puritan 'experimental' theologians than either Donne or Hooker. When travelling with others he 'begins good discourses, such as may edify,' like Bunyan's pilgrims (251). When visiting the sick he makes 'continuall use' of 'all the points of consolation' provided by scripture (249). On weekday rounds he preaches as his parishioners go about their work, admonishing 'that they so labour, as neither to labour anxiously, nor distrustfully, nor profanely' (247). This ideal of constant preaching may be understood as an answer to Hooker's ceremonialist argument that 'publique prayer is a dutie intire in it selfe, a dutie requisite to be performed much oftener than sermons can possiblie be made.'[102] Herbert might almost be said to substitute preaching, or perhaps more broadly, religious instruction, for public prayer in Hooker's formulation, asserting paradoxically (and perhaps disarmingly to both Laudian critics of Puritan sermonizing and Puritan pedants) that preaching must be performed 'much oftener than sermons can possibly be made.'

The politics of preaching between 1626, when Herbert entered deacon's orders, and 1632, when he finished *The Country Parson*, meant that such an ambiguous and evasive position might be the only safe alternative to an emphatically Laudian one, for a man who had not yet attained a secure position in the church or who hoped to advance. This was the period of the most momentous changes in George Herbert's life, and one of the most precarious in English ecclesiastical history. *The Country Parson*'s guarded ecclesiastical politics reflect the pressures of the moment. The 'Directions Concerning Preachers' had, in effect, restricted preaching on controversial subjects to the universities (leaving aside occasional sermons by higher clergy); in 1626 and again in 1628 royal proclamations extended the restriction to university preaching. At Cambridge, John Davenant's friend and successor as Lady Margaret professor of Divinity, Samuel Ward, had planned to defend a thesis on absolute predestination at the 1626 Commencement. He was prevented by Bishop Neile, who on 16 June transmitted to him the two-day-old royal proclamation for 'the establishing of the peace and quiet of the Church of England.' A month later, on 13 July, Herbert performed 'his last public act as orator' when he spoke at the York House ceremonies celebrating the installation of the Duke of Buckingham as Chancellor of Cambridge University.[103] According to Nicholas Tyacke it was this event more than any other that signalled the 'muzzling of Cambridge Calvinism.'[104]

The fact that Herbert made this oration himself deserves some scrutiny. For nearly two years, since he took leave from the University to sit in the Parliament of 1624, Herbert's Orator's duties were performed by deputies. His earlier performance before the Duke of Buckingham had been a particularly difficult one: the 1623 speech on the return of Prince Charles from Spain in which he 'courageously extolled the blessings of peace' to a prince and a chief minister who were, in the view of some commentators, already 'determined on war.'[105] Moreover, Herbert had good reason to be elsewhere in July 1626. His installation as Canon of Lincoln Cathedral on 5 July 'was ... carried out by proxy, perhaps because of his involvement in plans for the ceremonies honouring the Duke.'[106] No text of the 1626 oration survives, but the circumstantial evidence suggests that Herbert was taking advantage of the opportunity to make a good impression on the chief patron of the Arminian bishops and the chief advisor of the new king, before finally severing his university connections and embarking on a church career.[107] In doing so, Herbert was entering the world of everyday affairs rather than retiring to the countryside. Cambridge had been a haven of sorts, but no longer. With John Williams (a Calvinist conformist bishop) as a new ecclesiastical patron, and with influential family connections, George Herbert set out to make a career in the Church of England at the most difficult time imaginable. If *The Country Parson* – Herbert's idealized vision of the vocation he was embracing – is a perplexing book, it is perplexing in ways clearly connected to the perplexities of the early Caroline church. *The Country Parson* constructs an elusive, dynamic *via media* by setting opposing conceptions of the parish ministry into complementary and contradictory play, defending formalist practices in terms designed to appeal to the godly, defending Puritan practices in formalist terms, defending clericalist practices in lay-populist terms. It deliberately adopts and adapts the discourses of potential adversaries in an effort to secure an audience.

chapter three

The *Country Parson* and the
Enclosure of Professional Fields

THe Countrey Parson desires to be all to his Parish, and not onely a Pastour, but a Lawyer also, and a Phisician. Therefore hee endures not that any of his Flock should go to Law; but in any Controversie, that they should resort to him as their Judge. To this end, he hath gotten to himself some insight in things ordinarily incident and controverted, by experience, and by reading some initiatory treatises in the Law, with *Daltons* Justice of Peace, and the Abridgements of the Statutes, as also by discourse with men of that profession ... Now as the Parson is in Law, so is he in sicknesse also: if there be any of his flock sick, hee is their Physician, or at least his Wife, of whom in stead of the qualities of the world, he asks no other, but to have the skill of healing a wound, or helping the sick. But if neither himselfe, nor his wife have the skil, and his means serve, hee keepes some young practicioner in his house for the benefit of his Parish, whom yet he ever exhorts not to exceed his bounds, but in tickle cases to call in help. If all fail, then he keeps good correspondence with some neighbour Phisician, and entertaines him for the Cure of his Parish.

> *A Priest to the Temple, or The Country Parson*
> *His Character and Rule of Holy Life,*
> Chapter XXIII, 'The Parson's Completenesse'

In the last chapter, I described *The Country Parson* as an intricate texture of discursive appropriations in which Herbert deploys the customary terms, phrases, and ideological allegiances of various ecclesiastical and theological parties and postures in the service of a Jacobean-style Calvinist conformity. But as I also suggested, *The Country Parson* is no straightforward statement of certain ecclesiological and theological positions. What conclusions can be drawn in these areas must be extracted from the book's pursuit of its central objective: to describe the character of an emerging early-modern clerical profession. To better understand *The Country Parson* as an exercise in professional self-fashioning, it is vital, therefore, to situate it in the context of other professional discourses. Traditionally, in medieval and early modern European cultures, there were three 'learned professions,' law, medicine, and divinity, each ostensibly requiring either university study or other advanced academic training such as that provided at the Inns of Court (though in practice, only an upper stratum of practitioners in each profession had such training).[1] By the eighteenth century, these professions, along with the military officer corps, had emerged as the respectable career options for younger sons of the gentry and also as the occupations that conferred a certain honorary gentility on practitioners of humbler birth.[2] Yet these occupations were only gradually beginning to meet the criteria that modern sociologists use to define a profession: social prestige linked to a clearly delineated body of formal, specialized knowledge, and 'labour market shelters' or mechanisms of 'social closure' designed to restrict unauthorized practice.[3] As Michael A. Hicks writes, 'taking ... [the] criteria of "a clearly defined and delimited membership with a corporate identity and a clear detachment from the laity" there were clearly no professions in the later middle ages.'[4] All three learned professions were, in the early modern period, engaged in simultaneous, overlapping, and often competing processes of self-definition. Just as sixteenth-century landowners had begun to enclose traditional common fields in the name of agricultural 'improvement,' the emergent early modern professions sought increasingly to enclose areas of common human endeavour as exclusive professional 'fields.' The purpose of this chapter is to examine *The Country Parson* in the context of these social and discursive processes. What sort of social role did the members of each of these groups play? How did clergy, lawyers, and physicians define their roles in relation to the laity, to other acknowledged social and political authorities (church, crown, and local gentry), and to one another? To further specify the question, how did the clergy define its role in relation to that of lawyers and physicians? Herbert's *Country Parson* is a uniquely valuable book where these questions are concerned because it systematically employs the rival discourses of law and medicine in its attempt to delineate the country parson's 'Character and Rule of Holy Life.'

As a prelude to this investigation it is useful to reflect, at least briefly, on the situation of these three professional groups at the beginning of the twenty-first century. Lawyers, as reviled as ever, are nevertheless acknowledged to be central to the function of the industrial and post-industrial state. Most citizens in western liberal democracies assume, tacitly, that passing and enforcing legislation is the essence of what governments do, and legislation requires lawyers. Physicians are in a slightly different but no less central situation. When a contemporary Canadian, European, or American, turns to a member of one of the 'learned professions' for advice, it is more likely to be a medical doctor than either a lawyer or a member of the clergy. To take another sort of measure, the most popular book of advice on rearing children written in English in the second half of this century was written by a physician, Dr Benjamin Spock. It takes a slight mental adjustment to see just how extraordinary this is. In the seventeenth century (indeed, I suspect in any century before the twentieth) a book like Dr Spock's *Baby and Child Care*, written by a physician, would have been more or less unthinkable. Yet despite the commonplace notion that in times of greater generational continuity such information was passed on orally rather than in books, there were actually many books of advice on rearing children,[5] but such books were almost invariably written by clergymen, not by physicians. The clergy played a similarly prominent role in the business of the early modern state. When we think of the most influential advisers to English monarchs of the early modern period, churchmen are high on the list: More, Wolsey, Cranmer, and Laud. We would be hard pressed to name a member of the clergy who wields anything like this kind of influence today. Clearly, then, something quite dramatic has happened to the social prestige and influence of the clergy between the early modern and the modern world. The other two acknowledged learned professions, not to mention the others that have emerged in industrial and post-industrial societies, have almost entirely displaced the clergy from their position of influence in personal and civic affairs. It is important to recognize that it was not always so. Clearly, in the early modern period, the clergy were still contenders for the kind of influence from which they are now excluded, even if that position was becoming precarious.[6] One important objective of *The Country Parson* is to consolidate and extend that influence. That the struggle in which Herbert's book participates was eventually lost should not blind us to its importance at a time when the outcome was in doubt.

The study of professions and professional discourses has become

increasingly important to historians and literary historians of early modern England, professionals who are themselves jockeying for position on
the boundary between adjacent disciplines. The sceptical response of
many historians to literary 'new historicism,' with its heavy reliance on
the theoretical work of Michel Foucault, illustrates both late twentieth-
century professional jostling and the need for further research into professions and professionalism. David Cressy's charge of 'anachronism
and dislocation' against Foucaultian-influenced literary historical studies may be based on a misreading of Foucault, attributing to his work a
greater emphasis on centralization and state apparatus than it actually
displays.[7] But Cressy's charge also depends, at least implicitly, on the
view that the 'rise of professions' as instruments of social control is
closely linked to the beginnings of urbanization and industrialization in
the eighteenth century.[8] However, many historians of early modern
England have challenged this view in the last fifteen years or so, exploring the training, practice, and social role of the emerging professions in
the sixteenth and seventeenth centuries, in rural as well as urban areas.[9]
As Wilfred Prest writes, 'both the numbers and socio-economic impact
of ... professional occupations ... in England before the mid-eighteenth
century have been drastically underestimated.'[10] If the professions in
seventeenth-century England had not yet emerged as instruments of
social control, they were in the process of doing so.

The increasing prominence of what Lawrence Stone calls 'semi-
independent professional hierarchies' in the English social order is also
suggested by the sweeping ambitions registered in an idealized professional handbook such as Herbert's *Country Parson*.[11] Herbert's declara-
tion that 'The Countrey Parson desires to be all to his Parish, and not
onely a Pastour, but a Lawyer also, and a Phisician' is part of a web of
allusions to, and borrowings from, the burgeoning early modern discourse of callings and professions, out of which raw material he fashions
his portrait of an idealized rural clergyman.[12] Indeed the book implicitly remarks on its own composition when Herbert writes that 'The
Countrey Parson is full of all knowledg. They say, it is an ill Mason that
refuseth any stone: and there is no knowledg, but, in a skilfull hand,
serves either positively as it is, or else to illustrate some other knowledge' (228). Herbert puts this precept into practice, employing his
knowledge of law and medicine 'to illustrate some other knowledge,' in
this case the knowledge of 'the Dignity ... and the Duty' (225) of a parish clergyman in the Church of England. But Herbert's reliance on legal
and medical terminology does more than demonstrate a facility for

similitudes. The analogies and distinctions between the priest, the physician, and the lawyer register *The Country Parson*'s participation in a complex struggle for professional and discursive territory.

Ministering and Administering

Perhaps inevitably, the process of professionalization and self-definition entails a certain amount of aggrandizement at the expense of other established and emergent professional groups. Certainly the increasing prestige and influence of professions generally led, in the early seventeenth century, to interprofessional friction and competition. Herbert's participation in this spirit of aggrandizement is clearly evident in his suggestion that the pastor should 'be all to his Parish' and in the title of the chapter from which that phrase is taken, 'The Parson's Completnesse.' But it is more subtly evident throughout the book. In chapter XV, for example, Herbert remarks that a good pastor. '*in his visiting the sick, or otherwise afflicted ... urgeth ... especially: the participation of the holy Sacrament, how comfortable, and Soveraigne a Medicine it is to all sin-sick souls; what strength, and joy, and peace it administers against all temptations*' (249–50). On the surface there is nothing at all remarkable here. The metaphor of sin as sickness, and of God, Christ, the prophets, and the apostles as physicians, is a biblical and literary commonplace.[13] Moreover, as one who suffered a series of serious illnesses, Herbert was no doubt preoccupied with medical concerns for the most ordinary reasons.[14] As the 'Affliction' poems and 'The Crosse' suggest, this preoccupation seems noticeably to have shaped, and disturbed, his sense of pastoral vocation:

> One ague dwelleth in my bones,
>   Another in my soul (the memorie
> What I would do for thee, if once my grones
>   Could be allow'd for harmonie):
> I am in all a weak disabled thing,
> Save in the sight thereof, where strength doth sting.
>
> ('The Crosse,' ll. 13–18)

Expressing a similar thought more prosaically in a 1622 letter to his mother, Herbert remarks, 'For my self ... I alwaies fear'd sickness more then death, because sickness hath made me unable to perform those Offices for which I came into the world, and must yet be kept in it' (373).

There are additional reasons to linger over Herbert's treatment of the medical/clerical analogy. The specific image of the sacrament as a '*Soveraigne ... Medicine*' depends, at least in part, on the appropriateness of the verb 'administer' in both contexts. The Latin verb *administrare*, in the sense of dispensing or delivering, is used in connection with the sacrament at least as early as the thirteenth century, though I can find no comparably early reference to administering medication.[15] Curiously, however, the OED attributes the earliest English usage of the expression 'to administer the sacrament' to Archbishop Sandys in 1585 (s.v. administer 4a) and dates the idea of administering medication or medical treatment to 1541 (6a).[16] In English then, it looks as though the clerical usage borrows from the medical. Indeed, by the seventeenth century, the notion of administering medication is sufficiently entrenched in medical discourse that it appears in the 1617 charter of the Society of Apothecaries.[17] In this context, it is possible to see in Herbert's '*Soveraigne ... Medicine*' metaphor an attempt to reclaim a bit of discursive territory, by restoring 'administer,' in the sense of 'dispense,' to its 'proper' sacramental context. Herbert employs this strategy in the sanctification of secular love poetry, in the 'Jordan' poems for example. Moreover, he articulates it quite explicitly in the sonnets addressed to his mother, first published in Walton's *Life*:

> My God, where is that ancient heat towards thee,
>   Wherewith whole showls of *Martyrs* once did burn,
>   Besides their other flames? Doth Poetry
> Wear *Venus* Livery? only serve her turn?
> Why are not *Sonnets* made of thee? and layes
>   Upon thine Altar burnt?   (ll. 1–6)

If the language of secular love can be reclaimed for God's service, so too can the language of medicine, and indeed the language of all callings: 'it is an ill Mason that refuseth any stone.' This example is a mere hint, of course, and not a conclusive case, but that hint can be confirmed by exploring the ways Herbert's pastoral manual defines the relationship between priesthood, physic, and law.

The Cure of Bodies and the Cure of Souls

The contested boundary between medical and clerical discourses and duties invites more careful consideration of Herbert's claim that the pastor is 'a Phisician' to his parishioners. Herbert is emphatically not referring, figuratively, to the cure of souls: 'if there be any of his flock sick, hee is their Physician, or at least his Wife, of whom in stead of the qualities of the world, he asks no other, but to have the skill of healing a wound, or helping the sick' (260). Clearly gender roles are as much of an issue here as professional roles, but I want to concentrate first on the parson's participation in the treatment of bodily sickness and injury, and return to the gender issue later. There was, in Herbert's day, a long-standing traditional sanction for clerical medical practice. In the later middle ages 'all "orthodox practitioners" were clerks and came under episcopal jurisdiction, [and] the bishops exercised control over medical practice,' granting licenses to practice in their dioceses even after the College of Physicians had emerged as the professional regulatory body for London physicians.[18] Moreover, the parish church and the parish priest had always played central roles in caring for the sick, especially in times of plague and crisis. With the English Reformation and the disso-lution of the monasteries, most hospitals under the patronage of monas-tic houses were closed, further increasing the share of medical service for which parish clergy were, in effect, responsible.[19] While the majority of priests had no formal medical training, many others, especially the increasing numbers who attended university, do seem to have studied the subject, either formally or informally. Timothie Bright, for example, entered holy orders only after 'a formal medical education and service at St. Bartholomew's Hospital.'[20] By the late sixteenth century, 'a sub-stantial body of priest-physicians existed, who were beyond the control of the College [of Physicians], and who could compete effectively with specialist physicians,' a fact that caused more than a little friction over professional territory.[21]

Beginning with the first Medical Act of 1518, London's learned physi-cians had sought and received the assistance of Crown and Parliament in their efforts to establish a monopoly over medical services in the metropolis. By 1551 the Company of Physicians had received a royal charter and had become the Royal College of Physicians. The College functioned as an elite learned society, as a regulatory body with statu-tory authority to prosecute and fine unlicensed practitioners, and increasingly, as an advisory body on matters of social policy, especially in times of plague and dearth.[22] In its regulatory role, the College tried, in particular, to regulate the practice of apothecaries and surgeons, and to ensure that practising physicians were its members or licentiates.[23] In this they achieved only modest success in the years leading up to the

Civil War, in part because they failed to extend their regulatory activities beyond London. And even in London there were, in addition to holders of Bishops' licences, university graduates in medicine like Thomas Bonham, who refused to seek the College's authorization to practice their profession, sparking one of the most celebrated law cases of the age.[24] In addition, there were hundreds, even thousands, of untrained practitioners, urban and rural, male and female, educated and ignorant: far more than the College could hope to prosecute. Two points need to be made, therefore. The first is that the College and its members were jealous of their authority, prestige, and position, had clear monopolistic aspirations, and had considerable support from the Crown and the Privy Council in pursuing them. Under James and Charles 'a de facto corporate medical policy emerged,' as medical corporations (that is, the apothecaries' and surgeons' companies) were subordinated to the College, and it 'began to advise the Privy Council on matters concerning the health of the metropolis.'[25] The second is that 'the carefully constructed edifice of medical monopolies erected under the Stuarts was highly unstable.'[26] There were simply insufficient numbers of London physicians, with insufficient power, to enforce a true monopoly.

A similar blend of lofty aspiration and limited realization characterizes the public policy role of the early modern College of Physicians. From 1577 on, outbreaks of plague and periods of dearth were answered by the publication, on order of the Privy Council, of printed books of orders. These were compilations of existing statutes, and increasingly in 1630 and 1631, of executive orders instructing Justices of the Peace on measures to prevent the spread of infection and manage food supplies.[27] The plague orders also contained medical advice from the College of Physicians. During the early years of Charles's personal rule, as Paul Slack has shown, this medical advice took on an increasingly social and political cast, reflecting the influential views of Charles's French Royal Physician, Sir Theodore de Mayerne, and the notions of 'positive sovereignty' that were becoming increasingly common in Continental and English political thought.[28] Influenced by Parisian practices, Mayerne advocated new quarantine procedures and the creation of new medical institutions: not just hospitals, but also a twelve-member court or board of health, consisting of four medical advisors, two bishops, two privy councillors, and four officials of the City of London.[29] Prodded by the Privy Council, the College of Physicians endorsed Mayerne's suggestions, eager to extend their advisory role into the treatment of the body politic. In the end these initiatives came to little, but according to Paul Slack, Mayerne's ideas 'cannot be dismissed as the utopian dreams of a single alien physician; they were supported by other members of the medical elite, and they were taken seriously by influential figures at Court and in the Council.'[30]

The frustration resulting from the College's inability to establish either a firm monopoly or a secure advisory role on matters of social and health policy could only amplify physicians' resentment about clerical practitioners. It is no surprise, therefore, that medical men like James Hart and John Cotta, both contemporaries of Herbert, complained bitterly in medical books and controversial tracts that clergymen who practice medicine 'doe wrongfully and injuriously, both contrary to the Law of God and man, intrude upon another weighty profession.'[31] Cotta and Hart are noteworthy because they were neither Londoners nor members of the College of Physicians (both lived and practiced in Northampton), but both held the MD, and Hart at least, held a license from the College. Both men seem to have been as jealous of the privileges conferred by their qualifications as any London court physician. Complaints like Cotta's and Hart's seem to have been commonplace. In the preface to his *Anatomy of Melancholy*, Robert Burton addresses the anticipated objection of 'any Physitian ... grieved that I have intruded into his profession' with characteristic bluster, ridiculing the arbitrary distinction between professions and asserting that sufferers from melancholy 'require a whole Physitian. A Divine in this compound mixt Malady, can do little alone, a Physitian in some kindes of Melancholy much less, both make an absolute cure.'[32] Herbert, having opened the subject on a similarly assertive note, seems to reverse himself, and responds deferentially to such charges in the final lines of his chapter 'The Parson's Completenesse,' when he writes that 'it is a justice and debt to the Common-wealth he lives in, not to incroach on others ' Professions, but to live on his own' (262). In between the self-aggrandizing opening and the deferential close of this chapter, a good deal of professional jostling takes place.

On the subject of medical education, a subject of central importance for the College of Physicians in its attempt to establish a professional monopoly, Herbert insists that it is 'easie for any Scholer to attaine to such a measure of Phisick, as may be of much use to him both for himself, and others. This is done by seeing one Anatomy, reading one Book of Phisick, having one Herball by him' (261). After 1606, fellows of the College had to possess an MD, which required seven years of study beyond the MA, and were further subjected to a rigorous three-part oral examination on physiology, pathology and therapeutics, with questions drawn from a list of seventeen works of Galen and Hippocrates; licentiates of the College were 'only somewhat less academic in their training.'[33] In this context, Herbert's casual-sounding suggestion that 'any Scholer' might become skilled in medicine by perusing a couple of books and observing an anatomy lecture reflects a presumption that caused James Hart and his medical peers considerable distress. Hart might almost have Herbert's words in mind when he derides

> such novices as have perhaps attained to some few scraps of *Latine* in the Grammer-schoole; and perhaps proceeded yet further, to reside some space at the University; and afterwards by reading some Physicke books, take themselves to be sufficiently furnished for the performance of so great a taske, without either instruction or manuduction of able masters skilled in that profession.[34]

As Harold J. Cook has pointed out, the similarities in the humanistic training, professional authority, and practice of the learned physicians and the clergy made them natural rivals.[35] Humanist medical education was more literary than clinical, and both Physicians and Protestant clergy were largely purveyors of advice. Try as they might, neither group was likely to establish a monopoly on that commodity. Leaving aside its contentious preface, Hart's ΚΛINIKH or *The Diet of the Diseased* treats essentially the same subject as Luigi Cornaro's treatise *Temperance and Sobriety*, which George Herbert translated: the maintenance of health through judicious diet. In a sense, therefore, it is the lack of clear distinctions between the qualifications and prerogatives of these two adjacent professions that makes professional friction possible in the first place.

Having defined medical expertise as something 'easie for any Scholer to attaine,' Herbert compounds the insult by insisting on the subordination of medical to divine knowledge:

> Now both the reading of ... [physick], and the knowing of herbs may be done at such times, as they may be an help, and a recreation to more divine studies, Nature serving Grace both in comfort of diversion, and the benefit of application when need requires; as also by way of illustration, even as our Saviour made plants and seeds to teach the people. (261)

Not only is medical knowledge easy to acquire, according to *The Country*

Parson, its function is entirely secondary, as expressions like 'a recreation to more divine studies' and 'Nature serving Grace' clearly intimate. Even when he acknowledges the possibility that a parson may not be competent to treat his sick parishioners, Herbert subordinates the physician to the pastor:

> if neither himselfe, nor his wife have the skil, and his means serve, hee keeps some young practicioner in his house for the benefit of his Parish, whom he yet ever exhorts not to exceed his bounds, but in tickle cases to call in help. If all fail, then he keeps good correspondence with some neighbour Phisician, and entertaines him for the Cure of his Parish. (260–1)

There are two significant points here. The first is the preference for a 'young practicioner,' little better than a domestic servant, who can be directed by the parson even in areas of the parson's incompetence. The second is the suggestion that a 'neighbour Phisician' – who would, if he were well qualified or well known, carry his own social authority and prestige – should be consulted only 'if all fail.' As its opening chapter insists, Herbert's book is concerned to assert and protect the dignity, as well as to define the duty, of a priest in the Church of England. Just as the College of Physicians set out to subordinate and control apothecaries and surgeons as trades practiced under the oversight of a learned profession, Herbert's handbook seeks to subordinate medicine to divinity within a hierarchy of the learned professions.

The examples treated so far are *The Country Parson*'s most explicit challenges to the medical profession, but many of Herbert's professional-discursive border raids are more ambiguous or figurative in nature, as in this passage from chapter XXXIII, 'The Parson's Library':

> the Parson having studied, and mastered all his lusts and affections within, and the whole Army of Temptations without, hath ever so many sermons ready penn'd, as he hath victories. And it fares in this as it does in Physick: He that hath been sick of a Consumption, and knows what recovered him, is a Physitian so far as he meetes with the same disease, and temper; and can much better, and particularly do it, then he that is generally learned, and was never sick. And if the same person had been sick of all diseases, and were recovered of all by things that he knew; there were no such Physician as he, both for skill and tendernesse. Just so it is in Divinity. (278)

'Just so ... in Divinity'? Well perhaps not quite. In the case of the physician, Herbert implicitly argues against an exclusive definition of the medical profession. In this view, anyone who knows how to cure is a physician, 'so far as he meets with the same disease.' Not only is the exclusivity of medical practice under indirect attack, here; there is also a clear challenge to its integrity (in the sense of wholeness or indivisibility). It is possible, Herbert suggests, to be a physician in some cases and not in others, *and*, at least hypothetically, to be a complete physician without ever undertaking the formal study of medicine or obtaining a degree or a license to practice. Indeed the very meaning and application of the title 'physician,' which the College of Physicians would have liked to reserve for the exclusive use of its members and licentiates, is at issue here. But Herbert is not arguing, by analogy, that *anyone* who has conquered his own temptations is a pastor (notwithstanding the doctrine of the priesthood of all believers). Rather, he asserts that a *parson* who has conquered his own temptations will be a *better* parson. Herbert's similitude incorporates a careful differentiation that reinforces the clergyman's professional prestige at the physician's expense. Formal medical training and official sanction are incidental, rather than essential, to medical practice. Ordination, on the other hand, is an essential feature of membership in the clergy.

This sort of calculated slipperiness is evident in subtle ways throughout *The Country Parson*, as Herbert's text alternately collapses and expands the distinction between matters medical and matters spiritual. Consider, for example, Herbert's discussion of the sin of gluttony:

He that either for quantity eats more then his health or imployments will bear, or for quality is licorous after dainties, is a glutton ... so that men must eat neither to the disturbance of their health, nor of their affairs ... nor of their estate, nor of their brethren ... Many think they are at more liberty then they are, as if they were Masters of their health, and so they will stand to the pain, all is well. But to eat to ones hurt, comprehends, besides the hurt, an act against reason, because it is unnaturall to hurt ones self; and this they are not masters of. (266)

Herbert's casuistry here blurs professional boundaries in support of a broad construction of the parson's duties and prerogatives. The identification of the sin of gluttony depends, in large measure, on a medical (or social or economic) diagnosis, an assessment of the harm caused by the parishioner's eating habits. Spiritual harm, in this case at least, is observable in its bodily effects, so the parson becomes a custodian of the parishioners' health. Parishioners are not absolute 'Masters of their health,' and likewise, medical doctors are not absolute proprietors of the art of diagnosis. The terms of Herbert's account of gluttony are strikingly similar to those employed by Justice Walmsley in his opinion supporting the College of Physicians (as an agent of the Crown) in Bonham's case:

> It is the Office of a King to survey his subjects, and he is a physician to cure their maladies, and to remove Leprosies amongst them, and also to remove all fumes and smells, which may offend or be prejudicial to their health ... and so if a man be not right in his wits, The King is to have the protection and government of him, lest he being infirm, waste or consume his lands or goods; and it is not sufficient for him that his subjects live, but that they should live happily.[36]

Herbert, then, employs precisely the same type of argument in support of clerical prerogatives as the physicians and their supporters were using. The discursive struggle here is not merely a competition between a new professional elite and one of the traditional estates of a stratified society. It is also a struggle by an estate to retain its social power by appropriating the discourse of a professional rival, in an effort to transform itself into a professional elite. A similar, more playful transgression of professional boundaries occurs in the provocative title of chapter XXXIV, 'The Parson's Dexterity in applying of Remedies' (280). In this case, however, the teasing challenge is quickly withdrawn, as we discover that the chapter actually deals with spiritual remedies for temptation, and not with medicines in the ordinary sense. If the subtle argument about gluttony demonstrates Herbert's appropriation of the discourse and practice of medicine as part of the parson's professional territory, this witty skirmish suggests Herbert's consciousness of the game he is playing.

The discussion of gluttony points to a further irony in Herbert's construction of the priest-as-physician. On the one hand the role of the clergy in healing is merely one aspect of a very old tradition of non-professional medicine involving families, neighbours, local wise women and men, and aristocratic 'Ladies Bountiful.'[37] Typically, as Roy Porter notes, medicine was part of 'a body of lore that was in essence public, handed down orally, sometimes preserved in family manuscript recipe books, or culled out of printed volumes.'[38] And yet the seventeenth century also saw a burst of genteel intellectual interest in botany and herbal medicine, an enthusiasm that illustrates an 'active interest in natural philosophy and growing receptivity to recent developments in experimental science.' In 1621 Henry Danvers, the Earl of Danby and elder brother to Herbert's stepfather, had endowed England's first botanical garden, the 'Physic Garden' at Oxford, in order to create a 'nursery of simples [i.e., herbal remedies],' and other members of the Herbert network were serious gardeners as well.[39] *The Country Parson* contains a sample of this herbal lore, in a passage carefully calculated to undermine the medical-professional hierarchy:

> In the knowledge of simples, wherein the manifold wisdome of God is wonderfully to be seen, one thing would be carefully observed; which is, to know what herbs may be used in stead of drugs of the same nature, and to make the garden the shop: For home-bred medicines are both more easie for the Parsons purse, and more familiar for all mens bodyes. So, where the Apothecary useth either for loosing, Rhubarb, or for binding, Bolearmena, the Parson useth damask or white Roses for the one, and plantaine, shepherds purse, knot-grasse for the other, and that with better successe. (261)

In defending the pastor's right to heal with 'home-bred medicines,' Herbert is implicitly defending the 'wider social network'[40] of community medicine and self-treatment, and the traditional prerogative of the gentry to treat the ills of their tenants and dependants. On the other hand, the parson's 'diagnosis' of the sin of gluttony and its bodily effects is clearly an assertion of his own special professional competence, and Herbert's personal connections to the emerging genteel and quasi-scientific medical botany sets him slightly apart from traditions of folk medicine. Just as the parson is both aligned with and distinguished from the physician, the healing parson is both aligned with and distinguished from other non-professional healers, the midwives, and local cunning women (and men) about whom we read nothing in *The Country Parson*.

The irony of this omission is especially evident in the book's representation of the parson's wife as a healer. In two separate passages Herbert describes skill in healing as one of the primary qualifications for a parson's wife. Chapter X, 'The Parson in his house,' offers the fuller account of an ideal clerical helpmate:

> In stead of the qualities of the world, he requires only three of her; first, a trayning up of her children and mayds in the fear of God, with prayers,

and catechizing, and all religious duties. Secondly, a curing, and healing of all wounds and sores with her owne hands; which skill either she brought with her, or he takes care she shall learn it of some religious neighbour. (239)

To a considerable extent, it seems, the parson's duties as a healer are to be delegated to, or shared with, his wife. In the context of the gradual exclusion of women from medical practice in early modern Europe, this is worthy of comment.[41] On the one hand, a pastor's wife who treated the sick probably enjoyed a certain amount of protection from the harassment directed against 'empirics' and 'wise women' (including occasional charges of witchcraft and prosecution for unlicensed practice), but what the parson gives, he also takes away. In the preceding chapter, Herbert comments in more general terms on the authority delegated to the parson's wife: 'he gives her ... halfe at least of the government of the house, reserving so much of the affaires, as serve for a diversion for him; yet never so giving over the raines, but that he sometimes looks how things go, demanding an account, but not by the way of an account' (238–9). Presumably this principle of delegating and yet retaining authority applies to the wife's role as a healer as well. Just as she manages the household in her husband's name, so the parson's wife treats the sick in his name (and of course both do so in God's name: 'hee for God only, she for God in him'). The special professional dignity of the clergyman as Christ's deputy (225) serves both to open a social space for non-professional medicine, including that practiced by women, and to limit and enclose that space, placing it under the parson's patriarchal authority.[42]

   The Country Parson then, engages in a complex process of professional-territorial negotiation, competition, and expansion. Even as it contests acts of professional closure and enclosure by the medical profession, Herbert's pastoral manual seeks to enlarge and enclose its own professional field. In its main thrust toward clerical professionalization we might call it innovative, yet it consistently employs the discursive materials of tradition in pursuit of that objective.

The Law and the Gospel

Many of the observations made about medicine can also be made about Herbert's appropriation of legal discourse in *The Country Parson*. As with medical language it is clear that Herbert employs legal terms and ideas to enlarge and consolidate the authority of the clerical profession. Yet despite his conventional pairing of the physician and the lawyer as the pastor's kindred and rival professionals, Herbert plays a slightly different game with the law and lawyers, demonstrating a palpable ambivalence to the whole apparatus of law. Raised like other members of the English gentry in the conservative discourse and ideology of the common law, Herbert clearly reveres its traditions.[43] Heirs of the gentry have a duty, according to the advice of *The Country Parson*, 'to read Books of Law, and Justice; especially, the Statutes at large.' Moreover, 'they are to frequent Sessions and Sizes [i.e., Quarter Sessions and Assizes]; for it is both an honor which they owe to the Reverend Judges and Magistrates, to attend them, at least in their Shire; and it is a great advantage to know the practice of the Land; for our Law is Practice' (276–7). And yet alongside this reverence is a clear reluctance to embrace that ideology without qualification, a tendency to explore the limits and inadequacies of legal discourse. 'The Law' Herbert insists, citing a scriptural example, 'required one thing, and the Gospel another: yet as diverse, not as repugnant' (229). As Glenn Burgess has argued, the language of theology functioned, in early modern English social discourse, in tandem with the languages of common and civil law, to provide conventional ways of addressing social and political questions, particularly questions of order and hierarchy. Usually these parallel discourses appeared to operate harmoniously, since each was customarily applied to different sorts of questions. After 1625, however, Charles and his officials increasingly used the languages of common law, civil law, and theology in unconventional, or, to use Burgess's suggestive term, 'unidiomatic' ways, precipitating a 'crisis in the confidence which people were able to repose in the common law.'[44]

Burgess's account of the 'crisis of the common law' is drawn largely from parliamentary debates on issues related to non-parliamentary taxation. But doubts that the law provided 'a firm and reliable barrier against ... attacks on the liberties of freeborn Englishmen' may also be found in popular anxieties about the daunting scope and complexity of the legal system, or rather non-system, in early modern England, the vast and bewildering array of courts to which litigants might have recourse and before which alleged offenders might be 'presented.'[45] At the local level there were, as Herbert notes, the Quarter Sessions, presided over by a county Commission of the Peace, and the Assizes, which brought 'The King's Justice' from the courts at Westminster into the countryside. In London, by the seventeenth century, the three superior common-law courts (King's Bench, Common Pleas, and Exchequer) were engaged in vigorous competition for business, a situation that permitted, or even encouraged, litigants to play one court against another in the game of suit and counter-suit. This had not always been the case. The jurisdictions of the courts had been more or less settled in the late middle ages according to principles derived from Magna Carta. The Court of King's Bench dealt with trespass (a shared jurisdiction with Common Pleas), appeals of felony cases (heard in the first instance by the Assize judges), and most importantly, with cases in which the Crown had an interest; it was prohibited from hearing common pleas – that is, cases in which the Crown had no interest. The last made up the majority of cases in the medieval and early-modern judicial system, and in the fifteenth and sixteenth centuries Common Pleas was by far the busiest of the Westminster courts. The Court of Exchequer was, until well into the sixteenth century, similarly restricted, able to hear only cases involving debts to the Crown and its officers. In the fifteenth and sixteenth centuries, however, King's Bench introduced new procedures that expedited its business and enabled it to hear cases previously in the exclusive jurisdiction of Common Pleas. The Exchequer too, through a series of legal fictions, was gradually evolving into a court for common pleas (though the key developments in this evolution took place later, around the middle of the seventeenth century). Simultaneously the court of Chancery, a 'court of equity' rather than a 'court of law,' gradually evolved into a 'fourth major court of Westminster Hall.' Originally conceived as a source of extraordinary remedy in individual cases where the application of common law was demonstrably unjust, Chancery eventually became 'a court of constant resort for claimants to property.' While it retained its own distinctive (and increasingly cumbersome) procedures, the vast numbers of cases, and clashes between Chancery and the common law courts in the 1520s and again after 1610, led to the hardening of equity into law.[46] As the volume of litigation grew, the bureaucracy associated with the Westminster courts became quite staggering. In the Court of Common Pleas alone 'over thirty officials were associated with the procedural business ... there were also four cryers, two pursuivants, and a porter.' King's Bench was similarly complex, though different in structure, and by 1590 the Court of Chancery was beginning to assume Dickensian proportions, with 'at least forty-one different officials ... many of [whom] employed large numbers of assistants.'[47]

There were also the ecclesiastical courts, both episcopal and archidiaconal, with their own quite distinct system of law and legal training. By the early fourteenth century their responsibilities had solidified so that the church courts held 'a pervasive jurisdiction over the lives of most ordinary people: over family matters and wills, sexual offences, defamation and breach of faith.' The English Reformation did little to alter this jurisdiction or the procedures of the ecclesiastical courts, though it replaced the highest levels of appeal (to the Pope) with two superior ecclesiastical courts, the High Commission and the Court of Delegates. Canon law had been systematized and refined throughout the later Middle Ages, and one of the awkward effects of the English Reformation was to prohibit its study in the universities, while continuing its practice in the ecclesiastical courts. After the Reformation, advocates in the church courts were trained in civil law at the universities (since civil law principles underlay canon law), and as J.H. Baker suggests, 'the long survival of the wider jurisdiction of the church may be attributed to the existence of this small but persistent Civilian profession.'[48] Burgess argues that, along with theology and common law, civil law functioned as a third distinct and coherent language in which political questions might be addressed, a language more generalized, abstract, and logical than the historically grounded common law, and more deeply informed by continental humanist learning.[49] But in practice, as in theory, there were areas of adjacent or overlapping jurisdiction. Common law still governed inheritance of real property; civil law and the church courts had jurisdiction over moveables. Advowson (the system of lay ecclesiastical patronage) was, ironically, a temporal matter, justiciable at common law, whereas tithe disputes were sometimes matters for the ecclesiastical courts and sometimes for the common law. The result, in many people's minds, must have been confusion and a sense of the law's arbitrariness or inconsistency.

The local officials whose duty it was to enforce the laws were also in a vexed position, because the relationship of any individual to the legal system, or of officers within that system to each other, was fraught with uncertainty and ambivalence. Moreover, the competing functions subsumed under the administration of justice – adjudication, advocacy, prosecution, and enforcement – were, in practice, often intermingled. Justices of the Peace, for example, had wide-ranging responsibilities that included policing, adjudication (at the Quarter Sessions), and administration of county public works, not to mention collection of the Crown's forced loans and implementation of prerogative orders like those concerning plague and dearth.[50] Not surprisingly they tended to take a passive approach to the exercising of their duties. Confused by a proliferation of statutes and by overlapping and ambiguous jurisdictions, and torn between national-legislative and local-customary definitions of good order, the humble constables and churchwardens were even more inclined to avoid confrontation.[51] The best intentioned were rendered virtually powerless by their modest social rank; the worst used their positions to facilitate bullying and intimidation. With scoundrels in office, jurisdictional disputes were common. Hence Roger Pouncey, a Dorsetshire sheriff's bailiff (and therefore a county officer), frequently found himself in trouble with the civic authorities in Dorchester over the manner in which he performed his duties.[52] In his chapter on churchwardens, Herbert evokes the deep cultural reverence for the common law ideal in an effort to compensate for these handicaps and to build an impression of official dignity and authority. He insists that churchwardens derive their authority not

> from the Ecclesiasticall Laws only, since even by the Common Statute-Law they are taken for a kinde of Corporation, as being persons enabled by that Name to take moveable goods, or chattels, and to sue, and to be sued at the Law concerning such goods for the use and profit of their Parish: and by the same Law they are to levy penalties for negligence in resorting to church, or for disorderly carriage in time of divine service. (269–70)

The very need to articulate such an appeal suggests the fragility as well as the pervasiveness of the 'common-law mind.' Churchwardens bold enough to seize property in connection with, say, a tithe dispute were unlikely to be treated with reverence by the parishioners in question, and clergy willing to demand such action must have risked anti-clerical backlash.

It is therefore no surprise that when, in the opening lines of 'The Parson's Completenesse,' Herbert represents the parson as a lawyer, he abandons the notion of law as a source of stability and security. Instead, Herbert plays on the complexity and uncertainty of the early modern legal system, and on the imprecision of the word 'lawyer,' which can refer narrowly to a professional advocate, as in modern usage, or more generally to anyone learned in the law.[53] At first Herbert seems to have in mind the former, since advocacy is the legal function most easily assimilated into the clergyman/physician analogy. Pastor, physician, and legal advocate all attempt to intercede, with God, nature, or the court, on behalf of a parishioner, patient, or client. In addition, all three undertake to instruct and advise the parishioner, patient, or client on how to proceed in his or her own best interest: what to ingest, how to plead, how to pray.[54] But the discourse and practice of law in Herbert's day is at once so expansive and so diffuse that this narrow analogy is unsustainable. At least, Herbert introduces it only to abandon it. In the chapter's second sentence the parson's legal function shifts from advocacy to adjudication, from the narrower to the broader sense of 'lawyer': 'hee endures not that any of his Flock should go to Law; but in any Controversie, that they should resort to him as their Judge' (259). In a characteristically Herbertian rhetorical ploy, what seems an amplification is actually a striking reversal. Suddenly the issue is *elimination* of the professional advocate. Herbert's parson ceases to be someone who functions *like* a lawyer and becomes someone who functions *in place* of a lawyer. One doesn't have to think very long about literary representations of lawyers, or about lawyer jokes, to realize that Herbert is operating within a cultural *topos* here. As one of Herbert's proverbs runs, 'Lawyers houses are built on the heads of fooles' (352).

What this alternating identification and repudiation suggests, I think, is Herbert's ambivalence about the law as a social institution, an ambivalence fairly typical of both the early modern clergy and their parishioners. On the one hand, 'It was a shibboleth of English politics that English Law was the birthright of every citizen who, unlike many of his European counterparts, was subject not to the whim of a capricious individual but to a set of prescriptions that bound *all* members of the polity.'[55] On the other, 'for most villagers "the law" was something imposed on them from far away and high above. Statute law was made by representatives of a small section of the upper class, and related to their interests, rather than those of the populace.'[56] As Martin Ingram has shown in a study of legal records from early seventeenth-century Wiltshire – where Herbert's Parish of Bemerton is located – Herbert's contemporaries were well aware of the potential for vexatious litigation to serve as a source of disorder and discord among neighbours, for the law to exacerbate rather than resolve differences.[57] The same was true of statute enforcement: 'vigorous application of the laws could excite conflict within the local community.'[58] According to Wilfred Prest, the English clergy, in a 'twice-yearly barrage of assize sermons ... regularly castigated the corruption, avarice and injustice of ... [the legal] profession,' giving voice both to public dissatisfaction and to their own 'jealousy of the common lawyers' rising eminence and power since the Reformation.'[59] Hence, in the case of John Earle's 'Grave Divine,' 'the Lawyer is the onley man he hinders, he is spited for taking up quarrels.[60] By preventing recourse to the courts, Herbert and Earle imply, the parson might forestall the discord and resentment arising from judicial resolution of disputes. And if the eminence of the clergy was enhanced in the process, so much the better.

Herbert's participation in the popular ambivalence about law, lawyers, and courts leads him repeatedly to insist that no appearance of malice should taint the parson's exercise of the legal force at his disposal:

> Whensoever the Countrey Parson proceeds so farre as to call in Authority, and to do such things of legall opposition either in the presenting, or punishing of any, as the vulgar ever consters for signes of ill will; he forbears not in any wise to use the delinquent as before, in his behaviour and carriage towards him, not avoyding his company, or doing any thing of aversenesse, save in the very act of punishment. (263)

Similarly he strives to reconcile litigious parishioners, not merely to one another, but also to the impersonal nature of legal procedure: if they insist on their proverbial 'day in court,' 'he shews them how to go to Law, even as Brethren, and not as enemies, neither avoyding therefore one anothers company, much lesse defaming one another' (260). Implicit in these passages are two contradictory views of the law: on the one hand, a reverence for its supposed impartiality and detachment, and on the other, an anxiety about the pettiness and lack of neighbourly harmony it can engender. Here the reversal noted above – from pastor *as* lawyer to pastor *instead of* lawyer – is reversed again. Only by emulating the qualities associated with the English law in its positive aspects can the parson provide a viable alternative to the law and its negative attributes.[61]

Despite Herbert's evident participation in the popular English ambivalence to the legal system, *The Country Parson* occasionally expresses a surprising zeal for the less agreeable aspects of law: surveillance, enforcement, and coercion. In some chapters of the book, the ideal country parson functions less as a lawyer or judge, and more as a constable or prosecutor. This is clearest in Herbert's handling of 'presentment,' the term for laying charges during episcopal and archidiaconal visitations. Submitting bills of presentment in the ecclesiastical courts was a duty assigned to the churchwardens by the 1604 *Canons* of the Church of England, though it was a disciplinary option available to the parish priest as well.[62] As a rule, Herbert seems to prefer covert disciplinary strategies, and those that rely on the authority of the community: '*the Parsons punishing of sin and vice, is rather by withdrawing his bounty and courtesie ... or by private, or publick reproof ... then by causing them to be presented, or otherwise complained of*' (254). Nevertheless the churchwardens had their duty to perform, and informing on neighbours must have been an unpleasant and even at times hazardous task.[63] So it is perhaps no surprise that Herbert's ideal parson strives to ease this burden where he can. He celebrates communion

> if not duly once a month, yet at least five or six times in the year ... not onely for the benefit of the work, but also for the discharge of the Church-wardens, who being to present all that receive not thrice a year; if there be but three Communions, neither can all the people so order their affairs as to receive just at those times, nor the Church-Wardens so well take notice who receive thrice and who not. (259)

Sometimes, he admits, presentment is the only recourse:

> If there be any of the gentry or nobility of the Parish, who somtimes make it a piece of state not to come at the beginning of service with their poor neighbours ... [and] after divers gentle admonitions, if they persevere, he causes them to be presented: or if the poor Church-wardens be affrighted with their greatness ... he presents them himself, only protesting ... that not any ill will draws him to it, but the debt and obligation of his calling. (232)

Here, the element of compassion for the 'poor Church-wardens' in the parson's decision to perform their unpleasant task for them, and the common-law insistence that the law applies equally to 'the gentry or nobility,' merges with a stern sense of parish discipline and with the concern, already observed, to protect both the procedure and the parson himself from any suspicion of malice or partiality.

One reference to presentment seems to move beyond this stern impartiality. It deals with participation in Rogationtide processions, one of the traditional festive practices attacked by many godly reformers ('Puritans') as remnants of popery. The processions customarily involved feasting, almsgiving, and hospitality, revolving around a ceremonial perambulation of the fields to clear and review boundary markers and to ask blessings for the crops. Among other functions, 'beating the bounds' served to confirm the status and property rights of landowners.[64] The relevant chapter, entitled 'The Parson's Condescending,'

opens on a permissive note: 'The Countrey Parson is a Lover of old Customes, if they be good, and harmlesse; and the rather, because Countrey
people are much addicted to them, so that to favour them therein is to
win their hearts, and to oppose them therin is to deject them' (283).
Later in the chapter, however, permission becomes coercion, recreation
becomes an obligation, and the parson's reservations about presentment seem to vanish: 'he exacts of all to bee present at the perambulation, and those that withdraw, and sever themselves from it, he mislikes,
and reproves as uncharitable, and unneighbourly; and if they will not
reforme, presents them' (284). Despite anxiety about the exercise of
coercive authority elsewhere, here Herbert advocates its use in an
extremely subjective and controversial, and perhaps rather surprising,
area. A 1559 statute had restricted participation in Rogationtide processions to property owners, and while James's 1618 *Book of Sports* had
endorsed such festive pastimes, the battle between reformers and tradi-
tionalists was being fought locally and vigorously, especially in Wiltshire
and neighbouring Dorsetshire.[65] That battle is being fought discursively
here, as Herbert, ever fond of a pun, employs the language of ecclesiastical justice (a system despised by many of the hotter sort of Protestants)
as both a toy and a weapon – 'be present or be presented' – and turns
the discourse of the godly on its head by insisting that the reformers
'reform' themselves. One can imagine the response by an indignant
member of the puritan gentry, perhaps a reformulation of Sir Toby's
complaint to Malvolio: 'Dost thou think because thou art a lewd tippler,
that a godly man must stand for thy cakes and ale?'

It is in this debate about social order between systematic reformers
and advocates of a traditional ethic of neighbourly charity and hospitality that *The Country Parson* reveals its deep and rather confusing entan-
glement with issues of law, class, and social control.[66] Like Davenant in
the Sherfield case, Herbert's idealized parson is most willing to 'call in
Authority' when clerical influence seems threatened by competing lay
interests. This was clearly the case in Wiltshire in the early 1630s. Severe
economic depression throughout the 1620s was compounded by an outbreak of plague in 1627 and the resulting problems of poverty and
vagrancy continued to increase through the early years of the 1630s, just
as Herbert was beginning his pastoral rounds within sight of the spire of
Salisbury cathedral.[67] The Wiltshire countryside was similarly troubled:
between 1626 and 1628, and again in 1631, there were massive anti-
enclosure riots, first in Gillingham forest on the Wiltshire-Dorsetshire
border and then in Braydon Forest at the northern end of the county.[68]

Throughout England, and particularly in such troubled areas, the traditional classification of the poor, based on a distinction between the deserving and the undeserving, or more colloquially, between the impotent and the impudent poor, began increasingly to break down. No longer could the 'deserving' poor be limited to widows, orphans, and the aged and infirm among local residents. No longer could idleness be linked simply to vagrancy and criminality, and offenders stocked or whipped out of town. Increasingly, in Salisbury, in the industrial villages of north Wiltshire, and throughout England, whole families of able residents lived in poverty; skilled artisans with children to feed joined the proverbial sturdy rogues as potential threats to social order. In the 1620s and 1630s, led by men such as the lawyer Henry Sherfield, the puritan civic oligarchy of Salisbury responded with a series of ambitious, systematic, and controversial measures that retained and in some ways intensified the customary ideological distinction between impotence and indolence, attempting to eradicate the latter through positive (one might almost say proto-Keynesian) measures, as well as punitive ones. The vigour with which they set about their task marks Herbert's Salisbury as one of the centres of the 'transition from individual and ecclesiastical relief ... by alms and "hospitality" to increasingly complex regulation of the poor by statute, by-law and penal institution.'[69] Such measures probably tended to improve the quality, efficiency, and fairness of poor relief, but they were not universally welcomed. Beyond the predictable opposition from those with vested interests in the economic status quo, civic poor-relief schemes met with opposition from Herbert's Bishop, John Davenant, whose Calvinist theology might have led him to support the reformers had civic control of charity not seemed a threat to the church's social function.[70]

Given the intimate connection between poverty, lawlessness, and social control, and the precariousness of the church's claim to authority in these areas, it is not surprising that Herbert's chapter 'The Parson's Charity' should be suffused with legal language. The chapter begins by invoking, among a series of Christian commonplaces, the relationship between the Law and the Gospel, between charity and justice: 'To Charity is given the covering of sins, I *Pet.* 4.8. and the forgivenesse of sins, *Matthew* 6.14. *Luke* 7.47. The fulfilling of the Law, *Romans* 13.10' (244). Here the point seems a theological one, with 'Law' referring to Mosaic law, the law of the Hebrew Bible, rather than the law of England. But it is not merely coincidental that Herbert has chosen to cite the chapter that opens with the most famous Biblical legitimation of civil authority: 'Let

every soul be subject unto the higher powers' (Rom 13.1). Two senses of
the word 'law' are at work in Herbert's chapter, as in Paul's, and the slide
between them is a complex ideological gesture. In the body of the chapter Herbert shifts his focus away from Mosaic law to deal explicitly with
statute law and its complicated relationship to charity:

> in all his Charity, he distinguisheth, giving them most, who live best, and
> take most paines, and are most charged: So is his charity in effect a Ser-
> mon. After the consideration of his own Parish, he inlargeth himself, if he
> be able, to the neighbour-hood; for that also is some kind of obligation; so
> doth he also to those at his door, whom God puts in his way, and makes his
> neighbours. But these he helps not without some testimony, except the evi-
> dence of misery bring testimony with it. For though these testimonies may
> also be falsifyed, yet considering that the Law allows these in case they be
> true, but allows by no means to give without testimony, as he obeys Author-
> ity in the one, so that being once satisfied, he allows his Charity some blind-
> nesse in the other; especially since of the two commands, we are more
> injoyned to be charitable, then wise. But evident miseries have a naturall
> priviledge, and exemption from all law. (245)

Herbert is concerned about the distinction between the deserving and
the undeserving poor, and the statutory prohibition against giving to
vagrants.[71] The parson's first duty is to his own parish; only 'if he is able'
does he 'inlarge himself' by distributing alms to the poor of neighbouring parishes or to strangers at his door. The distinctions Herbert refers
to in the first sentence of the passage are just the kind the Poor Law
demanded, distinctions the reformers in Salisbury were attempting to
make much more rigorously and systematically than their predecessors
a generation earlier, but when the issue shifts from the impoverished
parishioner to the stranger, Herbert begins to depart from the reformist
program.[72] Strangers were required to give 'some testimony,' some
account of their place of residence and the cause of their distress, and
the able and the wandering poor were to be sent on their way. But Herbert points out a couple of important loopholes in this harsh policy. The
first is the repeated insistence that 'the evidence of the misery [might]
bring testimony with it,' that the need might be so serious and so apparent that no further 'testimony' would be required. The second loophole
is an intricate bit of casuistry designed to get around the probability of
false accounts. Herbert writes that the 'Law allows [testimonies] *in case
they be true*' (my italics); it requires the parson to obtain them, not to

verify them. And having satisfied the legal requirement to *ask* for a story, the parson 'allows his Charity some blindnesse' when he is presented with an improbable or incomplete account. This is where the initial slide from Mosaic law to statute law becomes important: if the parson permits a little 'covering of sins' in the name of charity, he will ultimately be 'fulfilling ... the Law,' even if he might be violating a statute, because Holy Scripture defines charity as a fulfilling of the law.[73]

The authorities in Salisbury were trying to minimize the kind of discretion Herbert describes. From their point of view it only led to inconsistency and injustice in the distribution of scarce resources. Herbert's defence of clerical discretion in this realm seems on the surface a matter of simple compassion and a mark of the difference in spirit between bureaucratic town parishes and traditionalist rural ones, but it is more than this. It is also a defence of the state church as an instrument of social control, a position that was being threatened by competing lay interests, precisely when the Church of England was creating the educated, activist clergy needed to oversee and regulate the lives of parishioners. The parson, as the first sentence of this long passage says, makes 'his charity in effect a Sermon' (245) indoctrinating by giving. Earlier in the chapter, Herbert's metaphor is even more graphic: 'the Parson ... making a *hook* of his Charity, causeth them still to depend on him' (244, my italics). Fishers of men indeed! 'So doth hee also before giving make them say their Prayers first, or the Creed, and ten Commendments, and as he finds them perfect, rewards them the more. For other givings are lay, and secular, but this is to give like a Priest' (245). In a curious twist, Herbert defines unconditional giving as secular; sacred giving, 'to give like a priest,' becomes a commercial transaction, a matter of exchange and reward. In the process, charity becomes a commodity. And as with any other commodity, the way to keep its price high is to limit supply. Hence the parson 'gives no set pension to any; for this in time will lose the name and effect of Charity with the poor people ... for they will reckon upon it, as on a debt' (244). As one of a number of emerging professions engaged in managing people's behaviour, the clergy had to compete for influence, and charity was a crucial arena for such competition. As a powerful means of generating dependence and compliance, charity was simply too valuable an instrument to be turned over from the state church to civic authorities, from the proprietors of the gospel to the proprietors of the disorderly law.

To return to the Weberian categories of 'traditional' and 'legal-rational' social order, it appears that *The Country Parson* at once contributes to and resists the increasingly legal-rational character of the English social order, or to be more precise, the book resists some manifestations of the transition in order to promote others. Even as it seeks to extend and consolidate the increasingly professional role of the clergy, it defends some traditional social practices, like folk medicine, seasonal festivity, and discretionary charity, because of their links to clerical authority and influence. In effect the book seeks to offer legal-rational justification for these traditional practices, appropriating them and so transforming their cultural meaning significantly. Herbert wants to enclose his own professional field, but he can only do so by defending the commons (or at least the portion of it that the church uses) against the encroachment of rival landlords.

chapter four

The Country Parson and the Parson's Country

God hath and exerciseth a threefold power in every thing which concernes man. The first is a sustaining power; the second a governing power; the third a spirituall power. By his sustaining power he preserves and actuates every thing in his being; so that corne doth not grow by any other vertue, then by that which he continually supplyes, as the corn needs it; without which supply the corne would instantly dry up, as a river would if the fountain were stopped. And it is observable, that if anything could presume of an inevitable course, and constancy in its operations, certainly it should be either the sun in heaven, or the fire on earth, by reason of their fierce, strong, and violent natures: yet when God pleased, the sun stood stil, the fire burned not. By Gods governing power he preserves and orders the references of things one to the other, so that though the corn do grow, and be preserved in that act by his sustaining power, yet if he suite not other things to the growth, as seasons, and weather, and other accidents by his governing power, the fairest harvests come to nothing. And it is observeable, that God delights to have men feel, and acknowledg, and reverence his power, and therefore he often overturnes things, when they are thought past danger; that is his time of interposing.

A Priest to the Temple, or The Country Parson
His Character and Rule of Holy Life,
Chapter XXX, 'The Parson's Consideration of Providence'

George Herbert's contradictory attempt to embrace a new clerical professionalism, while resisting the professional claims of law and medicine, is part of a larger pattern of ambivalence, contradiction, and paradox in early modern social discourse. Such paradoxes, even when they partake of both sides of a social debate, are seldom ideologically neutral. Often the forging of discursive links between the familiar and the disruptive serves to disable conservative resistance to social change. In 'The Parson's Consideration of Providence,' for example, Herbert creates a simultaneous sense of cosmic stability and uncertainty, attributing this paradoxical condition to the interplay between God's 'sustaining power' and his 'governing power.' Peter Laslett's influential book *The World We Have Lost* documents, without explicitly acknowledging, a different but related paradox in the social and ideological fabric of early modern England. On the one hand, Laslett's work in historical demography shows that people in sixteenth- and seventeenth-century England were more mobile, socially, geographically, and economically, than had commonly been assumed. Transience was the rule, not the exception, especially for young unmarrieds: 'most young people in service ... seem to have looked upon a change of job bringing them into a new family as the normal thing every few years.'[1] On the other hand, Laslett insists, as do most other commentators on social ideology, that the inhabitants of 'the world we have lost' shared a belief in the permanence of social institutions and relationships:

> The ancient order of society was felt to be eternal and unchangeable by those who supported, enjoyed and endured it. There was no expectation of reform. How could there be when economic organization was domestic organization, and relationships were rigidly regulated by the social system, by the content of Christianity itself?[2]

The social world of early modern England was, like the divinely ordered cosmos, characterized at once by permanence and uncertainty. What Herbert calls 'the references of things one to the other' was, paradoxically, both rigidly fixed and surprisingly fluid. Of course, there is always a gap between an ideology and the conditions it purports to explain and justify. What is remarkable is that even after more than three hundred years the gap or paradox should be more or less invisible (or perhaps merely uninteresting) to a distinguished social historian like Laslett.

Karl Marx saw the paradox, writing a century earlier about the process of 'primitive accumulation,' 'those moments when great masses of men are suddenly and forcibly torn from their means of subsistence, and hurled as free and "unattached" proletarians on the labour market.'[3] The quotation marks around 'unattached' emphasize the fictiveness of the freedom of the early modern worker (Marx refers specifically to workers driven off the land by enclosure, but the status of those who never had land to be driven from is little different). Released from a lifetime of obligation to a particular landlord or feudal master (indeed feudal land tenures had been largely eliminated in England by the early modern period), people were by no means released from the concepts of mastery and servitude. Legal definitions of vagrancy depended on the concept of 'masterlessness.'[4] Capitalism, even in its infancy, required a labour force at once mobile and submissive, paradoxically attached and 'unattached.' The paradox towards which Marx's quotation marks point is given explicit formulation in Michel Foucault's *Discipline and Punish*: 'discipline increases the forces of the body (in economic terms of utility) and diminishes these same forces (in political terms of obedience).'[5] Foucault, admittedly, is concerned with eighteenth-century France, not seventeenth-century England, but the paradox of freedom in bondage, evident in all three of these analyses, is a central *topos* of Protestant theology, already deeply embedded in English social discourse by the early seventeenth century.[6] It is evident in the words Walton attributes to Herbert when he sent the manuscript of *The Temple* to Nicholas Ferrar for publication: 'he shall find in it a picture of the many spiritual conflicts that have passed betwixt God and my soul, before I could subject mine to the will of Jesus my master, in whose service I have now found perfect freedom.'[7] This chapter will explore some manifestations of these paradoxes in Herbert's use of rural and agricultural discourse in *The Country Parson*.

Improvement

According to George Herbert,

> there are two branches of [a householder's] affaires; first, the improvement of his family, by bringing them up in the fear and nurture of the Lord; and secondly, the improvement of his grounds, by drowning, or draining, or stocking, or fencing, and ordering his land to the best advantage both of himself, and his neighbours. (275)

Elsewhere in *The Country Parson,* this paternalist rhetoric of spiritual and agricultural 'improvement' is extended to matters of parish discipline, for 'the Country Parson is ... a father to his flock' (250), and eventually, perhaps inevitably, to God's providential oversight of his creation, as 'the great householder of the world' (241). On the surface this seems a straightforward instance of the kind of analogical thinking that served to perpetuate a deference-based society of reciprocal hierarchical relationships in early modern England, a society founded on obligations that were, at least residually, feudal.[8] As Herbert writes, 'Gentlemen ... are to know the use of their Arms: and as the Husbandman labours for them, so must they fight for, and defend them, when occasion calls' (277). Clearly, Herbert's book strives to present a vision of seamless and harmonious social and cosmic order. There is, of course, no implication that this is a perfect or a fully accomplished order. Everywhere in Herbert's hypothetical parish, as in his poems, 'Gods goodnesse strives with mans refractorinesse; Man would sit down at this world, God bids him sell it, and purchase a better' (272). But there is a deep conviction that it is a right order, a just and good order.

Herbert's parabolic illustration of this injunction to 'purchase a better' world, and his characteristic adoption of scriptural modes and figures, implicitly asserts the timelessness of this order, and of the process of moral and spiritual 'improvement':

> Just as a Father, who hath in his hand an apple, and a piece of Gold under it; the Child comes, and with pulling, gets the apple out of his Fathers hand: his Father bids him throw it away, and he will give him the gold for it, which the Child utterly refusing, eats it, and is troubled with wormes: So is the carnall and wilfull man with the worm of the grave in this world, and the worm of Conscience in the next. (272)

This peculiar little narrative is a variation on the parable of the merchant and the pearl of great price, evidently one of Herbert's favourites, domesticated and recast in terms of another favourite Herbert *topos*, the biblically sanctioned parent-child analogy.[9] '[K]nowing that Countrey people are drawne, or led by sense, more then by faith, by present rewards, more then by future' (254), the parson acts as a wise parent who urges his wilful child (a child resembling the speaker of 'The Collar') to forego immediate gratification and seek the greater reward. But Herbert's recasting of the parable has some rather arresting features. As forcefully as the biblical original, Herbert's version figures the Christian's yearning for salvation in monetary terms: to put it starkly, devotion becomes a sort of spiritual avarice. At the same time, temperance of appetite, about which Herbert can sometimes be almost obsessive, becomes, in this instance, a metaphor for worldliness and complacency.[10] Astonishingly, the child who rejects 'Money ... [the] bane of blisse, & sourse of woe,' according to Herbert's poem 'Avarice' (l. 1), and chooses instead the wholesome fruit of God's earth, serves as an emblem of 'carnall and wilfull man.'[11] Childhood here is not, as in 'The Collar,' 'Holy Baptisme' [II], and Matthew 18:3 ('Except ye ... become as little children, ye shall not enter into the kingdom of heaven') a state to be recaptured; rather it is a state to be abandoned, as in I Cor. 13:11 ('When I was a child, I spake as a child, I understood as a child, I thought as a child: but when I became a man, I put away childish things'). But what *are* the childish things Herbert's parable would have put away? What is the apple he would have 'carnall and wilfull man' throw away?

For an answer to this question we must return to the analogy between moral and spiritual improvement and agricultural improvement. On reflection, the reference to 'drowning, or draining, or stocking, or fencing,' especially fencing, does not seem so clearly calculated to generate collective ideological assent. Rather, it opens up the debate on one of the 'regulated antagonisms' that define early modern English culture.[12] Complaints and confrontations over land enclosure are perhaps the most obvious example of a lack of consensus on issues of social good and the reciprocal obligations of superiors and inferiors. And as I have already intimated in my discussion of the early modern professions, enclosure is one of the most striking signs of the transition from a traditional social order to a legal-rational order – to use Weberian terms – and from a feudal to a capitalist mode of agrarian production – to use Marxist terms.[13] Herbert's own pronouncements reflect the fragmentation of early modern discourse on the subject.[14] Taken as instances of a single governing ideology, they seem incoherent. Taken as declarations of allegiance in a well-established controversy, they suggest that Herbert simply changed sides on one of the defining questions of his time.

In his early poem 'The Church Porch,' Herbert adopts the prevailing Tudor humanist posture, a posture hostile to enclosure and improvement:

O England! full of sinne, but most of sloth;
Spit out thy flegme, and fill thy brest with glorie:
Thy Gentrie bleats, as if thy native cloth
Transfus'd a sheepishnesse into thy storie:
    Not that they all are so; but that the most
    Are gone to grass, and in the pasture lost.   (ll. 91–6)

This is the same complaint voiced in Book 1 of More's *Utopia*, first published in 1516, where Hythloday observes that English sheep

> have become so greedy and fierce that they devour men themselves. They devastate and depopulate fields, houses and towns. For in whatever parts of the land sheep yield the finest and thus the most expensive wool, there the nobility and gentry ... are not content with the old rents ... they enclose every acre for pasture; they destroy houses and abolish towns, keeping only the churches – and those for sheep-barns.[15]

This complaint is repeated throughout the century, in sermons, pamphlets, parliamentary speeches, and in a series of Tudor 'depopulation' statutes. Particularly resonant is the preamble to the 1489 act, the first of many, which declares that

> great inconveniencies daily doth increase by desolation and pulling downe, and wilfull waste of houses and townes within this realme, and laying to Pasture Lands, which customably have been used in tillage, whereby idlenesse, which is the ground and beginning of all mischiefes, daily doth encrease. For where in some townes two hundred persons were occupied and lived by their lawfull labours, now there are occupied two or three heardmen, and the residue fall into idlenesse, the husbandrie, which is one of the greatest commodities of this Realme, is greatly decayed; Churches destroyed; the service of God withdrawn; the bodies there buried not prayed for; the patron and curate wronged; the defense of this land against our enemies outwards feebled and impaired; to the great displeasure of God, to the subversion of policy and good rule of this land.[16]

Enclosure, particularly where it involved conversion from arable to pasture, was linked, in Tudor humanist rhetoric, to depopulation of the countryside and creation of vagabonds.[17] Nearly a century later, the husbandman in Sir Thomas Smith's 1581 *Discourse of the Commonweal* reprises the complaint that

> enclosures do undo us all ... All is taken up for pasture, either for sheep or for grazing of cattle. So that I have known of late a dozen plows within less compass than six miles about me laid down within these seven years; and where forty persons had their livings, now one man and his shepherd has all. Which thing is not the least cause of these uproars, for by these enclosures many do lack livings and be idle.[18]

What is particularly noteworthy here is the convergence of official discourse and the literature of protest. In the traditionalist view of things, a view shared by the Tudor monarchs and by those who claimed to speak for the dispossessed, the common weal is defined not merely in terms of maximum productivity, but in terms of subsistence and employment for the largest population.[19] An England devoted to pasture rather than farming is an England 'full ... of sloth' and the greed of enclosers is a cause of idleness and 'uproars.' In this milieu, the child in Herbert's parable, who wants only the apple and not the piece of gold, might well have been the hero of the story. As Joan Thirsk writes, 'most people expected to get their living by farming, and ... the idea of an ordered society in which no man took advantage of his neighbours was regarded as the only philosophy by which communal farming could work.'[20] Agricultural 'improvement,' of which enclosure was the most visible form, was, at least for much of the sixteenth century, likely to be represented as detrimental to the functioning of a properly ordered society, not only in satire and popular protest but also in statutes, parliamentary speeches, and royal proclamations.

Toward the end of the century, however, positive representations of enclosure proliferate, just as the attitude to enclosure changes between Herbert's early poem and his later prose work.[21] According to Joan Thirsk,

> The 1590s mark a turning point in the agricultural history of this period. They include a run of bad harvests which caused grain shortages, plague, and near famine. Thereafter, profit margins no longer favoured grass at the expense of grain. The enclosure movement did not cease, but the conversion of arable to pasture did not hold out the attractive possibilities of two generations earlier.[22]

Instead, much seventeenth-century enclosure was accomplished by agreement (though agreement certainly cannot be taken to mean the absence of coercion) and was aimed at facilitating more intensive cultivation rather than conversion of arable to pasture. A shift in the prevailing social discourse surrounding enclosure and improvement accompanied these changes. In 1649, Walter Blith denounced open-field agriculture as a barrier to industry and prosperity in *The English Improver*. 'when all men's lands lie intermixed [as in traditional common field husbandry] ... the ingenious are disabled to the improving [of] theirs because others will not, neither sometimes can the improvement be made upon any unless upon all jointly.'[23] This had been the view of

English agricultural writers like Tusser and Fitzherbert even in the six-teenth century.[24] In his 'Comparison Between Champion Country and Severall,' from *Five Hundred Points of Good Husbandrie* Tusser writes:

> The countrie enclosed I praise,
>> the tother delighteth not me,
> For nothing the wealth it doth raise,
>> to such as inferior be.

He goes on to associate anti-enclosure sentiment with the very same social ills that protestors laid at the feet of rapacious enclosers:

> For Commons these commoners crie,
>> enclosing they may not abide:
> Yet some be not able to bie
>> a cow with hir calfe by hir side.
> Nor lai not to live by their wurke,
>> but theevishly loiter and lurke.[25]

Sixteenth-century advocates of enclosure still tended to associate enclosure with management of livestock. Nevertheless, their views gained ground by degrees, and by the seventeenth-century, with increased emphasis on arable enclosures, they became mainstream.

The shift towards acceptance of enclosure for cultivation is recorded even in the 1589 *Discourse of the Commonweal*, where the Knight argues that

> enclosures should be profitable and not hurtful to the Commonweal, for we see the counties where enclosures be are most wealthy ... And I have heard a civilian once say that it was taken for a maxim in his law this saying, 'That which is possessed of many in common is neglected of all,' and expe-rience shows that tenants in common be not so good husbands as when every man has his part in severalty.

This argument leads the Doctor, an opponent of pastoral enclosure, to qualify his own position:

> I mean not of all enclosures, nor yet all commons, but only of such enclo-sures as turn common arable fields into pastures, and violent enclosures of commons without just recompense ... For if land were severally enclosed to

the intent to continue husbandry thereon and every man had for his portion a piece of the same to himself enclosed, I think no harm but rather
good should come thereof, if every man did agree thereto.[26]

The *Discourse of the Commonweal* is concerned as much with grain short-
ages and rising grain prices as with enclosure per se. So while it represents 'violent enclosures' for pasture as a cause of dearth, it represents
enclosures of arable land, by agreement of the commoners, as a solution
to the same problem.

John Norden's 1607 *Surveiors Dialogue* dramatizes a similar persuasive
triumph for the cause of agricultural improvement and innovation. It
opens with an exchange between a diligent and upright land surveyor
and an impressionable young husbandman who complains of surveying
as a newfangled intrusion by which

millions [are] disquieted that might live quietly in their Farmes, Tene-
ments, Houses and Lands, that are now daily troubled with your so narrow
looking thereinto, measuring the quantity, observing the quality, recount-
ing the value, and acquainting the lords with the estates of all men's livings,
whose ancestors did live better with little, then we can now do with much
more, because by your meanes rents are raysed, and Landes known to the
uttermost Acre, Fines inhaunced far higher than ever before measuring of
land and surveying came in.[27]

Countering the husbandman's complaint with references to a host of
petty encroachments by unscrupulous tenants on their landlords' and
neighbours' privileges, the surveyor persuades the young fellow of the
necessity of true surveys for the maintenance of order in the 'little commonwealth, whereof the tenants are the members, the land the body,
and the Lord the head.'[28] In the eyes of Stuart officials, too, 'the *pros*
of enclosure were beginning to outweigh the *cons.*' There were more
commissions of enquiry into rural depopulation in 1607 and 1630, but
like the husbandmen's complaints in the *The Surveiors Dialogue* and *A
Discourse of the Commonweal,* and like Herbert's anti-enclosure stanza
from 'The Church Porch,' they had a slightly anachronistic flavour.[29]

There is no such anachronism in *The Country Parson.* Its forward-
looking model householder is not only an encloser, but, like the Knight
in *A Discourse of the Commonweal,* a local advocate for agricultural
improvement, one of the community leaders who stands to increase his
own revenues by spreading the gospel of improvement to reluctant ten-

ants.[30] Beyond his own land and family, he 'considers every one ... [in his Parish or Village] and either helps them in particular, or hath generall Propositions to the whole Towne or Hamlet, of advancing the publick Stock, and managing Commons, or Woods, according as the place suggests' (276). By the time he writes *The Country Parson* in the early 1630s, Herbert seems to have embraced the new orthodoxy of agricultural 'improvement.' Yet this transformation of the prevailing social discourse, and of Herbert's own position, does not imply the waning of the traditionalist vision of social order, on which anti-enclosure polemics had rested, and with which enclosure had once seemed irreconcilable. What is truly remarkable is the durability and malleability of this discourse, its capacity to absorb and accommodate initiatives and arguments previously seen as antithetical, even protorevolutionary. If traditionalist rhetoric was to survive changes in traditional patterns of life and of getting a living, ways had to be found to close this ideological rupture, to link the sense of a timeless, harmonious, and providentially ordained social order with an emergent rhetoric of change and with the practice of agricultural improvement and innovation.[31] This is one aspect of the cultural work undertaken by *The Country Parson* in its melding of several very different kinds of agricultural discourse.[32] Like the Doctor in *A Discourse of the Commonweal,* Herbert is constructing the 'common ground' previous treatments of enclosure lacked: a conflict-laden *via media.*[33]

Herbert's Versions of Pastoral

The Country Parson's agricultural language and imagery, its portrait of country life, country people, and country labour, is textually mediated; it reflects discursive convention at least as much as it reflects rural experience. But we need explicitly to consider the extent to which this is true. How 'literary' is *The Country Parson*? To what extent can Herbert be observed 'reading' the countryside itself, as he experiences it intimately for the first time as an adult between 1628 and 1633, the last five years of his short life? What sorts of continuities and contradictions does his account of country life display? These are the issues the remainder of this chapter will address. To begin, it is probably necessary to distinguish analytically the main strands of agricultural rhetoric woven into the book, while admitting that ultimately they may be impossible to disentangle.

First of all, there is virtually no trace in *The Country Parson* of what we think of as Renaissance literary pastoral, the diverse tradition that encompasses Marlowe's 'Passionate Shepherd,' Sidney's *Arcadia*, Spenser's *Shepheardes Calendar*, Shakespeare's *As You Like It*, and Milton's 'Lycidas.' For this reason, it is tempting to abandon the term 'pastoral' altogether and to speak of *The Country Parson* as a georgic, that genre of didactic literature in a middle style, based on Hesiod's *Works and Days* and Vergil's *Georgics*, which describes rural labour, as opposed to rustic leisure, in concrete detail, and celebrates its dignity.[34] Nevertheless, we cannot entirely avoid the designation 'pastoral' because Herbert uses it himself to indicate that *The Country Parson* is a book for and about pastors, in the ecclesiastical sense (224). Obviously, the word 'pastor' in this context is itself a metaphor (it's probably safe to call it a dead one) that evokes the parable of the good shepherd and links the clergyman's care of his congregation with a shepherd's care of his flock.[35] Herbert can make this linkage on the basis of scriptural authority and conventional wisdom: it requires no specific agricultural knowledge or experience to affirm that

> our Saviour made plants and seeds to teach the people: for he was the true householder, who bringeth out of his treasure things new and old; the old things of Philosophy and the new of Grace; and maketh the one serve the other. And I conceive, our Saviour did this for three reasons: first, that by familiar things hee might make his Doctrine slip the more easily into the hearts even of the meanest. Secondly, that labouring people (whom he chiefly considered) might have every where monuments of his Doctrine, remembring in gardens, his mustard-seed, and lillyes; in the field, his seed-corn, and tares; and so not be drowned altogether in the works of their vocation, but sometimes lift up their minds to better things, even in the midst of their pains. Thirdly, that he might set a Copy for Parsons. (261)

Here, Herbert affirms the conformity of the book of nature and the book of scripture. This is the symbolic vision of nature and agriculture we get in poems like 'Paradise,' a vision that depends very little on the actual experience of farming.[36] The passage is also an instance of the kind of deductive procedure Herbert's friend Francis Bacon scorns in *Novum Organum*, the kind of thinking that 'flies from the senses and particulars to the most general axioms, and from these principles, the truth of which it takes for settled and immovable, proceeds to judgement, and to the discovery of middle axioms.'[37] For the early modern Christian it is axiomatic that Christ is the 'true householder' and that

God is evident in his works, so in preaching to country people, the ideal parson presents the evidence most familiar to his parishioners. As Herbert writes in an earlier chapter, the parson 'condescends even to the knowledge of tillage, and pastorage, and makes great use of them in teaching, because people by what they understand, are best led to what they understand not' (228; see also 257).

In representing 'knowledge of tillage, and pastorage' as something achieved through condescension, however, Herbert suggests that the university-educated cleric may have to expend some effort to grasp the connections between divine providence and 'tillage, and pastorage.' He implies that there may be things the parson himself 'understand[s] not' about what a 'true householder' is and does, things the parson may have to learn if he is to communicate effectively with his parishioners. He may have to 'condescend' to acquire more particular 'knowledge of tillage and pastorage,' because, as Herbert says elsewhere, 'particulars ever touch, and awake more than generalls.' In other words, he may have to begin to think inductively about agriculture, beginning with the details in good Baconian fashion and 'rising by a gradual and unbroken ascent ... [to arrive] at the most general axioms last of all.'[38] Of course this is only a pseudo-inductive method, for the 'general axioms' of divine providence are still held to be 'settled and immovable,' but it is a hint that *The Country Parson* is informed by the interplay between two distinct kinds of agricultural discourse: a generalized and conventional set of agricultural tropes, largely biblical in origin, and a particular, local consideration of agricultural practices and concerns.

Perhaps the most delightful example of this interplay is the following argument for the benefit of weekday visits to parishioners: 'there he shall find his flock most naturally as they are, wallowing in the midst of their affairs' (247). Here, 'flock' is a dead metaphor for the congregation, just as 'pastor' is for the clergyman. The rather comic mixed metaphor, in which the sheep-parishioners suddenly become pig-parishioners 'wallowing in ... their affairs,' testifies to the opacity of the metaphorical term 'flock.' Even as the conventionality of flock links Herbert's agricultural discourse with a diffuse body of scriptural language and imagery, his use of 'wallowing' points in the opposite direction: towards the possibility that Herbert has indeed been watching farmers at work, digging the ditches so necessary for the 'drowning or draining' of their fields.[39]

Herbert's concrete experience of rural life was, however, quite limited, both temporally and geographically. This means that local and agricultural historians can give us a fairly detailed picture of the kinds of agricultural work Herbert would have observed and of the social and economic conditions in which his parishioners lived. His limited experience also makes it extremely likely that, as a scholar preparing to assume the duties of a country parson, he would have consulted the substantial vernacular literature of husbandry (books like Fitzherbert's and Tusser's) in search of those 'particulars' of rural life that 'ever touch, and awake more than generalls.' Herbert's family connections also point in both directions. As Cristina Malcolmson has noted, both Sir John Danvers (Herbert's stepfather) and William Herbert, third Earl of Pembroke, were formidable gardeners, and Herbert's poems bear many traces of his fascination with the achievements and ideology of English Renaissance gardening. But the Herberts of Wilton were also at the centre of one of the foremost literary patronage networks of the day, and agricultural writers such as Gervase Markham and Rowland Vaughan were among their many clients. Indeed Markham, the most prolific, if not the most innovative, agricultural writer of his day, has been described as one of the leading recipients of Herbert family patronage.[40] Given Herbert's friendship with Lady Anne Clifford, and her keen interest in land issues, it seems likely that the agricultural improvements being practiced in Wiltshire in the early 1630s would have been a topic of polite conversation on Herbert's visits to Wilton house.[41]

Herbert and the Wiltshire Farming Country

As I have mentioned already, the man who wrote *The Country Parson* was, in terms of life experience, an urbanite. He had been born, to be sure, in rural Montgomeryshire in the Welsh border country, and his grandfather, Sir Edward Herbert, was an important farmer and landowner.[42] Some sense of the scale of Sir Edward's farming enterprise on his extensive demesne lands may be gathered from his will, which lists a team of sixteen oxen – this at a time when most ploughing involved teams of horses or oxen two abreast and when the heavy trenching, requiring teams of eight or nine oxen plus two or four horses, was usually a matter of community expense funded by the whole township.[43] The poet's rural life was brief, however, as his grandfather died in 1593, the year George Herbert was born, and his father's death followed just three and a half years later. Magdalen Herbert moved with her family repeatedly in the years that followed, first to her mother's home at Eyton-upon-Severn, then, after the death of Lady Newport in 1599, to Oxford, and finally, in 1601, to the fringes of London, where she established her household at Charing Cross.[44] By the age of seven, therefore, Herbert was a town child. By the age of nine he was a Londoner. By the time of his admission to Trinity College, Cambridge in 1609, he had spent as much of his life in London as in the border country.

Amy Charles has suggested that 'the early years in his father's house ... and his grandmother's ... undoubtedly developed the sense of family and place that formed part of the continuing stability of his view of life.'[45] And yet, Herbert's sense of place (I will address his sense of family in the next chapter) does not seem to me remarkably stable or coherent. Without resorting to biographical determinism, one might argue that Herbert's view of rural life reflects the sense of rupture and dislocation so many deaths and removals would be expected to engender. In any event, no elaborate biographical or psychological argument is really necessary, because the fragmented and contradictory vision of rural life offered in *The Country Parson* corresponds to the larger instability of English agriculture in the early seventeenth century. We can describe this general instability primarily as a technological revolution, or as part of the transition from feudal to capitalist modes of production, or we can abandon terms like revolution and transition altogether, concentrating on the enormous regional variations in agricultural and social practice across England.[46] These approaches diverge on crucial questions, but none offers much support for the view that English rural life in the early seventeenth century exemplifies the continuity and stability that Charles suggests George Herbert drew from his early childhood.

Whatever impressions of country life Herbert may have carried forward from youth, he had a great deal to learn before he could begin writing *The Country Parson*. Most of that learning would almost certainly have taken place in Wiltshire between 1628 and 1632. Having lived at Cambridge and in and around London for twenty-six of his thirty-five years, Herbert moved in 1628 'from his stepfather's house at Chelsea to that of [his uncle] Henry Danvers, Earl of Danby, at Dauntesy, near Chippenham in Wiltshire.' After his marriage to his cousin, Jane Danvers, in 1629, Herbert and his new wife lived with Jane's widowed mother at nearby Baynton House 'for a year or more ... through the time of Herbert's hesitancy about accepting the rectory of Fuggleston-with-Bemerton, offered to him late in the winter or early in the spring of 1630.'[47] These moves involved comparatively short distances. Baynton House (near Edington) was about twenty-five miles from Herbert's parish – close enough that Charles believes he might have travelled the distance for Sunday services while the Bemerton rectory was being refurbished – and not much further from Dauntesy. Nevertheless, the character of the countryside changes markedly in this small space. To make the journey from Edington to Bemerton, Herbert would have begun by ascending the chalk escarpment of Salisbury plain just south of the village, crossing as he did so the boundary between two very different rural economies.

Edington is on the perimeter, and Dauntesy in the midst, of the Wiltshire 'cheese country,' a region devoted, in the seventeenth century, primarily to dairying and to cottage-based textile work. It was characterized by 'parishes of larger area, patterns of scattered settlement rather than nucleated villages, extensive tracts of woodland in Braydon, Chippenham and Melksham forests, and weaker manorial controls.'[48] Enclosure and disafforestation were making steady progress in this part of the county; by the seventeenth century about three quarters of the region was enclosed, and the disafforestation of Chippenham and Melksham forests was complete by about 1624. Since dairying was an enterprise most efficiently carried out on small enclosed farms, the number of independent small holders in cheese country actually increased as the region was farmed more intensively. Still, an increasing population and proliferation of small family holdings did not spell uniform prosperity. Disafforestation did mean dispossession or loss of subsistence for many forest cottagers, who became landless day-labourers, combining sporadic farm work with home-based industrial work for the depressed cloth industry.[49] Although there were no major disturbances here, as there were a few years later in Gillingham and Braydon Forests, there was still considerable social distress.[50]

The character of south Wiltshire, on the chalk downs of Salisbury Plain between Edington and Bemerton, is much different. Here people lived in nucleated villages under comparatively strong manorial controls. The landscape was mostly champion (that is, open fields), devoted, in almost equal proportion, to pasture and grain cultivation. Indeed the success of the system of 'sheep and corn husbandry' depended on this balance between pasture and arable field. Sheep were grazed in the day on the pasture and folded on the fields at night to manure them. As Herbert writes in the poem 'Providence': 'Sheep eat the grass, and dung the ground for more' (l. 69). The practice required very large flocks and a good deal of cooperation among villagers. Wealthy landowners had private flocks; tenants, small holders and middling yeomen combined their flocks and rotated the fold to ensure that

every farmer's land was manured at the proper time, a procedure over-
seen by a village shepherd, who followed rules established in the manorial court. The tendency was towards engrossing (amalgamation of small
holdings) and depopulation, but enclosure did not make the same
progress as in the cheese country, partly because the thin soil cover on
the chalk made hedging very difficult.[51]

Historian David Underdown has linked these differences in agricultural practice and social organization to the 'reformation of manners'
described by a number of historians of early modern England.[52] According to Underdown, the arable regions on the chalk downs and the forest
pasture region (cheese country) represent

> two quite different constellations of social, political, and cultural forces,
> involving diametrically opposite responses to the problems of the time. On
> the one side stood those who put their trust in the traditional conception
> of the harmonious, vertically-integrated society – a society in which the
> old bonds of paternalism, deference, and good neighbourliness were
> expressed in familiar religious and communal rituals – and wished to
> strengthen and preserve it. On the other stood those – mostly among the
> gentry and middling sort of the new parish élites – who wished to empha-
> size the moral and cultural distinctions which marked them off from their
> poorer, less disciplined neighbours, and to use their power to reform soci-
> ety according to their own principles of order and godliness. These two
> socio-cultural constellations can be observed in all parts of England, but in
> varied strengths in different geographical areas: the former more conspic-
> uously in the arable regions, the latter in the cloth-making wood-pasture
> districts. Two alternative societies existed side by side ... one relatively sta-
> ble and reciprocally paternalistic and deferential, the other more unstable,
> less harmonious, more individualistic.[53]

Herbert's experience in Wiltshire, limited as it was, brought him in
touch with both of these social 'constellations,' though it seems unlikely
that he would have distinguished them as clearly and sharply as this.[54]
Rather, he might have been troubled by conflicting elements of Wiltshire rural life: ambitious entrepreneurial small holders, impoverished
cottagers enduring deplorable lives, tenants and manorial lords clinging
(either heroically or stubbornly) to familiar ways. The harder we try
to look at the landscape and the issues without the schemata available to hindsight, the more contradictory things look. The sixteenth-
century anti-enclosure rhetoric Herbert echoed in 'The Church Porch'

had often identified the problem of enclosure with its most visible symbols – hedgerows, ravenous sheep, and the conversion of arable to pasture – and had identified the negative consequences as depopulation, elimination of small family farms, and especially vagrancy and crime. Seventeenth-century Wiltshire contradicted much of this. Where there were enclosures there were few sheep and there was little depopulation, but there was a proliferation of both comparatively prosperous small holders and impoverished cottagers. Where traditional open field husbandry was practiced, there were plenty of sheep, and there was also depopulation, but without any significant conversion of arable to pasture. These contradictions undermined the Tudor humanist critique of agricultural improvement, and in conjunction with the fact that the estates of Herbert's kinsman, the Earl of Pembroke, were the testing ground for major innovations in the practice of sheep and corn husbandry, they may help to account for Herbert's conversion to the cause of agricultural innovation, and for the generally contradictory character of his portrait of rural life.

Herbert's 'Country People'

> Now if a shepherd know not which grass will bane, or which not, how is he fit to be a shepherd? Wherefore the Parson hath throughly canvassed al the particulars of humane actions, at least all those which he observeth are most incident to his Parish. (230)

For all its insistence on particulars, Herbert's *Country Parson* is filled with generalizations, especially in its references to country life and country people. The impulse to make precise observations and comments coexists with the tendency (promoted by humanist education) to offer generalized precepts, maxims, aphorisms, and *sententiae* that can be adapted to a wide range of situations. The tension is one Herbert acknowledges himself as he cautions his clerical readers to illuminate precept with experience (with a passing shot at the problem of non-residency):

> And Scholers ought to be diligent in the observation of ... [petty injustices], and driving of their generall Schoole rules ever to the smallest actions of Life; which while they dwell in their bookes, they will never finde; but being seated in the Countrey, and doing their duty faithfully, they will soon discover: especially if they carry their eyes ever open, and fix them on their charge, and not on their preferment. (265–6)

This injunction places Herbert's own book in an ambiguous position, for it too contains 'generall Schoole rules,' and so long as readers 'dwell' in *it*, they are liable to neglect some more concrete aspects of their duty. In this sense *The Country Parson* resembles Herbert's poems, which repeatedly declare themselves superfluous. If we are looking in *The Country Parson* for evidence of the specific character of Herbert's rural experience, therefore, or for his 'true opinion' of country life and manners, we need to consider the interplay of conflicting images and the way in which what is present in the book gestures towards what is absent from it.

The first images Herbert offers of his parishioners, in chapter III, 'The Parson's Life,' are familiar stereotypes of rugged integrity, even moral precision, stereotypes with their roots in georgic literary traditions.[55]

> Because Countrey people live hardly, and therefore as feeling their own sweat, and consequently knowing the price of mony, are offended much with any, who by hard usage increase their travell, the Countrey Parson is very circumspect in avoiding all covetousnesse (227)

> Because Countrey People (as indeed all honest men) do much esteem their word, it being the Life of buying, and selling, and dealing in the world; therefore the Parson is very strict in keeping his word. (228)

These passages balance the emphasis on the parson as an observer, an emphasis reflected in chapter titles like 'The Parson's Eye,' 'The Parson's Surveys,' 'The Parson in Sentinell,' and 'The Parson in Circuit,' with reminders that the parson is also an object of community scrutiny.[56] If they reflect Herbert's experience, they also reflect the conventional expressions of rural morality found in the early modern agricultural handbooks. In Konrad Heresbach's *Foure Bookes of Husbandrie*, translated into English by Barnaby Googe, the authorial persona fondly recalls his father, a farmer and devotee of sermons who 'brought both preacher and priest into order, and caused them to frame their lives according to the rule of the Gospel.'[57] In such depictions the moral authority of the clergyman seems rather precarious, dependent on, and at times subordinate to, the comparatively secure moral authority of the community. Pastoral authority and community authority operate in a dialectic, each working to keep the other in its place.

As if to hold up his end of the mutual-scrutiny bargain, Herbert repeatedly tempers and even contradicts the georgic stereotype of rugged rustic integrity with images of country people more indebted to comic traditions. If country people are morally precise where others are concerned, they are nevertheless, according to Herbert, 'full of ... petty injustices, being cunning to make use of another, and spare themselves' (265). They are unresponsive to exhortations from the pulpit, 'thick and heavy, and hard to raise to a poynt of Zeal, and fervency, and need a mountaine of fire to kindle them' (233). The parson must reward and punish 'in Gods stead,' and in the here and now, because 'Countrey people are drawne, or led by sense, more then by faith, by present rewards, or punishments, more then by future' (254). Herbert seems almost to have in mind two distinct sorts of country people in these passages, though he nowhere makes such a distinction explicitly. Of course people *are* contradictory, even hypocritical, and it is entirely possible that Herbert saw, or thought he saw, all these qualities in his parishioners at Bemerton.

There is another possibility, however, equally plausible and attractive. Might not a man educated to think and write in *sententiae*, thrown into unfamiliar social and geographical surroundings, among people whose manners and modes of life varied widely even over comparatively short distances, respond to that experience by drawing from his stock of discursive conventions a series of contradictory generalizations, each 'true' for a significant group of people? Might not the precise observers of clerical conduct be found among the prosperous small holders of north Wiltshire, people Underdown characterizes as more inclined to Puritanism and 'gadding to sermons,' and more critical of the deficiencies of their clergy? Might not the pettiness, the indifference to preaching and theological persuasion, the insistence on immediate reward and punishment be more typical of the downland parishioners who clung to traditional festive customs and an 'older, more permissive concept of order'?[58] Might not *The Country Parson*'s treatment of country people be a record of social diversity and variability, cloaked in a rhetoric of typicality?

The contradictions in Herbert's treatment of rural labour and vocation do seem consistent with an attempt to frame generalizations about a diverse population. Chapter XV, 'The Parson in Circuit,' describes the parson's weekday visits to parishioners. Its descriptions correspond closely to the situation in the wood-pasture district of north Wiltshire, where differences between the industrious and the idle, the propertied and the landless, and the godly and the godless were especially pronounced.[59] The chapter itself is divided, treating first the parson's response to those he finds 'religiously imployed' or 'busie in the works of their calling' (247) and next his handling of '[t]hose that the Parson finds idle, or ill imployed' (248). The former invite praise, but also an extended cautionary discourse:

> he admonisheth them of two things; first, that they dive not too deep into worldly affairs, plunging themselves over head and eares into carking, and caring; but that they so labour, as neither to labour anxiously, nor distrustfully, nor profanely. Then they labour anxiously, when they overdo it, to the loss of their quiet, and health: then distrustfully, when they doubt Gods providence, thinking that their own labour is the cause of their thriving, as if it were in their own hands to thrive, or not to thrive. *Then they labour profanely, when they set themselves to work like brute beasts, never raising their thoughts to God, nor sanctifying their labour with daily prayer.* (247–8)

These cautions read like an account of the excesses incident to the 'Protestant work-ethic,' as seen from the standpoint of the established church, excesses to which only the most prosperous and individualistic of rural labourers would probably be liable.[60] In the second part of the chapter, when Herbert refers to the 'idle, or ill imployed,' he may have in mind the landless cottagers of north Wiltshire, whose living depended on domestic industry (chiefly spinning) and on the intermittent supply of raw wool from middle men.[61] After insisting that idleness in any parishioner be reproved, albeit in a manner consistent with the status and sensibility of the individual, Herbert urges an enquiry into domestic order, 'prayers ... reading of Scripture, catechizing, singing of Psalms at their work' (248). Like their more prosperous neighbours, though for very different reasons, impoverished cottagers probably needed to be reminded to '*sanctify* ... *their labour.*' The chapter closes with an emphatic assertion of the parson's duty to minister to the inhabitants of 'the poorest Cottage, though he even creep into it, and though it smell never so lothsomly' (249). On the one hand, there are clear signs of the prevailing early modern view of unemployment as a crime and idleness as a sin. On the other, there are hints, however slight, of recognition that idleness was, for many of these people, a product of circumstances over which they had no control.

Later, in chapter XXX, 'The Parson's Consideration of Providence,' Herbert returns to some of the same issues, only to treat them quite differently:

The Countrey Parson considering the great aptnesse Countrey people have
to think that all things come by a kind of naturall course; and that if they
sow and soyle their grounds, they must have corn; if they keep and fodder
well their cattel, they must have milk, and Calves; labours to reduce them
to see Gods hand in all things, and to beleeve, that things are not set in
such an inevitable order, but that God often changeth it according as he
sees fit, either for reward or punishment. (270)

The difference in tone suggests a geographical, biographical, and ideological shift. Despite the references to cattle and milk Herbert seems to
have shifted his gaze south, toward the chalk downs of Salisbury Plain,
where he moved in 1630, and where the long-established seasonal
rhythm of 'sow and soyle' must have seemed very much like 'a kind of
natural course.' In the north, cheese was the main dairy product, and
the labour-intensive cheese-making process would not seem likely to
promote the complacency of which Herbert complains. In contrast to
the earlier chapter, here the 'typical' vices of the farmer seem to arise
from insufficient, rather than excessive, anxiety about God's providence. The parson must urge such a man 'not to break off, but to continue his dependance on God, not onely before the corne is inned, but
after also; and indeed, to depend and fear continually (271). If hypoc-
risy among parishioners is one possible explanation for the moral and
spiritual inconsistencies Herbert catalogues, it is less persuasive as an
account of these divergent attitudes towards labour and providence.
People might well be simultaneously particular about others' trans-
gressions and blind to their own (Puritans, in particular, were often
condemned for such inconsistency), but they are less likely to be simultaneously anxious and complacent about the efficacy of their own
labours. Either Herbert is a poor observer of country people, or he is a
better observer than he realizes, registering subtle variations in attitude,
corresponding to variations in geography and agricultural practice,
without registering them *as* variations.[62] We might even speculate that
Herbert's comments on providence reflect his experience of the harvest
failures of 1630 and 1631, when even prosperous farmers in Wiltshire
had difficulty finding enough good seed to sow.[63]

If Herbert's generalizations offer a fragmented picture of the rural
parishioner, they nevertheless offer a fairly coherent portrait of Herbert's clerical audience. The conventional view of *The Country Parson* is
that it addresses the clerical 'old guard,' who were locally recruited, ill-
educated, and set in their ways. Yet, as I have suggested, it is hard to

imagine the old-guard clergy having much patience for or interest in a book written by a young gentleman-pastor of rather slight experience. On the contrary, the overwhelming assumption in these passages is that Herbert's readers will lack rural experience. Herbert imagines an audience of men much like himself: comparatively young and well educated, liable to be ambitious for preferment (or perhaps disappointed in their secular ambitions), and apt to behave in ways that might make them seem remote from rural parishioners. One objective of the book is perhaps to reduce the anticlericalism provoked by this new generation, by preparing naive university men for the realities of country life.

The chapters of *The Country Parson* considered in the preceding paragraphs also offer a consistent image of the clerical function. If the parishioners Herbert considers are susceptible to a wide range of weaknesses, Herbert's ideal parson offers correspondingly wide-ranging counsel, counsel that looks, at least on the surface, quite contradictory. Those who work hard and rely on their own labours are cautioned to trust in God. For them, the ideal parson represents providence in terms of constancy and reassurance. On the other hand, those who already equate providence with nature and its cycles, who are inclined to 'rest in Nature, not the God of Nature' ('The Pulley' l. 14), are urged to see things quite differently, to beware the sudden and unexpected catastrophes that make God's ways unknowable: 'God delights to have men feel, and acknowledg, and reverence his power, and therefore he often overturnes things, when they are thought past danger' (271). Common to both these strategies is the impulse to 'reduce' the parishioner to 'repining restlesnesse' ('The Pulley,' l. 18), by disrupting preconceptions, offering images of God and his ways that run contrary to habit or experience, insisting that God is always other. In reducing the parishioner, the parson elevates himself as the repository of a knowledge that is always contradictory, at once elusive and essential for the parishioner's 'improvement.' If it is axiomatic that 'God's goodnesse strives with man's refractorinesse,' then one of the central duties of God's deputy is to construct every human action as an instance of that 'refractorinesse,' thereby to magnify 'God's goodnesse.'

The bias evident here reveals the underlying economic ideology of Herbert's portrait. For Herbert, as for all the commentators on agricultural improvement, the key social problem and 'the great and nationall sin of this Land [is] Idleness' (274), and the reproof of this sin is always central to the parson's duty.[64] If, as the parable of the child and the apple suggests, one of the projects of *The Country Parson* is to reconcile an emergent rhetoric of agricultural and economic improvement and innovation with a traditionalist rhetoric of paternalistic social order, then it is in the interest of such a reconciliation to seem to temper the former with the latter. Conveniently for the cause of improvement, the sanctification of labour does not require any significant interruption in that labour; the industrious must guard against pride by 'raising their thoughts to God' *as* they labour. For those already immersed in the ideology of improvement, Herbert's ideal parson represents God as a comforter who will reward their labours, so long as those labours are performed in a spirit of devotion. On the other hand, for those too inclined to rely on providence and the natural course of things (probably those participating in traditional sheep and corn husbandry), Herbert's ideal parson urges not only a devotional state of mind, but a series of 'acts of dependence' – a euphemism, one suspects, for working harder. The traditional arable farmer, who follows in the footsteps of his father and grandfather is like the child who wants only the apple rather than the piece of gold underneath: his moderate ambitions are, paradoxically, a sign of carnality and wilfulness, and the parson is the 'worm of conscience' sent by God to trouble him.

Agricultural Improvement in Herbert's Wiltshire

There remains a slight biographical puzzle concerning Herbert's conversion to the cause of agricultural improvement. One might plausibly argue that despite ambiguities and contradictions, the conservative Tudor-humanist commonweal position to which Herbert seems to have subscribed as a young man would have been reinforced by the traditional community-based sheep and corn husbandry practiced on the open fields of Salisbury Plain. Many commentators have assumed that this view stayed with Herbert throughout his life.[65] What forces precipitated his change of heart? Perhaps he came to admire the spirit of the more individualistic smallholders of the cheese country when he lived at Dauntesy and Edington, and hoped to disseminate their ideology among his more conservative parishioners at Bemerton, and even more widely through his book. But Herbert's time in North Wiltshire was a brief interval, and it is hard to imagine such a conversion would be possible without continuing reinforcement of the new posture after his move to Bemerton. Some of that reinforcement may well have come from the agricultural handbooks that celebrated the virtues of industrious husbandry, and that probably contributed to the Herbert's idealizations of rural character. Even more may have come from the agricultural practice of south Wiltshire, which was not so rigidly traditional as Underdown's sketch seems to suggest.[66] As Buchanan Sharp has pointed out, the farming culture of arable regions was increasingly market-oriented in the early seventeenth century: the 'main road to maximization for every landholder, whether king or middling sort, was through sponsoring or engaging in enclosure or other improvements.'[67] And as I have already mentioned, the prevalence of engrossing meant that Bemerton and the surrounding countryside suffered many of the negative consequences of enclosure – depopulation, elimination of small family farms – without actually experiencing enclosure. Indeed the structure of sheep and corn husbandry, with its dependance on very large flocks and community cooperation, lends itself to engrossing. A farm had to be very large to support a private flock and a shepherd; even substantial yeomen like the Wansboroughs of Shrewton, who owned about 160 acres and about 400 sheep and lambs, folded their sheep with the common flock.[68] As Eric Kerridge observes, 'the lower proportional working cost of the large farm ... whether accompanied by the extinction of common rights or not, encouraged ... amalgamation.'[69]

Beyond this, the chalk downs of Herbert's Wiltshire were, in the second quarter of the seventeenth century, the proving ground for the floated flowing water meadow, an innovation that was to become 'the crowning glory of [English] agricultural technique' for the subsequent two hundred years. Specifically, there is a record of a contract in 1632 for the floating of meadows at Wylye, on the estates of the Earl of Pembroke, an agreement that 'shows floating was well understood in the district ... and that farmers, tenants, and manorial Lord ... were all aware of the innovation's advantages.'[70] This technique, a significant refinement of the irrigation methods developed in the sixteenth century, employed elaborate systems of trenches to keep large expanses of meadow under a blanket of flowing water throughout the winter, which protected the grass from frost. This provided abundant fresh grass for sheep in April, when winter fodder was beginning to run out, and a rich hay crop later in the season.[71] As a result, much larger flocks could overwinter, and since the yield of grain depended on the size of the flock manuring it, the technique eventually led to substantial increases in grain production. Of course, contouring the land to facilitate the flow of water, and constructing the necessary weir and trenches, were expensive propositions, and while in the instance cited tenants shared the expenses and the manual labour, opportunities for the sometimes spectacular increases in profit must have been weighted heavily towards landlords with substantial capital.[72] That Herbert knew of, and was impressed by this practice is suggested not only by his reference to 'drowning and draining' of lands in *The Country Parson*, but also by his poem 'The Water-course,' and stanza four of 'The Invitation':[73]

> Come ye hither All, whom joy
> > Doth destroy,
> While ye graze without your bounds:
> Here is joy that drowneth quite
> > Your delight,
> As a floud the lower grounds.   (ll. 19–24)

In the second half of the stanza, Herbert figures the Eucharist as a meadow enriched by flooding, capable of sustaining the flock that has succumbed to the temptation to 'graze without ... bounds.'[74]

The two forms of reinforcement to which Herbert might have been exposed – material practice and literary propaganda – converge in one remarkable little book, Rowland Vaughan's *Most Approved and Long Experienced Water-Workes*. It was published in 1610, with a lengthy dedication and plea for patronage addressed to William Herbert, third Earl of Pembroke, to whose ancestors (who are also George Herbert's ancestors) Vaughan claims kinship ties.[75] Unlike other agricultural handbooks, *Water-Workes* does not survey techniques of ploughing and soil improvement, crop varieties and planting schedules, or methods of breeding and maintaining livestock. Rather, it offers an extended account of the author's experiments with water meadows on his own estates in Herefordshire, the earliest known description of the practice. Vaughan's book also offers a vivid glimpse of the link between agricultural improvement and the transition to capitalism, and of the ideological manoeuvres that reinforce the transition.[76] Like so many agricultural projectors, Vaughan links his schemes of improvement to the quest for social order. In Herefordshire, where Vaughan lived, engrossing had pushed an unusually large number of small farmers off the land, creating a crisis of poverty and vagrancy.[77] Vaughan complains of 'five hundred poore habitations; whose greatest meanes consist in spinning ... [T]hese Idelers live intollerablie by other meanes, and neglect their painfull labours by oppressing the neighbourhood' with begging, gleaning (which Vaughan denounces as a cover for robbing orchards and gardens), and time-wasting trips to the market and mill.[78] What Vaughan is attacking here is, of course, the remnant of an integrated system of traditional (pre-capitalist) production in which 'economic organization was domestic organization.'[79] With the all-important patronage of the Earl of Pembroke, and with the success of the water works as testimony to his ingenuity, Vaughan proposes 'to raise a golden world (for common-wealth) in the *Golden Vale* of Herefordshire.' He will build a community of artisans, diverting the labour released from agricultural production into concentrated capitalist cottage industry – a sort of country sweatshop. There 'my *Mechanicals* ... shall never lose an houres time to provide for such *meanes* as the *backe* or *belly* requires: *bread, beefe, mutton, butter* and *cheese* of mine own provision, shall attend their appointed hours without the trouble or losse of labor to any Market or other place.'[80] Bentham and Foucault would surely be impressed: Vaughan's discourse renders these workers 'mechanical' in a sense that reaches far beyond the usual early modern sense of the term.

Nevertheless, Vaughan is far from a thoroughgoing utilitarian or venture capitalist. He appeals to an aristocratic patron because he has been treated badly by 'usurers,' who have been so indelicate as to ask for sureties, and so presumptuous as to expect payment at the appointed time. Anxious to defend himself against charges of 'ambition,' he couches his project in the traditionalist rhetoric of charity, good works, and devotion to the commonweal:

> if any ... should be so injurious to say so, then (my LORD) they may say the Clothier; the habitation for *Artificers* the *Chappell,* and *Preacher, Curate, Almeshouse*; My Table for the benefit of poore *Artificers,* and whatsoever else is good (yea a *common-good*) is out of ambition.[81]

Ironically, given the importance of weirs in the construction of water meadows, and his frustration with his own tenants' resistence to their construction, Vaughan explicitly invokes traditional common rights and the obligations of deferential hierarchy in pleading for the destruction of a series of weirs on the river Wye in order to 'make the *River* Navigable, Portable ... [and] Sammonable': 'Remember the love your Father and Grand-father bare their-our *Countrey*: remember wee were their *kinsmen* and *servants*.' All this might be dismissed as contradiction, but such contradictions have a certain utility. Articulated as compromises they give a veneer of moderation, good sense, and common purpose to even the most radical (harebrained?) projects. In this context, it is not surprising to find Vaughan invoking the theological *via media*: 'Your Lordship doth see I am no *Papist*, nor *Puritane*, but a true *Protestant* according to the Kings Injunctions.'[82] The strategy of the Elizabethan compromise, retaining the rituals of an old faith while consolidating a new theology, is mirrored in Vaughan's economic project, which clings to elements of tradition, and uses them to prop up a terrifyingly 'rationalist' agenda.

Herbert's Nationalism and Ruralism

In returning from Vaughan to Herbert, we leave behind an economic visionary who invokes the *via media* in defence of his schemes to rid 'the *Golden Vale* of Herefordshire' of 'Idelers,' and rejoin a moderate clergyman who seeks solutions to 'the great and nationall sin of Idlenesse.' Herbert's concern for this subject hints once more at the divergent senses of the word 'country' in *The Country Parson*. Each of these writers pursues the betterment of his country, yet Vaughan's concerns are largely parochial, while Herbert's book is often deeply concerned with the parson's and the parishioners' patriotic duty to the nation. If the country parson is a rural pastor, he is also an English pastor:

> His children he first makes Christians, and then Commonwealths-men; the one he owes to his heavenly Countrey, the other to his earthly, having no title to either, except he do good to both (239);

> it is a justice and debt to the Common-wealth he lives in, not to incroach on others Professions (262);

> it is ... a debt to our Countrey to have a Calling, and it concernes the Common-wealth, that none should be idle, but all busied. (274)

The expression 'country parson,' then, bears some of the nationalistic overtones of countryman, as we have come to understand the term, just as 'countryman,' in Herbert's usage, often designates social status rather than a national affiliation: 'a plaine countryman, he reproves ... plainly' (248). Similarly, 'country' used as a noun need not refer to the nation; it can also have narrower regional associations, as in 'the Wiltshire cheese country.' Herbert uses the word this way when he remarks that service as a Justice of the Peace is 'an honorable Imployment of a Gentle, or Noble-man in the Country he lives in' (276). The word 'country' shifts its geographic associations from large to small, and from national to parochial, as occasion requires.

Those shifts correspond, at least approximately, to variations in the cultural and ideological valence of 'country.' Where the term refers to the nation, as in most of the examples listed above, it is linked to emergent discourse of commerce and property through terms like 'owe,' 'debt,' 'title,' and 'incroach.' In these passages Herbert's conception of the 'common-wealth' and the 'country' (both heavenly and earthly) seems thoroughly commercialized: there is little residue of the old notions of commonweal associated with traditional subsistence agriculture. Herbert's England is, increasingly, a trading nation. So the nation's model parson 'commends the study of Civill Law' not, as one might expect, because it is the basis of Ecclesiastical law, but 'because it is the key of Commerce, and discovers the Rules of forraine Nations' (277).[83] Herbert's enthusiasm for commerce and trade is almost prescient given that exports in goods other than cloth do not become a significant element in the English economy until late in the century. A 1688 estimate puts goods for export at about 7 per cent of England's total production.[84] Nevertheless, the rhetoric of commerce, like the rhetoric of agricultural improvement, suffuses Herbert's account of pastoral duty:

> The Country Parson, as soon as he awakes on Sunday morning, presently falls to work, and seems to himselfe so as a Market-man is, when the Market day comes, or a shopkeeper, when customers use to come in. His thoughts are full of making the best of the day, and contriving it to his best gaines. (235)

Even in a region utterly dependent on sheep for economic survival, the 'good shepherd' is transformed into a merchant. This is where *The Country Parson*'s 'knowledge of tillage and pastorage' leads: even in the most 'traditional' parts of Wiltshire, agriculture is commerce by Herbert's day.

With both Herbert and Vaughan, there are contradictions, or remnants of an alternative discourse. If Herbert's parson is the zealous, spiritual entrepreneur, he also plays the cautious, locally minded husbandman, suspicious of innovations and 'outlandish' commodities. Vaughan wants to tear down weirs on the river Wye to preserve a common fishery and transportation artery, while he builds weirs on its tributaries to flood his meadows; Herbert praises the study of trade and commerce, while he inveighs against the lure of imported luxuries. Speaking of medicines, he urges his readers to 'make the garden the shop: For home-bred medicines are both more easie for the Parsons purse, and more familiar for all mens bodyes' (261). He goes on to extend the point, amplifying the nationalistic tone:

> As for spices, he doth not onely prefer home-bred things before them, but condemns them for vanities, and so shuts them out of his family, esteeming that there is no spice comparable, for herbs, to rosemary, time, savoury, mints; and for seeds, to Fennell, and Carroway seeds. Accordingly, for salves, his wife seeks not the city, but preferes her garden and fields before all outlandish gums. (261–2)

Here the concepts of the native and the rural seem entirely to have merged. The city is associated with the 'outlandish,' its Englishness tainted by foreign influences. Only the garden and fields are reliably English. The same spirit is evident in Herbert's account of the parson's domestic comforts:

> The furniture of his house is very plain, but clean, whole, and sweet, as sweet as his garden can make; for he hath no mony for such things, charity being his only perfume, which deserves cost when he can spare it. His fare is plain, and common, but wholsome, what hee hath, is little, but very good; it consisteth most of mutton, beefe, and veal, if he addes any thing for a great day, or a stranger, his garden or orchard supplyes it, or his barne, and backe-side: he goes no further for any entertainment, lest he goe into the world, esteeming it absurd, that he should exceed, who teacheth others temperance. But those which his home produceth, he refuseth not, as coming cheap, and easie, and arising from the improvement of things, which otherwise would be lost. (241)

In this passage, the parson's 'country' seems to have contracted even further, to the narrow compass of his glebe lands; to stray farther in search of luxury items is to risk going 'into the world.'[85] Herbert counters his own tendency to magnify the clergy's social role with a traditionalist discourse calculated to curb clerical ambition and aspiration.

Like the displaced rural worker and the traditional farmer too reliant on providence, Herbert's pastoral audience is disoriented and controlled by these shifting constructions of duty and belonging. The contradictions serve to establish and limit what Michel Foucault would call the 'disciplinary space' in which the pastor operates. Discipline, says Foucault, requires 'Docile Bodies'; Herbert's parson 'keeps his body tame, serviceable, and healthfull; and his soul fervent, active, young and lusty as an eagle' (237). Discipline seeks 'at each moment to supervise the conduct of each individual, to assess it, to judge it, to calculate its qualities or merits'; the chapters of Herbert's book – chapters with titles like 'The Parson in his House,' 'The Parson Comforting,' 'The Parson in mirth' – situate the parson temporally, physically, and spiritually, prescribing the correct activity and feeling for every moment, the moment and feeling for each activity, and the moment and activity for each feeling.[86] Yet the chapters often achieve that precise placement through disruption, displacement, or destabilization: 'The Parson in mirth' begins: 'The Countrey Parson is generally sad' (267). Like the parishioners whom the ideal parson disciplines with contrariety and contradiction, the clerical reader is to be an anxious *self*-disciplinarian. His duty is clear, and the standard uncompromising: 'he *fils that which is behinde of the afflictions of Christ*' (225). The parson's 'Mark to aim at' is set beyond reach (224) to provoke continual striving, or in the words of 'The Pulley,' 'repining restlesnesse.' As both the instrument and the object of disciplinary surveillance, loyal to a sense of country at once local and national, elevated to a place of dignity and constrained by an ideology of duty, the county parson is, rather like one of Vaughan's 'mechanicals,' fixed in his place of work, the parish.

Discussing the flood of maps and chorographic books in late Elizabethan and early Stuart England, Richard Helgerson has traced the emergence of an antidynastic nationalism in which '[s]ervice to the country alone ... was displacing service to king *and* country.' According to Helgerson, 'the nation, unlike the dynasty, is ... strengthened by ... receptiveness to ... individual and communal autonomy. The dialectic of general and particular that is built into the structure of a chorography in the end constitutes the nation it represents.'[87] This 'dialectic of general and particular' operates in *The Country Parson* as well, though rather differently than in the chorographic works that undoubtedly constitute some of its subtexts. Despite its repeated insistence on the importance of particularity, not just geographic, but also hierarchical – the country parson must take account of local custom, age, and social status in dealing with his parishioners – Herbert's book moves relentlessly towards generalization. Even when describing features of country life that seem to reflect local variations, Herbert refers to 'country people' in general. The result is a fiction of homogeneity and typicality that resolves diversity, difference, and contradiction into an ideology of common purpose, quite distinct from old-fashioned commonweal but sharing its reassuring rhetoric.

One ambiguous instance of the word 'country' encapsulates this strategy. In chapter IIII Herbert remarks by way of analogy that 'as one Countrey doth not bear all things, that there may be a Commerce, so neither hath God opened, or will open all to one, that there may be a traffick in knowledg' (229). The word 'country' in this analogy is ambiguously regional and national, just as Herbert's stance is ambiguously traditional and commercial. The traffic in knowledge may be likened to the trade of nation states and emerging empires, or to the necessary cooperation and complementarity of specialized agricultural regions. The ideological posture sanctioned by the analogy may be ambitious and entrepreneurial or humble and parochial. Indeed given these two almost diametrically opposed readings, we might well tease out a third: 'one [definition of the word] countrey doth not bear all things': one's country is both one's region and one's nation. This amounts to an argument for a 'commerce' or a 'traffick' between modes of expression and understanding, a cultural/economic/discursive *via media* composed of traditional and commercial elements. But 'traffic' and 'commerce,' the controlling terms in this analogy, are not quite the same as synthesis and compromise, the usual connotations of the *via media*. Instead they imply an adversarial vision in which trading partners are also competitors. The operation of Herbert's text as an arena for the competitive traffic in ideologies is perhaps the clearest sign of its specific ideological character, its embrace of an agrarian capitalism sustained and rendered palatable by a residue of traditionalist commonweal rhetoric.

chapter five

Pastor as Patriarch: Gender, Family, and Social Order in *The Country Parson*

> The Countrey Parson is not only a father to his flock, but also professeth himselfe throughly of the opinion, carrying it about with him as fully, as if he had begot his whole Parish. And of this he makes great use. For by this means, when any sinns, he hateth him not as an officer, but pityes him as a Father: and even in those wrongs which either in tithing, or otherwise are done to his owne person, hee considers the offender as a child, and forgives, so hee may have any signe of amendment; so also when after many admonitions, any continue to be refractory, yet hee gives him not over, but is long before he proceede to disinheriting, or perhaps never goes so far; knowing, that some are called at the eleventh houre, and therefore hee still expects, and waits, least hee should determine Gods houre of coming; which hee cannot, touching the last day, so neither touching the intermediate days of Conversion.
>
> *A Priest to the Temple, or The Country Parson*
> *His Character and Rule of Holy Life,*
> Chapter XVI, 'The Parson a Father'

As I suggested in chapter 4, and as critics from Leah Marcus to Jeffrey Powers-Beck have noticed, Herbert understands his place in the social and cosmic hierarchies, and communicates that understanding, through the discourse of parent-child relations. Not surprisingly, this understanding permeates his account of pastoral dignity and duty: 'the Countrey Parson is ... a father to his flock.' But Herbert's parable of the child and the apple in chapter XXX of *The Country Parson* also reveals a bifurcation in that ideology. As Marcus observes, contending forces in Herbert's culture both idealized and repudiated childhood: 'Conservative Anglican and royalist theorists ... advocated childish submission ...

in order to restore an idealized – and very selective – vision of what medieval England had been.' At the same time, the self-consciously godly rejected the 'liturgical and festival survivals of medieval Christianity ... [as] in a very precise sense of the word, childish.'[1] Drawing illustrations primarily from the poetry, Marcus places Herbert squarely in the 'conservative Anglican' camp, arguing that for him, 'becoming the child of God meant replacing his adult intellect and inclinations with total dependence on the wisdom and will of his heavenly Father.'[2] Yet in the apple parable Herbert seems much closer to what Marcus would call the 'Puritan' version of patriarchy, in which an ideal father cultivates the child's 'adult intellect and inclinations,' promoting social and spiritual maturity. On the questions of land management and farming practice, I argued that Herbert appears to change his mind, as he becomes increasingly exposed to both the practice and the discourse of agricultural 'improvement' in the last years of his life. Even on these questions, however, the social power of traditionalist rhetoric impels or permits him (and others) to understand and to represent innovation as continuity. This tendency is even more evident in the realm of patriarchy, the cornerstone of traditionalist social discourse. The bifurcation Marcus describes was probably a good deal less evident to Herbert and his contemporaries than it is to commentators writing at the turn of the millennium. Despite some differing conceptions of childhood and human development, early modern representations of the family, and the social roles of parent and child, present these roles as the most stable and constant elements in a sometimes inconstant world. But how well did the early modern family correspond to these images of stability and constancy? In Herbert's writing we face a central problem in studies of the early modern family: the problem of disentangling representation and 'reality,' convention and observation. Before exploring in detail Herbert's handling of patriarchal discourse in *The Country Parson*, therefore, it is necessary to make a detour into the controversial history and historiography of the early modern family.

The Debate over Early Modern Patriarchy

It has become customary for studies of the family in early modern England to open with an implicit or explicit critique of Lawrence Stone's sweeping study *The Family, Sex and Marriage in England, 1500–1800.*[3] Scholars from all sides have challenged Stone's key propositions, his account of the oppressively patriarchal character of the sixteenth

and seventeenth century family, his claim to discern a profound transformation in the structure of the English family (from the 'open lineage
family' to the 'restricted patriarchal nuclear family'), and eventually, to
the 'closed domesticated nuclear family,' and his account of the gradual
emergence of affection and choice as guiding forces in courtship, marriage, and child rearing. Historical demography has demonstrated with
some certainty that the nuclear family was firmly established as the prevailing English model, and indeed the prevailing model throughout
Northwest Europe.[4] Analysis of diaries and autobiographies, along with
Christian domestic advice literature, has led some to paint a portrait of a
benevolent, nurturing patriarchy.[5] And it has become clear that, with
certain important exceptions (for heirs and heiresses and for the very
poor), young men and women had a good deal of freedom in the realm
of courtship and marriage and typically delayed marriage many years
beyond the time of sexual maturity for economic reasons.[6] If the weight
of rebuttal a work attracts is a measure of its influence, then Stone's
book is influential indeed, albeit mostly in generating misconceptions
for other historians to correct. And yet in comprehensiveness and ambition Stone's study has no rival. The historiography of the early modern
English family is the story of Stone and his critics.

    There are clearly political and ideological undercurrents to some of
this criticism, extending beyond the realm of family history. Stone's *The
Causes of the English Revolution* has been described as representing 'a
stage in historical analysis which may have peaked in the early 1970s, but
which has been in retreat for more than a decade,' an old orthodoxy
displaced by revisionist accounts stressing 'stability and continuity in
Early Stuart England.'[7] The same emphasis on stability and continuity is
evident in much of the work on the family that sets out to counter
Stone's. Alan Macfarlane's *Marriage and Love in England, 1300–1840*,
for example, resembles 'those sociological tomes of the 1950s which
explained all social and economic relations in terms of a harmonious
homeostatic functionalism. Inevitably, since he has not paid due attention to dissonant elements, his methodology leads to a portrait of egali-
tarian family harmony.'[8] At stake in the debate about the early modern
family are major issues of historical methodology and emphasis:
whether to concentrate on the 'normal' functioning of a society and its
members, or on the 'dissonant elements,' the strains and tensions that
lead to change (though not inevitably to particular changes), and
whether England in the decades before 1640 should be seen as a pre-
revolutionary or a transitional society, or whether the Civil War should

be seen (as many contemporaries undoubtedly saw it) as an extraordinary disruption in a more or less smoothly functioning political order. It might at first seem odd that notions of family structure should be so central to a major debate about historiography and about the political and constitutional history of a nation, but the account of early modern English society as essentially stable and 'unrevolutionary' (to borrow Conrad Russell's phrase) depends, at heart, on a vision of the stable and harmonious early modern family. Hence Peter Laslett's *The World We Have Lost* moves from an account of the family structure of a typical London baker to an argument for the abolition of the phrase 'English Revolution.'

In many accounts of Tudor and Stuart history, the family functions, as it did for contemporaries, as a central explanatory metaphor, the locus of a system of analogies that extends from the level of psychology and physiology to the level of national politics.[9] This is the familiar model of the 'Great Chain of Being' with its intricate 'System of Correspondences' that was so succinctly expressed in E.M.W. Tillyard's now decidedly unfashionable *Elizabethan World Picture*. The family, in this picture, is the cornerstone of a social system of deferential hierarchy, authoritarian and highly stratified to be sure, but more important, divinely ordained and almost universally accepted.[10] People defined themselves and their places in terms of their duties to superiors and inferiors, and of the treatment to which they were entitled by virtue of their status. Class affiliations and antagonisms did not exist any more than affiliations existed among children of different families, or antagonisms between children collectively and parents collectively. What conflict there was should be seen as local and factional, contained within the structures of family, village, and county, and never as offering an alternative vision of social order.

Nevertheless there were exceptions and challenges to the notion of a smoothly graduated and widely accepted social hierarchy. In terms of social status, the emerging professions were among the most obvious exceptions. The status of a lawyer, physician, or clergyman was partly a function of birth, partly a function of income, and to some degree independent of these conventional measures of social hierarchy. Each professional group was, itself, hierarchically organized, yet as I argued in chapter 3, the status relationship of any one to the others was uncertain, as was the relationship between professionals and the traditional hierarchy based on land ownership and labour. A growing number of people, though still a small number in terms of the overall population, fit uneasily into the conventional, vertically integrated hierarchy. To put the matter in terms of the governing analogy of family, there were a growing number of influential people whom we might describe metaphorically as societal bastards, orphans, adoptees, and step-children. This is important because the very texts that disseminate and perpetuate the ideology of deferential hierarchy on a familial model, and make it available to historians and literary scholars, are often written by members of these semi-autonomous professional groups, especially clergymen. Paradoxically, those people whose social position is most anomalous are the source of many of our accounts of social norms.

Foremost among these sources are the sermons and domestic advice books that represented the family figuratively as a human body, in which 'the *Husband* is as the head, the wife as the body or the rib,' or as a little commonwealth, where just 'as a King is to see that land well governed where he is King, so he [i.e., the father] that is the chiefe ruler in an house.'[11] In the structure of the family, conventional opinion held, everyone could see his or her duty in macrocosm and in microcosm. As Thomas Gataker put it in *Marriage Duties Briefely Couched Togither,* 'where dutie faileth betweene man and wife it causeth a neglect of all other good duties in the family that dependeth upon them, yea of dutie oft even to God himselfe in them.'[12] Herbert's *Country Parson* occupies a distinctive if not a unique position in this literature, as a systematic extension of the familial analogy into the professional sphere. In proclaiming 'The Countrey Parson ... a father to his flock,' Herbert follows the lead of writers such as Gataker, who also likened fathers to priests: 'as ... the priests lips should preserve knowledge for the people, and they are to aske the law of him: so the husbands head should preserve wisedome and counsell for his wife, and she is to take advice of him.'[13] These two passages also suggest, however, that the very texts that transmit, extend, and reinforce the ideology of familial hierarchy also display the inadequacy of that ideology as an account of the social world in which their readers operate. They offer support for a more nuanced account of domestic life, an account in which authority and submission, affection and oppression operate in tandem and in tension.

As Susan Dwyer Amussen notes, 'Political theorists [using the family as a metaphor] believed they were dealing with natural and immutable relations; writers of household manuals knew they were dealing with social and mutable ones,' in which all superiors were also inferiors.[14] Hence William Gouge cautioned that 'men must first learn to obey well, before they can rule well: for they who scorne to be subject to their governours while they are under authority, are like to prove intolerable insolent when they are in authority,' and more broadly, that '*they which are in authority, are also under authority*: masters have a master. For God is *Lord of Lords,* Master of Masters.'[15] To be sure, the prevailing tenor of early modern domestic advice books is absolutist: 'Though an husband in regard of evill qualities may carry the Image of the divell, yet in regard of his place and office, he beareth the Image of God: so doe Magistrates in the Common-wealth, Ministers in the Church, Parents and Masters in the Family.' Nevertheless, most authors acknowledged some limits to paternal authority. According to Gouge, in those rare cases (perhaps not so rare in reality?) where a man is 'destitute of understanding...stupid; unfit to manage his affaires ... the whole government lieth upon the wife, so as her Husbands consent is not to be expected.'[16] Beyond the confines of the household such exceptions and qualifications proliferated. So despite his insistence that the parson is a father to his parish, and his implicit claim to explore pastoral duty in those terms, Herbert does not offer an integrated and unproblematic picture of his ideal parson's social world through the application of the familial analogy. The parson's domestic hierarchy, so carefully detailed, offers much less insight into the dynamics of his delicate social and political position than one might expect. The anomalous social position of the early modern clergy, and the tensions in the social milieu in which families existed and which familial order was held to explain, must inevitably have strained the explanatory force of the analogy.[17] Those, like George Herbert, who continued to use the image of the patriarchal family as a social-structural paradigm had to find new ways of doing so.

Though we can no longer proceed according to Stone's view that momentous changes in family structure were taking place in George Herbert's lifetime, we probably can make the more modest claim that patriarchalism as a systematic social and political theory emerged and died in Herbert's century. The work most commonly cited as the central articulation of that theory, Sir Robert Filmer's *Patriarcha*, is almost exactly contemporaneous with Herbert's *Country Parson,* and the two books share similar early publication histories.[18] Moreover, Filmer is reported as describing Herbert as 'my intimate friend' in an unpublished manuscript.[19] *Patriarcha* offers a defence of divine right monarchy, grounded in a genetic theory of history and built on the assumption that the family was both the first and the most perfect society. Kings, Filmer insisted, 'ruled as successors to the power God had given to Adam at the creation.'[20] In Filmer's own words, 'I see not ... how the children of Adam, or of any man else, can be free from subjection to their parents. And this subjection of children is the only fountain of all regal authority, by the ordination of God himself.'[21] This argument gave an anthropological cast to the theological commonplace that the Biblical commandment, 'Honour thy Father and Mother,' encompassed a subject's duties to his or her sovereign, to officers of the crown, and indeed to all social superiors. In the words added in 1604 to the Catechism in the *Book of Common Prayer*, the commandments teach that

> My duty toward my neighbour is to love him as myself, and to do to all men as I would they should do unto me: to love honour and succour my mother and father: to honour and obey the King and all that are put in authority under him: to submit myself to all my governors, teachers, spiritual pastors and masters: to order myself lowly and reverently to all my betters.

Filmer's ideas received their most famous response in John Locke's *Two Treatises of Government*, and it is probably fair to say that with the ascendancy of contractual thinking about government, patriarchalism as a political theory (though certainly not patriarchy as an ideology) was dead. As Gordon Shochet has pointed out, '[t]he irony [about patriarchalism] is that the careful and self-conscious working out and enunciation of this view signalled the beginnings of its demise rather than its validity, for it is now clear that the social and political presumptions to which patriarchalism belonged were even then losing their relevance.'[22] Under these circumstances, early modern patriarchal thought begins to look much less like an overwhelming orthodoxy that was universally held to explain all social relations, and more like a tenuous yet tenacious ideology (it is, after all, still with us), straining under its own contradictions and remaking itself in the face of new social realities.

Pastor as Patriarch

There can be no question that Herbert falls within the tradition of patriarchal thought, broadly defined. As Leah Marcus has observed, commenting on *The Temple*, 'the lowly role of child and servant, though he cannot always sustain it, is the role which most consistently gives him respite from his spiritual struggles.'[23] Chapter XVI of *The Country Parson*, 'The Parson a Father,' offers us another side of the analogy (quoted in full, as the epigraph to this chapter):

> The Countrey Parson is ... a father to his flock ... when any sinns, he hateth
> him not as an officer, but pityes him as a Father: and even in those wrongs
> which either in tithing, or otherwise are done to his owne person, hee con-
> siders the offender as a child, and forgives, so hee may have any signe of
> amendment; so also when after many admonitions, any continue to be
> refractory, yet hee gives him not over, but is long before he proceede to dis-
> inheriting. (250)

If Herbert the poet finds solace in imagining himself as a child, Herbert
the priest represents himself primarily as a father. Neither role quite
captures his social identity. This is but the first and most obvious ripple
in the not-so-smoothly graduated social hierarchy of which the early
modern family is an emblem. Perhaps as a result of this uncertainty, the
patriarchal model does not function for Herbert in quite the way it does
for Filmer. Here, the fatherhood metaphor serves not as an argument
for pastoral authority, but as an argument for the exercise of forbearance, persistence, and forgiveness, qualities Herbert presumptively
attributes to fatherhood when he urges their extension to the quasi-
political realm of pastoral discipline. Working against the traditional
line of patriarchal political theory, which extended the honour due to
parents to officers of the state, Herbert insists on a distinction between
'officer' and 'father,' articulating 'the separation between state and society that was implicit in compact [i.e., contractual] doctrine,' even while
arguing that state affairs, like tithe disputes (often a matter for common-law litigation), should be handled in a familial manner.[24] If patriarchal discourse serves here to temper state authority, it also serves to
establish the autonomy of that authority. It is only when an officer is
clearly understood not to *be* a species of father that he can be enjoined
to *act* like one. Such a position clearly separates Herbert from a theoretical patriarchalist like Filmer, even as it confirms the extent to which
patriarchal assumptions shape his thought.

  Such an apparently benign posture might at first seem to make Herbert's idealized pastor one of Shuger's 'Nursing Fathers,' loving uncon-
ditionally if firmly. Indeed, the Priest's infantilized relationship with
God, through scripture where he 'sucks and lives' (228), perhaps helps
to explain the power of the image of benevolent fatherhood.[25] Consciousness of human subordination to a divine father virtually demands
such an image. Shuger argues that 'textual representations of the duti-
ful child and loving father symbolize the desire to establish a relationship exempt from coercion, mutability and struggle.'[26] This view is

complicated, however, by Herbert's account of household order, where the authoritarian cast is slightly more evident: the parson 'keeps his servants between love, and fear, according as hee findes them; but generally he distributes it thus, To his Children he shewes more love then terrour, to his servants more terrour then love; but an old good servant boards a child' (241). Here, even as Herbert treats children and servants in the same sentence, the emphasis on degree and differentiation reveals the inherent tensions of the patriarchal analogy (as does the paradoxical suggestion that age and duration of service make a servant more childlike!). Servants, in this view, are not the same as biological children; to be sure, they are entitled to a measure of paternal (or rather paternalistic) affection, but a different measure. Moreover, in every case, including the case of children, 'love and terrour' are to be rather carefully apportioned, according to a complex formula that takes into account the nature of the relationship (biological or economic), as well as its duration and quality. *The Country Parson* does not even try to imagine 'a relationship exempt from coercion, mutability and struggle,' let alone advocate one. The parson's fatherly love is emphatically conditional and calculating. In this Herbert echoes the standard posture of contemporary advice books. As John Dod and Robert Clever wrote, 'all in the family are not to be governed alike. There is one rule to govern the wife by, another for children, another for servants.'[27] Despite the elements of idealization in his portrait of the parson, Herbert's concerns are very much centred on the social realities of struggle and mutability in the household.

Marriage

Herbert's concern for the realities and exigencies of domestic life is even more tellingly revealed in *The Country Parson*'s discussion of marriage. Perhaps surprisingly, given the firmly Protestant cast of his theology and the fact that his own decisions to marry and to be ordained as a priest came so close together, Herbert apparently follows Queen Elizabeth in clinging to an ideal of clerical celibacy: 'The Country Parson considering that virginity is a higher state than Matrimony, and that the Ministry requires the best and highest things, is rather unmarryed, then marryed' (236–7). When he comes to consider the arguments in favour of marriage, however, Herbert represents the inconveniences of life as an unmarried clergyman as virtually overwhelming:

But yet as the temper of his body may be, or as the temper of his Parish may be, where he may have occasion to converse with women, and that among suspicious men, *and other like circumstances considered,* he is rather married then unmarried. Let him communicate the thing often by prayer unto God, and as his grace shall direct him, so let him proceed. If he be unmarried and keepe house, he hath not a woman in his house, but findes opportunities of having his meat dress'd and other services done by men-servants at home, and his linnen washed abroad. If he be unmarryed, and sojourne, he never talkes with any woman alone, but in the audience of others, and that seldom, and then also in a serious manner, never jestingly or sportfully. (37; italics in orig.)

Celibacy might remain a theoretical ideal, even for some Protestants, but godly marriage held a position of dignity in the entire Christian tradition, and its advantages were so numerous as to seem decisive.[28] In chapter 3 I touched on the protection that marriage to a clergyman might offer a female medical practitioner in early modern England. Here it is clear that such protection might be reciprocal. Herbert's vision of an activist ministry virtually demands the sort of intimate contact with parishioners that the godly might consider unseemly or suspicious in a bachelor.

Herbert's acceptance of marriage as a *de facto* norm may also reflect the realities that marriage was the threshold of social maturity and autonomy for men below gentry status, and that the lower clergy were balanced rather precariously on the outer margins of gentility. Apprentices and journeymen in their twenties were not considered fully adult, and a young unmarried curate or a priest of modest means would be in a socially ambiguous position. The roles of householder and husband were nearly inseparable.[29] Moreover, the expense of employing male servants, who earned much more than girls and women, to do work that might be done by an unpaid wife or a poorly paid maidservant might well be prohibitive for poorer clergy.[30] Such considerations, along with the urgings of nature, may have prompted Essex clergyman Ralph Josselin to do as Herbert had done, remaining unmarried during the time when his employment was unstable, but becoming engaged soon after accepting a curacy.[31]

Herbert's cautious injunctions about contact with women may, as Michael Schoenfeld suggests, imply 'acute nervousness about female company,' but such anxieties can hardly be attributed to Herbert as distinctive psychological characteristics.[32] Rather, they seem symptomatic of a broad pattern of increasing scrutiny of and anxiety about sexual conduct and public morality in early modern England and perhaps throughout Europe – anxiety registered powerfully in Shakespeare's *Measure for Measure*, for example.[33] Though there is a great deal of regional variation, records of civil and ecclesiastical courts demonstrate increasing public scrutiny of sexual conduct in the late sixteenth and early seventeenth century, scrutiny manifested by 'a hardening attitude to bastardy; some decline in tolerance towards bridal pregnancy; [and] tighter public control over marriage entry.'[34] In some places, such as Terling, Essex, there is reason to link the increase in prosecutions for sexual offenses to an even broader campaign for godly discipline, led by a small puritan oligarchy.[35] In Salisbury, similarly, there is clear evidence of a campaign of moral reformation, though in rural Wiltshire such a case is hard to make.[36] There, as in many places, anxieties about the social costs of loose sexual conduct were probably distributed throughout the middling and upper ranks of the communities, however intense their religious convictions. Actually, in light of the social history of marriage and sexuality in early modern England, *The Country Parson* devotes remarkably little attention to the topics of adultery, fornication, and lewd behaviour, all key objects (along with vagrancy) of early modern morality campaigns. For Herbert, these sins seem almost too obvious to be worthy of extended treatment: 'There are some vices, whose natures are alwayes cleer, and evident, as Adultery, Murder, Hatred, Lying, &c. There are other vices, whose natures, at least in the beginning, are dark and obscure: as Covetousnesse, and Gluttony' (264). Herbert, on the whole, seems much more interested in the parson's management of those dark and obscure vices, an issue to which I return at the end of the chapter.

Like the choice of whether to marry, the choice of whom to marry, for Herbert's idealized country parson, is imbued with the spirit of calculation:

> If he be marryed, the choyce of his wife was made rather by his eare, then by his eye; his judgement, not his affection found out a fit wife for him, whose humble, and liberall disposition he preferred before beauty, riches, or honour. *He knew that (the good instrument of God to bring women to heaven) a wise and loving husband could out of humility, produce any speciall grace of faith, patience, meeknesse, love, obedience, &c. and out of liberality, make her fruitfull in all good works.* As hee is just in all things, so is he to his wife also, counting

nothing so much his owne, as that he may be unjust unto it. Therefore he gives her respect both afore her servants, and others, and halfe at least of the government of the house, reserving so much of the affaires, as serve for a diversion for him; yet never so giving over the raines, but that he sometimes looks how things go, demanding an account, but not by the way of an account. And this must bee done the oftner, or the seldomer, according as hee is satisfied of his Wifes discretion. (238–9)[37]

Again, there is no doubt that Herbert's vision of courtship and marriage is a patriarchal one. A husband is God's instrument 'to bring women to heaven'; a wife, having the requisite qualities of liberality and humility, is a lump of clay to be moulded into a particular form by her husband. And those essential qualities, humility and liberality, are the ones best suited to ensure the bride's willing acceptance of her subordinate status. Such an account seems at first to offer unqualified evidence for the view of early modern marriage as harsh and oppressive, a manifestation of the restrictive social paradigms of a traditional order, but the sort of calculation Herbert advocates, as Alan Macfarlane argues, is also evidence of a significant degree of choice.[38] Herbert presents this as a simple matter of the man's choice of a bride, but in practice things were probably more complicated. Clear demographic evidence for the prevalence of late marriage among women, especially in the lower ranks of society, leads to the conclusion that women too had significant freedom in the selection of a mate.[39] Within a framework of patriarchal discourse, Herbert's emphasis on the bride's 'disposition' could imply a cautious celebration of the 'inner' as opposed to the 'outer' woman, a tacit acknowledgment of the necessity of the bride's consent, and of the possibility of refusal or incompatibility. Nuances of language are both important and potentially deceptive here. To a twenty-first-century ear the sentence 'I chose my wife because of her disposition' might imply loveless calculation, while the phrase 'I love my wife because of her disposition' might suggest mature love, free from mere lust or infatuation. In this context it helps to remember that Herbert's term 'affection,' juxtaposed as it is to 'judgement,' carries its obsolete negative sense of irrational passion. The point here is not to label Herbert's view of love and marriage as modern and 'enlightened' as opposed to outmoded and patriarchal. Patriarchy operates in 'enlightened' societies as surely as it operates in more traditional ones, but it functions differently. Fatherly rule serves Filmer as the foundation and rationale for state authority; that same state authority comes eventually to function behind a screen of supposed individual autonomy, as subjects become citizens. Herbert's patriarchal ideology is caught between these two positions, clinging to a patriarchal model despite its dubious explanatory force, and striving to assimilate it into a new paradigm.

Patriarchal and Pastoral Authority

Some sense of the ideological tension in Herbert's patriarchal thought is evident in two passages in which he takes pains to describe the bounds of the authority of the head of a household. In the first passage, quoted above, Herbert insists that a wife is entitled to fair treatment, but his argument for domestic justice is a curiously limited one: '[a]s he is just in all things, so is he to his wife also, counting nothing so much his owne, as that he may be unjust unto it' (238). Here a wife is virtually a piece of property, whose rights rest not on her special relationship with her husband, but on a generalized doctrine of stewardship, which places limits on all forms of ownership. On such questions, however, Herbert's thinking is distinctly unsystematic. Elsewhere, addressing the treatment of servants, he insists on a distinction in kind, rather than merely in degree, between servants and ordinary property:

> if God have given me servants, and I either provide too little for them, or that which is unwholsome ... and so not competent nourishment, I am Covetous. I bring this example, because men usually think, that servants for their mony are as other things that they buy, even as a piece of wood, which they may cut, or hack, or throw into the fire, and so they pay them their wages, all is well. (265)

These two instances of patriarchal authority and its limits illustrate the ideological divide *The Country Parson* straddles. The first is the inheritance of a narrowly constructed hierarchical doctrine that seeks to offer a single explanation for all relationships, an explanation based on the notion of a continuous cosmic hierarchy of which the family is the earthly model. The second has greater affinities with contractualist thinking, which, without abandoning hierarchy, insists on the distinctiveness of particular hierarchical relationships.[40] This emphasis on particulars, evident throughout *The Country Parson* (the word appears twenty-three times in various forms) is a crucial element in Herbert's preservation and transformation of patriarchal discourse.[41]

In terms of domestic affairs, the reconciliation of patriarchy and particularization is especially evident in Herbert's remarks on the properly differential treatment of heirs and younger sons. As Joan Thirsk has observed, this is a sore spot in early modern domestic politics among the gentry and aristocracy. The entrenched custom of primogeniture created a pattern in which elder brothers retained and enhanced familial holdings, while the wealth and status of younger brothers tended to decline with succeeding generations.[42] This is clearly the trajectory along which George Herbert was headed, as the fifth son of the minor branch of a great family. Even with the advantages of intelligence, a superb education, and influential family and friends, he ended his life as a rural clergyman of limited means. His own children, had he fathered any, might well have had to live even more modestly, judging from the advice he offers his clerical brethren. Herbert's model pastor 'turns his care to fit all ... [his children's] dispositions with some calling, not sparing the eldest, but giving him the prerogative of his Fathers profession, which happily [i.e., haply – perhaps] for his other children he is not able to do' (239). Here, the legacy of the clergyman's eldest son is the university education (increasingly a requirement for ordination) that had been Herbert's entitlement as the younger son of an aristocratic family. And that son, unless he was unusually prosperous, might have been hard pressed to continue the tradition for another generation.

Herbert's recognition of this pattern is confirmed in chapter XXXII, 'The Parson's Surveys,' when he addresses the parental obligations of the parish gentry. Heirs are to be prepared to assume their fathers' roles in the community, as landlords, Justices of the Peace, and Members of Parliament.

> As for younger Brothers, those whom the Parson finds loose, and not ingaged into some Profession by their Parents, whose neglect in this point is intolerable, and a shamefull wrong both to the Common-wealth, and their own House: To them, after he hath shew'd the unlawfulness of spending the day in dressing, Complementing, visiting, and sporting, he first commends the study of the Civill Law [and then mathematics, navigation, fortification, colonization, and trade]. (277–8)

Never in Herbert's comments on children's education and inheritance is there a trace of the critique of primogeniture, which, according to Thirsk, began to emerge between 1600 and 1650 as the proverbial resentment of younger brothers gained polemical focus.[43] Nor is there any hint of lingering resentment about Edward Herbert's unwillingness to pay in full the annuities their father had intended for the younger brothers.[44] Rather, there is a vigorous affirmation of the ideology of vocation. Parents, of whatever station, are to provide younger sons with an education that will allow them to make their own way in professions and trade, promoting independence and discouraging idleness and self-indulgence. Having done so, they have sufficiently discharged their parental obligations. The pastor, acting *in loco parentis*, is to reinforce the message: shape up or, 'if the young Gallant think these Courses dull, and phlegmatick,' ship out to the colonies (278). Cognizant of the social and domestic stress created by ill-employed young gentlemen (the gentry's equivalent of the vagrancy crisis), and committed to an ideology of agricultural and economic 'improvement,' which demanded the concentration of rural capital associated with primogeniture, Herbert actually intensifies the prevailing differentiation between heirs and younger sons. The solution to the problem of idle younger sons is not, as some pamphleteers would suggest in the 1650s, to reintroduce the ancient customs of partible inheritance (still practiced widely in Kent, and occasionally elsewhere), but to disabuse younger sons of the notion that birth in a landed family would automatically entitle them to continue in the lifestyle to which they had become accustomed.[45]

If the parson's quasi-parental role in the instruction of younger sons illustrates the persistence of patriarchal thinking, it also illustrates the limitations of that mode of thought. A parish clergyman of modest means and birth might offer paternalistic advice, but could not really function *in loco parentis* for the younger son of an aristocratic or gentry family. To pretend to such authority would be to undermine that of the natural parent.[46] Moreover, he would have neither the means nor the authority to establish such a young man in a suitable position. According to patriarchal theory, at least in its most extreme form, relationships of subordination, 'master and servant, teacher and student, employer and worker, landlord and tenant, clergyman and congregant, and magistrate and subject – were *all* understood as *identical* to the relationship of father and children.'[47] But anyone contemplating the situation Herbert describes – including the 'young Gallant' – would immediately see that the supposed identity is, at best, a rather strained analogy. The distinctive social position of the clergyman, far from consolidating his quasi-patriarchal authority, actually restricted that authority to the narrow sphere of matters within the scope of the church courts.[48] Outside this sphere, perhaps the most he could hope for was to exercise influence in proportion to the respect he had earned from his parishioners.

The problem of the 'young Gallant,' owing deference to his pastor in respect of the dignity of clerical office, yet simultaneously entitled to deference himself by virtue of birth and family status, becomes much more apparent when Herbert considers the relationship between a pastor and the leading gentry of the community. Here two contradictory applications of the patriarchal analogy clash, for if the vicar is a father to the gentleman, his parishioner, he might also be the 'child' of that same gentleman's ecclesiastical patronage. He might also, like Ralph Josselin in 1646, be financially indebted to his patron.[49] Even as he denounces 'over submissivenesse, and cringings' on the part of the clergy, and urges chaplains of noble families 'to keep up with the Lord and Lady of the house, and to preserve a boldness with them' (226), Herbert hints at the prevalence of the former posture and the difficulty of the latter. In a chapter fittingly entitled 'The Parson in Contempt,' he acknowledges 'the generall ignominy which is cast upon the profession,' but urges that his clerical readers procure respect 'by a bold and impartial reproof, even of the best in the Parish, when occasion requires' (268). The very structure of this chapter seems to record Herbert's frustration at the parson's position, simultaneously exalted and humble, authoritative and powerless. In the first half of the chapter he considers an ascending scale of responses to contempt of pastoral authority, culminating in the recourse to ecclesiastical justice. Then, acknowledging that contempt may be 'not punishable by Law' or that 'the Parson [might] think it in his discretion either unfit, or bootelesse to contend,' he turns to describe 'the five shields, wherewith the Godly receive the darts of the wicked' (269). If, as Amussen argues, domestic advice books acknowledged that paternal authority, absolute in theory, is in practice contingent and mutable, *The Country Parson* makes the same admission about pastoral authority.[50]

This is true not merely in the pastor's interactions with those who would consider themselves his social superiors, but with the whole parish. If '*in rewarding virtue, and in punishing vice, the Parson endeavoureth to be in Gods stead*' (254, italics in orig.), his parishioners play much the same role in monitoring his virtues and vices. Hence, in endeavouring to be 'holy, just, prudent, temperate, bold, grave in all his wayes,' the parson 'labours most in those things which are most apt to scandalize his Parish' (227). As Christopher Hodgkins points out, the parson 'must run a virtually epic gauntlet of scrutiny' as his parishioners monitor

every aspect of his behaviour. His relationship with his parish is characterized by the fact that he is at once 'observer and observed.'[51] To put
the point in terms of patriarchal analogy, the parson is 'not only a father
to his flock,' nor even a father to some and a child to others; he is
always, and to everyone, *both* father and child at once. For Hodgkins this
ambiguity is one manifestation of Herbert's commitment to a doctrine
of limited authority. I would suggest, however, that it marks the inadequacy of the juridico-political concept of 'authority' as an account of the
social relations in which the parson is enmeshed, and leads in the direction of the elusive and ambiguous notion of 'power' articulated by
Michel Foucault in *Discipline and Punish* and *The History of Sexuality*.
In this model, power is 'not ... a general system of domination exerted
by one group over another,' but rather 'the moving substrate of force
relations which, by virtue of their inequality, constantly engender states
of power ... always local and unstable.'[52] The displacement of Filmer's
vision of patriarchal authority by Foucault's 'power' in Herbert's character of the pastoral household is the subject of the remainder of this
chapter.

The Laboratory of Social Control

The refinement of patriarchal thinking evident in *The Country Parson* is
the key to its persistence in the face of the demonstrable incoherence of
Filmer's simple 'identity' model. Understanding one's social place is not
a simple matter of identifying the father figures to whom one owes deference, and from whom one claims sustenance. Rather, it is a matter of
identifying the particular *sense* in which one plays the father in a given
social situation, and the sense in which one plays the child, and of learning how to play both roles simultaneously. While Herbert and the writers of domestic advice books might be less systematic than Filmer in
their analysis of patriarchal structures, their thinking is arguably more
refined in its attention to the facts of the situation: flux, not stability,
characterized hierarchical relations. In such a paradigm, the ideological
function of the patriarchal family is quite different from the one
assigned to it by commentators on traditional hierarchy: the family functions not so much as an exemplary model for stable power relations, but
as a laboratory in which techniques for managing inherently unstable
relations can be tested, refined, and disseminated. The family becomes
less important as the *content* of ideological indoctrination (though Herbert continues to assign it that role) than as the *means* and the major *site*
of that indoctrination.[53]

This alternative patriarchal paradigm is evident even within the individual consciousness, at what Tillyard, and others subscribing to the 'great chain' metaphor, would probably call the microcosmic level. Herbert's ideal parson exercises 'Mortification in regard of lusts and affections, and the stupifying and deading of all the clamorous powers of the soul, therefore he hath throughly studied these, that he may be an absolute Master and commander of himself, for all the purposes which God hath ordained him' (227). Elsewhere Herbert explicitly feminizes the soul and its 'clamorous powers' in his account of temptation: '*for the humane soule being bounded, and kept in, in her sensitive faculty, will runne out more or lesse in her intellectuall*' (238). This observation falls between Herbert's account of the advantages of the unmarried state and that of the qualities to be sought in a wife, should the pastor choose to marry. Even the unmarried clergyman, it appears, has (or is) a wayward woman on the *inside*. Of course the feminization of the soul and its faculties is a philosophical and iconographic convention, and traditional hierarchical theory also applies to those faculties.[54] Authoritarian thinkers from Plato onward have insisted on the subordination of the 'lower' to the 'higher' faculties. Nevertheless, the notion of the human soul divided against itself, subjecting its own 'clamorous powers' to 'mortification,' permits Herbert to present a regime of self-discipline that attenuates and sometimes displaces overtly authoritarian structures. Such a regime requires calculated inversions of hierarchy. The parson 'sometimes purposely takes [poor parishioners] home with him, setting them close by him, and carving for them, both for his own humility, and their comfort' (243). Such exercises of 'humiliation' resemble both the courtly techniques of seeking advancement through self-abasement and the festive practices of early modern culture, consolidating the power they temporarily subvert.[55]

Reproducing and disseminating this exemplary self-discipline is a central object of domestic spiritual instruction, and the techniques of that reproduction are the main subject of chapter X, 'The Parson in his House.' Subordinate members of the parson's household are to become, as much as possible, the agents of their own subordination. They must learn to subdue the 'clamorous powers' of their own souls. Hence, Herbert insists on the importance of 'voluntary' 'private' prayer:

> besides the common prayers of the family, he straitly requires of all to pray by themselves before they sleep at night, and stir out in the morning, and knows what prayers they say, and till they have learned them, makes them kneel by him; esteeming that this private praying is a more voluntary act in

them, then when they are called to others prayers, and that, which when they leave the family, they carry with them. (240–1)

In the calculated movement from coercion to voluntarism, from surveillance to privacy and eventual autonomy, Herbert shifts the emphasis of household discipline from overt exercise of patriarchal authority to covert procedures of social control. As Susan Amussen has argued, the 'mechanism that coerces by means of observation,' which Michel Foucault associates with penal theories of the eighteenth and nineteenth century, is already 'in place in early modern villages,' and, one might add, in early modern families.[56]

Herbert's paradigm of family discipline as the inculcation of self-discipline does not apply uniquely to the pastoral household. The exemplary life of the pastor and his intimate knowledge 'of the faults of his own Parish' serves to establish his influence over other householders (274). '[F]amily is [every married man's] best care, to labour Christian soules, and raise them to their height, even to heaven; to dresse and prune them, and take as much joy in a straight-growing childe, or servant, as a Gardiner doth in a choice tree' (275). The duty to exercise family discipline also establishes the disciplinary space within which fathers operate. 'Could men finde out this delight, they would seldome be from home; whereas now, of any place, they are least there' (275). Properly instructed, fathers will delight in their role and confine themselves to it. Here, the parson does not exercise the quasi-paternal authority of clergyman over parishioner – Herbert defines this relationship largely in terms of forgiveness and forbearance – but rather engages in a lateral dissemination of power, observing and influencing as a householder the conduct of other householders. Parishioners 'of higher quality' in particular are 'very tender of reproof: and therefore he lays his discourse so, that he comes to the point very leasurely, and oftentimes, as *Nathan* did, in the person of another, making them to reprove themselves' (248). This delicacy in attempting to influence domestic order while affirming the autonomy of each nuclear family is especially clear in the discussion of the parson's conduct when visiting relations:

When he comes to any other house, where *his kindred, or other relations give him any authority over the Family*, if hee be to stay there for a time, hee considers diligently the state thereof to Godward ... And accordingly, as he finds any defect in these, hee first considers ... what kind of remedy fits the temper of the house best, and then hee faithfully, and boldly applyeth it; yet seasonably, and discreetly, by taking aside the Lord or Lady, or *Master* and *Mistres* of the house. (251; italics in orig.)

The parson professes no 'authority over the family' by virtue of his office. Whatever authority he assumes is delegated by the '*Master* or *Mistres* of the House,' with whom he must negotiate 'seasonably and discreetly.'

Herbert expects each member of the pastoral household to participate in the lateral dissemination of the ideology of self-discipline. Though the priest's authority over subordinate members of other households in his parish is much clearer than his authority over the heads of those households, he exercises this authority circuitously and indirectly, through his own wife, children, and servants:

all in his house are either teachers or learners, or both, so that his family is a Schoole of Religion, and they all account, that to teach the ignorant is the greatest almes ... And when they go abroad, his wife among her neighbours is the beginner of good discourses, his children among children, his servants among other servants; so that as in the house of those that are skill'd in Musick, all are Musicians; so in the house of a Preacher, all are preachers. (240)

Moreover, since the preacher plays so many roles – physician, lawyer, distributor of charity, teacher, advocate of moral and economic improvement – 'all in his house' share to some extent in each of these functions.[57] The parson's wife shares her husband's work not only in healing the sick, but also in the spiritual surveillance and maintenance of the parish. She 'takes account of Sermons, and how every one profits, comparing this yeer with the last' (240). His servants may teach neighbours' servants to read 'on holy dayes' (248). His children are expected to keep busy 'visiting other sick children, and tending their wounds' (239). Herbert even makes a distinction between 'sending his charity by them to the poor, and sometimes giving them a little mony to do it of themselves, that they get a delight in it, and enter favour with God' (239). As with the compulsory/voluntary, supervised/private prayers, the aim in giving children money that is at once their own and earmarked for charitable purposes is clearly to establish a sense of constrained autonomy or willing subjection. In each of these examples, Herbert advocates circumventing the overt vertical conduits of hierarchical power, and cultivating, instead, covert, horizontal means of shaping social behaviour.

Herbert's argument for the diffusion of disciplinary power throughout the community is clearest in the final chapter of *The Country Parson*, 'Concerning Detraction.' The chapter addresses the issue of libellous gossip: 'most, when they are at leasure, make others faults their entertainment and discourse' (286). Here Herbert enters into an area of some contemporary disagreement. Such 'entertainment,' especially when women indulged in it, was often categorized as scolding, and subject to communal sanctions.[58] But as Martin Ingram and others have shown, the production of libels, often in verse form, could also be a form of communal discipline, as well as a way of pursuing feuds, protesting injustices, and stirring up trouble. The practice can be linked, generically, to other forms of festive and ritual social inversion, including the 'ridings' used to humiliate and chastise scolds and cuckolds.[59] Detraction, then, could be either a violation of social order or a mechanism for reinforcing it. Many ordinary people seem to have viewed the practice with ambivalence, while 'the authorities took a wholly condemnatory view. The church courts had always regarded such productions as defamations, or breaches of Christian charity.'[60] Herbert's ideal parson, rather surprisingly in this context, weighs carefully the merits of detraction, and defends it. On the one hand gossip and detraction are effective means of surveillance and discipline in the parish: 'if he absolutely shut up mens mouths, and forbid all disclosing of faults, many an evill may not only be, but also spread in his Parish ... On the other side, if it be unlawful to open faults, no benefit or advantage can make it lawfull: for we must not do evill that good may come of it' (286–7). Here, as in the discussion of discretionary charity, 'lawfulness' is an intentionally ambiguous concept. Its primary sense seems ethical, given the gloss 'we must not do evil that good may come of it.' Nevertheless, Herbert's choice of the term allows him to slide from a broadly ethical to a more strictly legal sense of the term, when he goes on to argue that disclosing faults is indeed 'lawful,' 'because infamy is part of the sentence against malefactours, which the Law intends ... [and] in infamy, all are executioners' (287). Herbert answers the view that 'church courts and other official agencies existed to exercise such moral discipline' by assimilating the customs of popular ridicule into the 'official' framework.[61] To grasp the full import of Herbert's position with respect to patriarchy we need to return to Herbert's earlier assertion that 'when any sinns, [the parson] hateth him not as an officer, but pityes him as a Father' (250). If this sort of benevolent patriarchal rhetoric serves to temper the overtly authoritarian dynamics of a traditional hierarchical society, it does so, in part, by sanctioning a division and distribution of the coercive authority of the state and its officers throughout the society. When 'all are executioners' the temporal sword becomes a network of tiny needles. Herbert's defence of detraction, and his distribution of patriarchal authority throughout the social order, reflects the comparatively modern recognition that consent and conformity can be secured not just by persuading people that they are powerless, and that they owe obedience to their superiors, but also by persuading them that they are powerful, and that the good order of society rests on their proper exercise of that power.

That this authority remains, in important respects, state authority, or at least the authority of traditional superiors, momentarily delegated to members of the community, is suggested by the careful analysis and regulation to which Herbert would subject popular discipline. In good Baconian fashion, Herbert categorizes offenses, distinguishing between notorious and private faults, and among notorious faults, between those 'made known by common fame,' and those that 'have passed judgment, & been corrected' (287). Both sorts of notorious faults are fit subjects for public discourse, though the former should be treated 'not with sport, but commiseration' (287). As for 'private' faults, Herbert's position is rather evasive. The argument that disclosure is the first step towards remedy implies that these too should be open to public scrutiny; nevertheless, Herbert invokes the legal principle of the presumption of innocence, that 'all are honest, till the contrary be proved,' presumably as an attempt to check malicious gossip (287). If 'detraction' is, as Herbert argues, not a form of extra-legal social control, but an extension and application of legally authorized power, then it must be exercised within a legitimating framework of legal discourse.

Providing this legitimating framework is the work of a professional specialist like the priest, whose duty it is to make the fine distinctions that will 'lead his people exactly in the wayes of Truth, so that they neither decline to the right hand, nor to the left' (230). For this reason, Herbert's ideal country parson

> greatly esteemes ... cases of conscience, wherein he is much versed ... For every one hath not digested, when it is a sin to take something for mony lent, or when not; when it is a fault to discover anothers fault, or when not; *when the affections of the soul in desiring and procuring increase of means, or*

honour, be a sin of covetousnes or ambition, and when not; when the appetites of the
body in eating, drinking, sleep, and the pleasure that comes with sleep, be sins of
gluttony, drunkenness, sloath, lust, and when not, and so in many circumstances of actions. (230)

The parson's expertise is wasted on the ethics of the forbidden, on
'vices, whose natures are alwayes cleer, and evident, as Adultery, Murder,
Hatred, Lying, &c.' (264). These can be left to the comparatively blunt
instruments of the law and popular disapprobation. The educated
cleric's special expertise consists in destabilizing his parishioners' sense
of the permitted, just as he disrupts their reliance on the bounty of providence, so as to retain a measure of control over that delegated authority.[62] This is the same principle that governs his relations with his wife, to
whom he delegates 'halfe at least of the government of the house ... yet
never so giving over the raines, but that he sometimes looks how things
go, demanding an account, but not by way of an account' (238–9). Herbert's assertion that the parson is 'A father to his parish' needs, finally,
to be seen as another instance of this simultaneously constrained and
delegated authority. Like the deputized wife, child, and servant, the parson is represented as having more power than he really has. Herbert
echoes the commonplaces of authoritarian patriarchal theory, and flat-
ters his clerical readers by offering an elevated sense of their social prestige and responsibility. Meanwhile, the parson's household becomes the
arena for the strategic delegation and diffusion of his own limited
authority, allowing the pastor/father to capitalize on, rather than suffer
from, the intrinsic mutability and instability of that authority.

chapter six

The Country Parson and *The Temple*: Enabled Readings

Now I am here, what thou wilt do with me
        None of my books will show:
I reade, and sigh, and wish I were a tree;
        For sure then I should grow
To fruit or shade: at least, some bird would trust
Her houshold to me, and I should be just.   'Affliction' [I], ll. 55–60

Yet have I often seen, by cunning hand
And force of fire, what curious things are made
Of wretched earth. Where once I scorn'd to stand,
That earth is fitted by the fire and trade
Of skilfull artists, for the boards of those
        Who make the bravest shows.   'The Priesthood,' ll. 13–18

George Herbert's 'Affliction' [I] and 'The Priesthood' are both vocation poems. Both express a speaker's yearning to be useful to God and
to his fellow creatures, or in the resonant word from 'Love' [III],' to
'serve.' 'Affliction' [I], probably an early poem, is overwrought with the
anxieties for which Herbert is famous. It concludes with a desperate
prayer, the cryptic and arresting couplet: 'Ah my deare God! though I
am clean forgot, / Let me not love thee, if I love thee not.' Everything is
in God's hands, and everything remains uncertain. 'The Priesthood,'
probably composed much later, is very different. Its extended conceit
figures God as a potter, a craftsman who 'doth often vessels make / Of
lowly matter for high uses meet' (ll. 34–5). While the speaker's posture
is no less humble than that of 'Affliction' [I], it is, perhaps, a good deal

more trusting, and as a result, more self-assured. The speaker of 'The Priesthood' resolves to

... throw me at his feet.

There will I lie, untill my Maker seek
For some mean stuffe whereon to show his skill:
Then is my time.   (ll. 36–39)

Unlike the speaker of 'Affliction' [I] he seems certain that his 'time' will come.[1] The readings of Herbert's poems in this chapter seek to explore more fully the vocational sensibility displayed in 'The Priesthood,' a sensibility intimately connected to *The Country Parson*'s ideology of clerical and social 'improvement.'

One of the working premises of this study has been that *The Country Parson*, as Herbert's last substantial work, represents, albeit in a limited sense, the culmination of his literary effort. While it will never be seen as his most important work, it does represent the point at which Herbert had arrived by the end of his life, as a participant in the social discourse of his age. It shows his rejection or attenuation of some available positions, and his embrace of others. If one accepts that claim, at least provisionally, then a reconsideration of some issues in the study of Herbert's poetry may be possible. To embark on that reconsideration, we need to pay more than the customary attention to what we know about the poems' order of composition (without, of course, pretending to know more than we do). As Mary Ellen Rickey documented, in one of the early masterpieces of Herbert criticism, poems likely to be comparatively early – those included in the Williams manuscript – differ markedly in tone, mode of address, metaphorical technique, and prosody from poems found only in the later Bodleian manuscript (and, one might add, from *The Country Parson*, with which the later poems have many affinities).[2] For the latter group, admittedly, we have no dates; nevertheless they do seem to reflect a different stage in the development of Herbert's thought and expression. Most of Herbert's critics have made general remarks on this subject. Amy Charles, for example, argues that 'the changes between the two manuscripts [of the poetry] are surely our most important evidence of Herbert's development as a poet.'[3] Many readers, however, have de-emphasized change and process, or have concentrated on the changes dramatized in individual poems (in revision or in the unfolding), attempting to treat *The Temple* as a complex whole that embodies, if not an achieved poetic and religious vision, at least a definite problematic. However historically informed such discussions may be, they tend to reduce differences between poems, differences which may reflect specific historical conditions, to the tensions inherent in the poet's vision, or to the ideological contradictions of his epoch.

Herbert, of course, invites this distortion himself. By arranging his poems into a book, he sets them into play against one another in particular ways, emulating the way biblical texts echo, anticipate, and challenge each other, even when separated by many pages or by many centuries: 'This verse marks that, and both do make a motion / Unto a third, that ten leaves off doth lie' ('The Holy Scriptures' [II]). Just as the Bible, a composite of distinct texts, has come to function for Christian literary culture as a monolithic text – a single 'great code,' in Northrop Frye's phrase – the construction of *The Temple* implicitly asserts that its multiple voices and perspectives somehow coexist in the mind of the poet at a single moment of composition. But we know this is a fiction. The real value of such a fiction, in suggesting the complexity of consciousness, should not preclude consideration of the historical processes by which that consciousness is constructed.

What is needed, then, is an investigation of Herbert's poems as artifacts historically and biographically situated, an investigation that nevertheless avoids George Herbert Palmer's procedure of dismantling Herbert's carefully constructed poetic sequence and substituting a speculative biographical one. There are important limits to the degree of precision that can be brought to bear in such a discussion. The number of poems for which even a reasonable conjecture can be formed about the precise date of composition is very small.[4] Even if we accept Charles's persuasive argument for an early date for the Williams manuscript, we cannot be sure how much later the poems eventually added to form the original of the Bodleian manuscript were composed.[5] Some of the ninety-odd additional poems may even have existed in draft when the Williams manuscript was prepared and yet been omitted for one reason or another. There is some reason to think, though, that Herbert arrived at his final plan for *The Temple* relatively late.[6] Moreover, Charles suggests, quite plausibly, that Herbert's only period of leisure extended enough for the composition of a substantial number of new poems was the period spent in Wiltshire between 1628 and 1630, when he lived first with the Earl of Danby at Dauntsey house, and then with his new bride and mother-in-law at Baynton house near Edington.[7] Some few poems may reflect his experience as a parish priest, but the number is likely to be quite small. Nevertheless, it seems probable that traces of Herbert's last five years in Wiltshire are to be found in the final design of 'The Church,' even if specific poems cannot be said to be 'about' that time and place in quite the sense that Jonson's 'To Penshurst' is 'about' Penshurst.

Recently, critics have explored Herbert's revisions with renewed interest. Sidney Gottlieb sees a move towards a '"plateau of assurance," [which] corresponds to the ... painstaking achievement and confirmation of ... Herbert's Anglicanism' in the reworked ending of *The Temple*.[8] Janis Lull's excellent study offers the persuasive, yet rather tentative, observation that the changes between the Williams manuscript and the Bodleian involve a 'progression away from lyric individualism.'[9] Cristina Malcolmson offers the most definite thesis about Herbert's revisions, linking the reworking of the Williams manuscript to Herbert's forsaking the pursuit of high office around 1627. Malcolmson argues that, abandoning 'the original structure of identity that authorized social mobility through its performative gentility "without" and its poverty of spirit "within," ... the revised *Temple* tries to purify itself of a "selfnesse" associated perjoratively both with high status and profit seeking.'[10] The revised *Temple* is, according to these readings, more 'Anglican,' less 'personal,' and less concerned with 'social mobility' than the Williams manuscript. Each of these commentators, I think, neglects to state the obvious, and to pursue the conclusions that follow: that in the final version of 'The Church' we have the work of a clergyman in the making, a writer imaginatively 'trying on' the definite social role and voice of a spokesman for the state church.[11]

In 'The Church,' it is possible to chart a progressive, if halting, drift from ascetic inwardness toward evangelical, pastoral, liturgical, and homiletic modes of discourse. Herbert's poems fall into a handful of rather broad discursive categories. First are his many poems of prayer and praise addressed directly to God. These represent about 40 per cent of the poems in 'The Church,' though it is difficult to arrive at a precise count.[12] The remainder are framed as apostrophes, dialogues, narratives, and quasi-liturgical celebrations, involving a wide range of speakers and audiences, internal and external. By a conservative count, about half of the poems carried over from the Williams manuscript are prayers, whereas only about a third of the new poems are prayers. Moreover, eight of the 'new' prayers are inserted among the poems from the

Williams manuscript that make up most of the first half of 'The Church' in its final form. This leaves only twenty prayers (about a quarter) in the large group of seventy-six non-Williams poems in the second half of 'The Church.' Moving through the volume, then, the prevailing axis of communication tilts increasingly from the vertical (human to divine) towards the horizontal (human to human) plane. The proportion of poems addressed directly to God diminishes; later poems are more often addressed to human audiences, treating either human situations, or the intersection of the mundane and the divine, in what we might take to be a pastoral or evangelical voice.[13]

'The Water-course' and Covenant Theology

We can begin sharpening the historical focus on Herbert's later poems by juxtaposing the views of two important Herbert scholars on the perennial question of Herbert's theology. Richard Strier sees Herbert clinging, in his poems, to 'the original theology of the Reformation,' attempting to steer a course between 'Arminius' rationalized view of predestination' and the Puritan 'covenant theology' associated with Cambridge theologians like John Preston and Richard Sibbes, 'a rationalistic development parallel to the Arminianism which it opposed and as deeply subversive of the initial emphases of the reformation.'[14] Both movements attenuated the strict Calvinist doctrine of 'double predestination' by introducing elements of voluntarism, moralism, and contractualism into a theology that, at its core, is hostile to such notions. Both emphasized the Christian's duty in the world, and described that duty in the 'worldly' language of contracts, business transactions, and physical labour. Preston, for example, preached that 'if a man will take CHRIST, it is a laborious worke, as laborious as husbandrie, as laborious as putting the hand to the Plow, as taking the yoake.'[15] In contrast to Strier, Sidney Gottlieb sees in Herbert's revisions and additions to the Williams manuscript a movement away from 'the kind of severe understanding of God and human incapacity that we usually associate with Puritanism.' In these poems, more than in the Williams poems, 'man plays a role in [the] elevating action.'[16] Gottlieb, in other words, sees Herbert moving from the Calvinist position towards the Arminian one, even if he has not quite arrived there by the end of his life.

For both critics the argument turns on an understanding of 'The Water-course,' one of the poems not included in the Williams manuscript.

The Water-course

Thou who dost dwell and linger here below,
Since the condition of this world is frail,
Where of all plants afflictions soonest grow;
If trouble overtake thee, do not wail:

For who can look for less, that loveth $\begin{cases} \text{Life?} \\ \text{Strife?} \end{cases}$

But rather turn the pipe and waters course
To serve thy sins, and furnish thee with store
Of sov'raigne tears, springing from true remorse:
That so in purenesse thou mayst him adore,

Who gives to man, as he sees fit, $\begin{cases} \text{Salvation.} \\ \text{Damnation.} \end{cases}$

For Strier, as for Joseph Summers, Barbara Lewalski, and Gene Veith, the ending of 'The Water-course' is the clearest evidence of Herbert's adherence to strict predestinarian doctrine. Strier insists that 'Herbert ... accepted the 'capricious' God of Augustinian and Nominalist piety.'[17] For Gottlieb, the 'The Water-course' and a handful of other poems 'very much in accord with key Puritan positions,' like 'Dotage,' 'Home,' and 'The Glance,' compel a retreat from the otherwise 'tempting' conclusion that the 'late Herbert [is] the flexible and secure Anglican.'[18] Unable to deny the Calvinist posture of 'The Water-course,' Gottlieb argues that the poem is nevertheless an incomplete reflection of Herbert's vision. He perceptively suggests that the closing lines of 'The Banquet' – 'Hearken under pain of death, / Hands and breath; / Strive in this, and love the strife' (ll. 52–4) – recall and amplify 'The Water-course,' with its identification of life and strife. Strife becomes striving, strenuous activity in the service of God, a source of joy even 'under pain of death.' As Herbert remarks more prosaically in the preface to *The Country Parson*: 'it is a good strife to go as farre as we can in pleasing of him, who hath done so much for us' (224). Both poems, and *The Country Parson*, hearken back to the opening of Hesiod's georgic *Works and Days*, with its myth of two races of strife, 'The one supports evil war and contention ... The other ... rouses a man to work even if he is shiftless.'[19]

The difficulty with Gottlieb's attempt to qualify Herbert's Calvinism may be that he seeks to qualify it in the wrong direction, in the direction of what, using the anachronistic term, is called Anglicanism, and would

Water meadows near Britford, Wiltshire, from the Cambridge University Collection. © Crown Copyright 1954/MOD. Reproduced with the Permission of the Controller of Her Majesty's Stationery Office.

have been called, in contemporary terms of abuse, Arminianism or Laudianism. In fact, it seems clear from *The Country Parson*, with its emphasis on strenuous activity by the godly for the moral and economic 'improvement' of the land, the family, and the nation, that in the last years of his life, Herbert's theological Calvinism is augmented, not softened, and not by an Arminian or 'Anglican' moral theology, but by elements of Puritan covenant theology. These elements include the emphasis on calling and service, and the use of commercial, legal, and contractual discourse in so many of Herbert's poems.[20] The conceit of God the potter from 'The Priesthood' echoes Preston's explication of Ephesians 2:10 ('We are Gods workmanship') in *The Breastplate of Faith and Love*: 'God is the workeman, we are the materials, as the clay, and the wood, that he takes into his hands ... to cast us into a new Mould, to give us a new heart, and to frame a new spirit within us, that so we may walke in good workes before him.'[21] As Herbert the scholar and student of divinity becomes Herbert the country parson, his Calvinism becomes increasingly social and worldly in its preoccupations, but it becomes no less Calvinist.[22]

Herbert's engagement with the underlying principles of covenant divinity is evident in poems like 'Lent' and 'A true Hymn,' which might be read as a poetic exposition of the 'covenant of grace.' According to Perry Miller, 'The essential concept [in the covenant of grace] was obligation to the law along with commutation of its sentence; the saint may be very imperfectly sanctified and still assured as long as his heart is sealed.'[23] Echoing Davenant's 'hypothetical universalism,' Preston preached, in addition to the absolute covenant of grace between God and his elect, 'a conditionall Covenant of Grace, which is common to all.' Everyone is obliged to 'lead a holy life, a religious, sober, and righteous life ... yet ... we cannot worke in ourselves this holinesse, this religious and sober conversation, that must be Gods worke altogether.'[24] Paradoxically, the sanctified heart might, indeed must, be 'perfectly holy,' despite the persistence of sin:

> except the heart were perfectly holy, it could not keep the whole Law, there were an impossibility, we should not reach every Commandment. And therefore there must be integrity and entyrenesse in the heart, that we may be able to keep them, at the least in an Evangelicall sincere manner, though wee cannot perfectly keepe the whole law of God.[25]

Herbert's persona grapples with these paradoxes of duty and deficiency in 'A True Hymn':

He who craves all the minde,
And all the soul, and strength, and time,
If the words onely ryme,
Justly complains, that somewhat is behinde
To make his verse, or write a hymn in kinde.

Whereas if th' heart be moved,
Although the verse be somewhat scant,
God doth supplie the want.
As when th' heart sayes (sighing to be approved)
O, could I love! and stops: God writeth, *Loved.*   (ll. 11–20)

God craves perfection, and when he finds deficiencies, he himself 'supplie[s] the want.' This is assurance, as distinct from complacency. The heart that yearns for God's approval is keenly aware of its own insufficiency. As Michael McGiffert puts it, 'the covenant of grace admitted its members to the privilege of bearing Christ's yoke.'[26]

Illuminating as Gottlieb's link between 'The Water-course' and 'The Banquet' is, there is no need to qualify or amplify 'The Water-course' by comparing it to other poems to see Herbert paradoxically emphasizing godly human striving alongside absolute divine authority. 'The Water-course' itself contains this double emphasis. As Veith points out, 'the human being is said to "turn the pipe,"' yet in the final line it is God's exercise of will 'as he sees fit' that is decisive. But despite his initial emphasis on the paradox Herbert's poem shares with Calvin's theology – in affirming both human choice and God's election – Veith sees the ending of 'The Water-course' as corrective: 'in the final line it is stated that the tap is actually controlled by God.'[27] The poem actually says something slightly different however. There is no mention of a tap in the final line, which offers an explicit theological statement contained in a relative clause, a construction that implies amplification rather than retraction:

Who gives to man, as he sees fit, $\left\{ \begin{array}{l} \text{Salvation} \\ \text{Damnation} \end{array} \right.$

Nor does the line contain a corrective rhetorical link, a 'but rather,' between lines 9 and 10. Herbert uses that gesture of redirection to *introduce* the element of human initiative into the poem in line 6: 'But rather turn the pipe and waters course / To serve thy sinnes.' If the last line of the poem seems incompatible with the emphasis on human initiative in the rest of the second stanza, readers are compelled not to abandon the notion that people can strive for good as well as for ill, but to ponder the mysterious interaction of the human and divine wills.

The importance of human striving in 'The Water-course' becomes clearer when we consider the movement of the entire poem. The first stanza is a classic exposition of the medieval *contemptus mundi* theme, consistent with Protestant theology in its assessment of this 'frail' world, but antithetical to the entire Protestant tradition in its implied preference for ascetic retreat.[28] The characteristic Protestant response to the corrupt world, an active but critical engagement in its affairs, is summed up in Raphael's advice to Milton's Adam: 'Nor love thy Life, nor hate; but what thou livst / Live well' (*PL*, 11.553–4). It is this posture that Herbert's poem adopts in its second stanza. Suddenly technology and ingenuity, the human exercise of God-given talent, seem to play a role in the redemptive process. That role is a mysterious one throughout the second stanza: if the turning of the pipe is a human action, the waters which 'course / To serve thy sinnes' seem to come from an external source, at least until their figurative transformation into the sinner's own tears. The spring of 'true remorse' may be divine, but the tears, which are both Christ's and the sinner's, signify God's action *through* an active human agent, not merely his action *upon* a passive human object.

So much, I think, can be argued on the basis of a close reading of 'The Water-course.' A fuller and more historically precise account of the poem's conceit offers important corroboration and elaboration. Readers of the poem have traced its central figure to images of fountains and flowing water in Calvin's *Institutes*, and to the Old Testament books of Joel (3:18) and Zechariah (13:1).[29] While it is safe to assume the relevance of these sources, Herbert's exposure to innovative irrigation techniques in Wiltshire in the early 1630s and the pervasiveness of the literature of agricultural improvement may have offered a more immediate inspiration, whose aptness was reinforced by its consonance with passages in Calvin and in Scripture. The *OED* offers, as its first definition of 'water-course,' 'A stream of water, a river or brook; also an artificial channel for the conveyance of water,' citing specifically agricultural examples (albeit examples from later than the seventeenth century). It seems likely that the title of the poem is meant to imply not a fountain or 'branching pipes,' but rather the branching streams or trenches of an irrigation system (see page 141).[30] This reading is supported by the fact that the two instances of the word 'watercourse' in the authorized version of the Bible both apply the term to irrigation channels.[31] The first passage recounts the piety and prosperity of Hezekiah, who 'stopped the upper watercourse of Gihon, and brought it straight down to the west side of the city of David. And Hezekiah prospered in all his works' (2 Chronicles 32:30). The second passage is from God's challenge to Job:

'Who hath divided a watercourse for the overflowing of waters, or a way for the lightning of thunder;

To cause it to rain on the earth where no man is; on the wilderness, wherein there is no man;

To satisfy the desolate and waste ground; and to cause the bud of the tender herb to spring forth?'   (Job 38:25–7)

In these two passages, as in Herbert's poem, diverting the flow of water to promote fertility and prosperity is, paradoxically, both the unique act of an omnipotent God and the devoted work of his faithful human servant.

Once it becomes clear that the poem's conceit links grace primarily and specifically with agriculture and irrigation, rather than generally with baptismal and cleansing images of 'the water of life,' it also becomes clear that this conceit operates throughout the poem, rather than merely in the second stanza.[32] The poem imagines its Christian addressee as one of those farmers inclined to 'dive ... too deep into worldly affairs' (*Country Parson*, 247). But he is farming in the desert of 'this world ... / Where of all plants afflictions soonest grow.' How, then, can he prosper? Helen Vendler sees 'no comfort to the troubled soul' in the poem, but in the turn from the first to the second stanza the speaker advocates an activist posture that is less bleak than she thinks.[33] The solution is not renunciation, but rather spiritual and agricultural 'improvement.' The second part of the poem offers not an alternative to the strife of living in this world, but an alternative understanding of that strife, an alternative way of living in the world, '*raising their thoughts to God, [and] sanctifying their labour with daily prayer*' (*Country Parson*, 248). The husbandman who, in the words of 'The Collar,' reaps 'no harvest but a thorn' (l. 7), must 'turn the pipe,' divert the stream into a different channel, and his grounds will become fertile, flooded with 'sov'raigne tears' (a nice redeployment of the familiar Petrarchan conceit). Readings of 'The Water-course' that neglect or underemphasize its specifically agricultural frame of reference tend to see a corrective redirection of attention away from human endeavour and towards the divine source of the water. But if, as seems likely, Herbert really has in mind a water-meadow, the massive human undertaking that promised, through diversion of waters, a near-miraculous transformation of Wiltshire's geography and economy, then sanctified human labour assumes much greater prominence in the poem's account of salvation than otherwise. The scriptural example of Hezekiah looms much larger, even as the poem's final line asserts God's omnipotence in tones reminiscent of the Book of Job. And if the metaphor for salvation is an agricultural mega-project involving large investments of capital, land, and labour, then the vision of salvation conveyed by that metaphor looks increasingly like the social and political vision of godly community advanced by covenant theologians and local moralists in the early seventeenth century.

Even as their subject continues to be personal salvation, as understood by the Protestant Church of England in which Herbert was raised, poems like 'The Water-course' take on a more determinedly social character. This, then, is Lull's 'progression away from lyric individualism,' as reflected in one of the poems added to the early Williams manuscript.[34] Without abandoning theology these poems increasingly devote particular attention to practical questions of piety, morality and ordinary human affairs, and to godly conduct in the world. The general point has been made before that Herbert's poems accord 'with a general shift in the seventeenth century from speculative meditation to practical divinity,' and that even the theological poems 'are firmly tied to exact observations drawn from actual experience,'[35] but it has not often been pointed out that this is increasingly the case in what are likely to be later poems.

The difference between earlier and later poems is sometimes evident in the way they either endorse or undermine their own discursive procedures. 'Redemption,' a poem included in the Williams manuscript under the title 'The Passion,' shares with 'The Water-course' a conceit in which the Christian is a farmer, 'Not thriving' because of the harsh conditions (spiritual conditions, allegorized) under which he works.

Redemption

Having been tenant long to a rich Lord,
  Not thriving, I resolved to be bold,
  And make a suit unto him, to afford
A new small-rented lease, and cancell th' old.

In heaven at his manour I him sought :
   They told me there, that he was lately gone
   About some land, which he had dearly bought
Long since on earth, to take possession.
I straight return'd, and knowing his great birth,
   Sought him accordingly in great resorts;
   In cities, theatres, gardens, parks, and courts:
At length I heard a ragged noise and mirth
   Of theeves and murderers: there I him espied,
   Who straight, *Your suit is granted*, said, & died.

In 'Redemption,' as Richard Strier points out, 'the syntax of the poem enacts the breakdown of the speaker's world picture' and of the conceit likening God to a landlord. Far from rendering God's behaviour in familiar and comprehensible terms, 'Redemption' explores 'the strangeness' and 'the strange *givenness*' of divine grace.[36] Its conceit, while it does not evaporate entirely by the end of the poem, steadily loses explanatory force as the poem progresses.[37] In this regard, 'Redemption' resembles 'Prayer' [I] in its restless struggle with the inadequacy of figurative language. 'The Water-course,' by contrast, is one of those Herbert poems that asserts the worthiness, if not exactly the sufficiency, of human enterprise, and of poetic discourse as a form of enterprise. Unlike so many of the Williams manuscript's poems, it is not a 'self-consuming artifact,' and its conceit does not collapse under the pressure of the realization that God's 'word is all.'[38]

Reconsidering the 'Anti-Court Sequence'

The problems of living in the world of strife and the world of discourse are central to the group of poems Sidney Gottlieb has identified as an 'anti-court sequence,' extending from 'Content' to 'Affliction' [III], or perhaps to 'The Starre' (which Gottlieb omits from the group). In creating this sequence in *The Temple*, Herbert rearranged four poems carried over from the Williams manuscript, removed one ('Affliction' [I]) to another location, and added two or three new poems at the end of the group. Gottlieb's analysis, persuasive in the main, sees this sequence of poems working to 'dismantle a court,' and to 'anatomize ... certain kinds of court behavior, virtue, notions of self, and definitions of poetry.' Even as they 'attempt to envision alternate styles of behavior,' argues Gottlieb, they 'testify to the fact that the court is immanent, and perhaps irrepressible.'[39] But the fact that the last poems in this sequence are not included in the Williams manuscript, and that they make few explicit references to courts and courtly behaviour, invites an alternative reading, in which the sequence moves, like 'The Water-course,' away from denunciations of courtliness and towards a vision of godly activism in a world that is not constructed primarily in the image of a court.[40] As one might expect, the poems that are less likely to reflect Herbert's youthful ambitions and frustrations offer fewer signs of the immanence and irrepressibility of the court.

The first four poems partake of the medieval *contemptus mundi* tradition evident in the opening of 'The Water-course.' They identify worldliness with courtliness in order to renounce both. Having begun by attempting to silence his own 'mutt'ring thoughts,' the speaker of 'Content' prays:

> Give me the pliant minde, whose gentle measure
>   Complies and suits with all estates;
> Which can let loose to a crown, and yet with pleasure
>   Take up within a cloisters gates.   (ll. 13–16)

He closes in the same vein, renewing the injunction to silence found in so many of Herbert's poems, and framing it in terms of a rustic ideal that stands opposed to urban conceptions of elegance and eloquence: 'cease discoursing soul, till thine own ground' (l. 33). 'The Quidditie' concentrates on the link between poetic discourse and courtliness, attempting to sever that link, much as Herbert's early sonnets to his mother seek to sever the link between secular love and poetry:

> My God, a verse is not a crown,
> No point of honour, or gay suit,
> No hawk, or banquet, or renown,
> Nor a good sword, not yet a lute.   (ll. 1–4)

The rhetorical strategy of 'The Quidditie' also resembles that of 'Prayer' [I]:

> Prayer the Churches banquet, Angels age,
>   Gods breath in man returning to his birth,
>   The soul in paraphrase, heart in pilgrimage,
> The Christian plummet sounding heav'n and earth.   (ll. 1–4)

Both poems seek to define a mode of discourse (prayer, verse) through a succession of metaphors, or in the case of 'The Quidditie,' anti-metaphors. Whether the strategy is one of successive identification (which may imply either amplification or erasure and substitution) or of successive differentiation, the result is similar: an assertion of the futility of metadiscourse. Like 'Prayer' [I], 'The Quidditie' closes with an elliptical gesture that invokes the divine *logos*, outside of human discourse, as a guarantee of poetic meaning: [verse] is that which while I use / I am with thee, and *most take all*' (ll. 11–12). The attempt, in 'The Quidditie,' to detach verse from the court succeeds only by identifying the court and the world and detaching verse from the world. This leaves inwardness and otherworldliness as the only options for true poetry. In both these poems, as Gottlieb argues, 'Herbert reaches the limits of language.'[41]

'Humilitie' and 'Frailtie' develop the critique of courtliness and worldliness initiated in 'Content' and 'The Quidditie,' by anatomizing each in turn. In 'Humility' the allegory of court corruption ends with a subtle intimation that 'the law is hardly distinguishable from the crime.' It is, in part, the remarkably unspecific character of the allegorized court that makes this such a broad condemnation. Despite his reference to law and crime, Gottlieb seems to have in mind the royal court when he envisions a situation in which 'The Vertues ... act like highly-placed, rank-conscious Jacobean patrons ... [and the animals, like] ambitious and incipiently riotous courtiers.' But these patrons and courtiers were, after all, members of the same class, whatever their distinctions in influence. More consistent with the allegory of beastly supplicants and presiding virtues might be a local court, perhaps a quarter session, but more likely a manor court, which combined the functions we associate with a royal court – administration and the dispensing of patronage – with those we associate with a court of law – resolving disputes and punishing offenders, and where the gap in social status between those presiding and those appearing before the court was much wider. In such a context, the threat of 'crumbling social hierarchy' from the reversal of places is much more substantial.[42] The key point, however, is that nothing in the poem tells us whether we are dealing with a royal court or a local one: the imprecision of the allegory is characteristic of the poems of the Williams manuscript, which tend to direct attention away from the specifically material and social, and towards the spiritual. The precise nature of the concrete image is not especially important to the success of the poem. If the court stands for the world, any court, or a compendium of courts, will serve. 'Frailtie' resembles 'Humilitie' in its brisk movement from worldly externals to their inward analogues. The poem is not so much a denunciation of 'What upon trust / Is styled *honour, riches,* or *fair eyes*' (ll. 2–3) as of the speaker's inconstant responses to them – hence, perhaps, its placement immediately before 'Constancie.' Despite repeated and emphatic assertions of a 'spiritually correct' *contemptus mundi* sentiment – 'I despise'; 'I surname them *guilded clay*'; 'my foot doth ever tread / Upon their head' – the speaker is still tempted: 'That which was dust before, doth quickly rise, / And prick mine eyes' (ll. 15–16). We learn very little about *what* tempts him, because the focus is on the spiritual dynamics of temptation. Both of these poems stand in sharp contrast to a poem like 'The Water-course,' where the sort of watercourse that embodies the poem's theological ideas is crucially important.

'Constancie,' the first poem in the 'anti-court sequence' not included in the early Williams manuscript, is very different in this respect, and much closer to 'The Water-course' in its view of the world of human affairs. For one thing, the poem is not one of criticism, confession, satire, or complaint, but of praise. More than this, it is a poem in praise of *human* virtue. Its movement, unlike the others, is from the inside out, from constancy as a generality and abstraction, towards its manifestations in social conduct. Given its placement, following a group of rather pessimistic poems, '"Constancie" seem[s] naive.'[43] Nevertheless, its resonance with the pragmatic moralism of *The Country Parson* makes it typical of the posture towards which Herbert moves in his later writing. Moreover, if the poem's moralism is optimistic, it is far from simplistic, and, I would suggest, far from naive. More than any of its immediate predecessors, 'Constancie' abandons the agonizing polarities of *contemptus mundi* and sinful indulgence, striving to contextualize its subject, and to imagine virtuous action in a changeable world that 'now rides by, now lags behind' (l. 10). In such a world, the Christian's duty to love and serve 'God, his neighbour, and himself' is not satisfied by treating everyone the same, or even by treating everyone according to a single inflexible rule: constancy must be distinguished from uniformity or rigidity. Hence, the constant man weighs 'the thing and the example,' and 'All being brought into a summe, / What place or person calls for he doth pay' (ll. 3, 13, 15). In a society profoundly stratified by gender and rank, and increasingly stratified according to presumed moral criteria (as, for example, in the distinction between the deserving and the undeserving poor) the Christian's duty to his neighbour varies according to who that neighbour is and the circumstances under which the duty is performed. The honest man, 'when he is to treat / With sick folks, women, those whom passions sway, / Allows for that, and keeps his constant way' (ll. 26–8).[44] In the final stanza of 'Constancie' an alternative is offered for the polar opposites of worldliness and withdrawal that animate 'Content,' 'The Quidditie,' 'Humilitie,' and 'Frailtie.' What had been presented as a choice between two 'Regiments; / The worlds, and thine' ('Frailtie, ' ll. 9–10) becomes a choice between two ways of living *in* the world, to 'share ... [or] mend the ill.' The idealized 'honest man' presented in the opening line of 'Constancie' becomes a 'Mark-man,' not merely an archer (a marksman), as Hutchinson's gloss suggests, but also a target (a marked man).[45] The final line of the poem places this idealized yet pragmatic moralism in a context more Calvinist than Arminian. The ultimate test of an 'honest man' is that he attributes his perseverence in virtue not to his individual will, but to God's grace: he 'still is right, and prayes to be so still' (l. 35).

'Constancie' says virtually nothing about the court. Indeed, it breaks the figurative identification of the court and the world common to the more critical and satirical poems that precede it. This break allows for a more nuanced account of the world and its moral vagaries. It also opens the way for a reconsideration of the poetic issues treated in 'Content' and 'The Quidditie,' notably of the drift towards a 'rhetoric of silence' that proves impossible to put into practice. The next poem in the group, 'Affliction' [III], offers a reconciliation with the materiality of language and of the world, a reconciliation grounded in the recognition that though Christ's 'life on earth was grief' he was 'Constant unto it' (ll. 13–14). The poem opens with an 'unruly sigh' which might, under some circumstances, be taken as profane and blasphemous: '*O God!*' In 'Content' the speaker had tried to contain such 'private ejaculations' Within the walls of [his] own breast (l. 2), but here, as in 'Constancie,' context is everything. Immediately, the speaker moves to reconstitute his own barely articulate expression of grief as evidence of divine protection: 'Hadst thou not had thy part, / Sure the unruly sigh had broke my heart' (ll. 5–6). Even the most unpoetic utterance may be inspired. The playful rehearsal of conventional images of *spiritus* in the second stanza – 'thy breath gave me both life and shape' (l. 7) – implies that a sigh may be the most elemental form of inspiration. The sigh, which the speaker recognizes as 'a gale to bring me sooner to my bliss' (l. 12), expresses a human response to the trials of life in the world, and both the expression and the trial are to be endured, even embraced, rather than avoided. 'The Starre,' which Gottlieb does not link to the 'anti-court sequence,' despite its courtly plea for patronage – 'Get me a standing there, and place' (l. 21) – completes this movement of reconciliation. Indeed, with 'The Starre,' Herbert might almost be said to conclude the 'anti-court sequence' with a pro-court poem, abandoning the *contemptus mundi* posture in which 'court' symbolizes all the worst attributes of the world, for one in which it symbolizes the earthly manifestation of heavenly glory.[46]

'My busie heart shall spin': Praise and the Cloth Industry

'The Water-course' is only one of many Herbert poems to draw a metaphor for God's dealings with humanity from the stuff of ordinary material culture.[47] A considerable number of Herbert's poems draw from the cloth industry a pervasive body of homespun images. In 'The Pearl' (l. 38) and 'Providence' (ll. 57–9), God is, among other things, a spinner whose 'twist' joins heaven and earth. Similarly 'Man's Medley' (and perhaps, to stretch the point a little, 'Joseph's Coat'), draws on textile imagery to illustrate humanity's unique and ambivalent situation, 'with one hand touching heav'n, with th'other earth' ('Man's Medley,' l. 12), while 'Jordan' [II], 'The Glimpse,' 'Assurance,' and 'Praise' [III] use weaving and spinning, both positively and negatively, as figures for human ingenuity and discourse. Of these poems only two ('Jordan' [II] and 'The Pearl') are included in the Williams manuscript, and these employ textile images fleetingly. Four of the others ('The Glimpse,' 'Assurance,' 'Praise' [III], and 'Joseph's Coat') appear in a cluster that suggests, if not a clearly defined textile sequence, at least an effort to direct attention to this body of imagery and the issues it serves to illuminate.[48]

The most important of these poems is 'The Glimpse,' which addresses 'delight' as a departing visitor who leaves too soon and comes too infrequently. As Helen Vendler notes, the poem 'bears a resemblance to 'Love' [III] in its vying of reproach with courtesy,'[49] but the host-guest relationship portrayed here is rather perplexing. Why does the host seem to depend on the guest for food (ll. 11–12; 16–17)? This question anticipates others, prompted by the final stanzas, on which Vendler, like the other critics who have treated the poem, is silent:

> Yet if the heart that wept
> Must let thee go, return when it doth knock.

Although thy heap be kept
For future times, the droppings of the stock
May oft break forth, and never break the lock.

If I have more to spinne,
The wheel shall go, so that thy stay be short.
Thou knowst how grief and sinne
Disturb the work. O make me not their sport,
Who by thy coming may be made a court!   (ll. 21–30)

These lines are even more difficult to assimilate into the departing guest scenario. Who is this visitor and what sort of 'heap' is he keeping 'for future times' (ll. 23–4)? What do his comings and goings have to do with the reference to spinning in the last stanza? The answer turns on an understanding of lines 26 and 27, 'If I have more to spinne, / The wheel shall go,' which, I suspect, is usually read as expressing 'the speaker's resignation.'[50] The speaker seems at first to be saying 'very well, if more is expected of me, I'll do my best.' I would suggest, however, that these lines need to be read as a plea for 'more' from the 'heap' that is being 'kept for future times.' The lines might then be paraphrased: 'If you'll just let me have some more (that is, more wool to spin), I'll get to work right away, but please promise not to stay away so long the next time.' There is, at least in terms of the vehicle here, no resignation. Rather the speaker becomes increasingly desperate and explicit in his demands, or perhaps *her* demands, since so many spinners were spinsters.

A review of the state of the Wiltshire woolen industry in the 1620s reveals the precise knowledge that informs Herbert's poem. Wiltshire, particularly the northern part where Herbert lived from 1628 to 1630, was a key centre of the woolen industry that was the cornerstone of England's economy. The landless (or nearly landless) cottagers of the region survived by agricultural day labour (when they could get work) and by spinring yarn on the 'putting-out' system for two sorts of middlemen: clothiers, who supplied spinsters with wool and wove the cloth, and independent yarn merchants (known colloquially as 'wool broggers' and 'yarn badgers'), who traded in wool and yarn, but not in finished cloth. Spinners, who normally bought their wool from suppliers in small batches, were utterly dependent on these middle men for their 'stuff.' The infamous Cockayne project of 1614–16, a scheme ostensibly aiming to increase employment by prohibiting the export of unfinished cloth, virtually destroyed the continental market for English cloth, devastating the domestic textile industry. Clothiers, unable to sell their finished goods, dismissed weavers and hoarded their raw wool, refusing to supply spinners. 'At Easter quarter sessions [in 1620] the justices were petitioned by workless spinners and weavers and upon inquiry they learnt that over a hundred and thirty looms were known to be standing idle; so that the number of unemployed could be no less than two thousand six hundred.' The Privy Council, in the early 1620s, repeatedly commanded 'the justices of the peace in the clothing countries to see that wool was not hoarded, that clothiers did not dismiss their workfolk, and that public stocks of wool and yarn were provided for the unemployed.' Though the depression was most severe in the early years of the decade, the presence of large amounts of wool, yarn, and unsold cloth in the estates of Wiltshire clothiers who died in 1628 and 1630 suggests that these problems persisted into Herbert's Wiltshire years.[51]

This, then, is the metaphorical situation that emerges in the last stanzas of 'The Glimpse.' The poem figures 'Delight' as the middleman who supplies the spinner/speaker with the raw material necessary for subsistence. The middleman visits rarely, however, because he is hoarding his stock, waiting for the market to improve, while the destitute speaker struggles to survive:

> Thy short abode and stay
> Feeds not, but adds to the desire of meat. (ll. 11–12)

> In hope of thee my heart
> Pickt here and there a crumme, and would not die. (ll. 16–17)

This is not to insist that the poem is a sustained and unwavering exploration of the spinning conceit; also embedded in it is the curious parable of 'Lime' and the 'neighbour spring' that heats instead of cooling (ll. 13–15). Rather, the textile conceit develops progressively, as the poem struggles to find figurative terms in which to express the inconstancy of spiritual delight. The host/guest relationship seems predominantly social in the opening stanzas, but it becomes increasingly economic, and increasingly strained, as the poem progresses, and the theological point of the poem seems increasingly tied to the economic conceit.

These economic undercurrents become clearer when we consider the ideology of 'The Glimpse.' By using the plight of an impoverished pieceworker to explore spiritual distress, Herbert invites us to find, in the poem, an incipient working-class consciousness, associated later with the Diggers and Levellers. Such a reading seems to set 'The Glimpse' in opposition to *The Country Parson* and to poems like 'The Water-course,' which promote a kind of spiritual entrepreneurialism. The opposition is largely illusory, however, because the poem's account of the causes of spiritual distress accords so closely with the official explanation of economic distress in the cloth industry, an explanation that was distinctly *moralistic* in tone, rather than economic. If nobody wanted English broadcloth anymore, conventional wisdom held that something *must* be *wrong* with the cloth, and if something was wrong with the cloth, someone must be to blame. In the early 1630s the Privy Council appointed one Anthony Wither to investigate deficiencies in west country cloth manufacture and inspection, deficiencies which were presumed to be the cause of the declining reputation of English cloth in the European marketplace.[52] The established clothiers attributed these deficiencies to the adulteration of wool by their competitors, the independent yarn merchants or 'market spinners,' who dominated the trade in coloured Spanish wool, the only prosperous sector of the cloth trade at the time.[53] Indeed, the competition created by the success of 'Spanish Medleys' had begun to drive up the wages of spinners, much to the distress of the clothiers. So while there may have been some truth in the clothiers' charges, they seem to reflect economic self interest, propped up by familiar commonweal rhetoric. In 1633 (the year George Herbert died), a proclamation against frauds in cloth-making was issued, supported by Wither's investigations and the report of a special committee. But provisions for the suppression of independent yarn merchants were removed at the last minute, apparently through the intervention of the earl of Danby, acting on behalf of his brother (and Herbert's step-father), Sir John Danvers, now also resident in Wiltshire and struggling to keep his finances in order.[54] Evidently the interests of the Danvers family, of which Herbert was now a member, were linked more strongly to the emerging entrepreneurs in the yarn trade than to the declining clothiers in the white broadcloth sector. The effect of the amended report was not to replace the moralistic account of the problem with an economic one, however, but merely to restrict the scope of the moralistic explanation to those at the bottom of the socioeconomic pyramid: the spinners, the weavers, and the 'searchers' (inspectors) who were often ignorant of their duties or intimidated by the clothiers. This is the economic context for the confessional note on which 'The Glimpse' closes:

> Thou knowst how grief and sinne
> Disturb the work. O make me not their sport,
> Who by thy coming may be made a court!   (ll. 28–30)

These lines register the spinner's acceptance of the moral explanation for his or her plight. Indeed, only the common root of spiritual *and* economic distress in 'grief and sinne' makes the spinning conceit work. But the closing lines of the poem also contain a last desperate attempt to turn this explanation to the spinner's advantage: 'if you leave me in distress,' the spinner seems to say, 'the work I do for you will be second-rate and you'll suffer too.' The spinner emulates his masters, declaring his allegiance to their ideology, by fusing traditional moralism and economic rationalism in an effort to strengthen his bargaining position.

The advantages of this sort of strategic ideological compliance are explored in another spinning poem, 'Praise' [III]:

> Lord, I will mean and speak thy praise,
>   Thy praise alone.
> My busie heart shall spin it all my dayes:
>   And when it stops for want of store,
> Then I will wring it with a sigh or grone,
>   That thou mayst yet have more.   (ll. 1–6)

Here the focus of the spinning conceit has shifted, from delight as a yarn trader to praise as the thread spun by the speaker. But the basic situation is identical. Again the speaker/spinner worries about what will happen 'when it stops for want of store.' Lacking raw wool (joy?) out of which to spin praise, the speaker wrings his heart for 'a sigh or grone' that will become the stuff of praise. His resolution to wring his heart, 'That thou may'st yet have more,' repeats the moralization of an economic problem found in 'The Glimpse.' The spinner/speaker blames himself for the lack of 'store,' but retains his commitment to supply finished product to a supplier/customer who will not provide him with raw material.

The middle stanzas of the poem become the additional praise that the spinner manages to produce by wringing his heart. They also continue to reinforce the poem's figurative conflation of the economic and the spiritual:

> When thou dost favour any action,
>   It runnes, it flies: (ll. 7–8)

But when thou dost on businesse blow,
                    It hangs, it clogs.   (ll. 13–14)

In a stanza Helen Vendler finds 'strangely materialistic,' the tears of grief out of which the speaker spins his praise become charitable donations:[55]

    I have not lost one single tear:
                    But when mine eyes
Did weep to heav'n, they found a bottle there
        (As we have boxes for the poore)
Readie to take them in; yet of a size
                That would contain much more.   (ll. 25–30)

If this is grief as charity, it is also charity as investment. Christ, the 'King of grief' ('The Thanksgiving,' l. 1), augments the speaker's meager donation with a kind of 'matching grant' of superabundant grace: 'after thou hadst slipt a drop / From thy right eye,/ ... The glasse was full and more' (ll. 31–6).[56] Applying the same logic, Herbert's country parson 'resolves ... never to omit any present good deed of charity, in consideration of providing a stock for his children; but assures himselfe, that mony thus lent to God, is placed surer for his children's advantage, then if it were given to the Chamber of *London*' (p. 240). Ultimately, Herbert promises, the sacrifices of Christ's members in his name will be rewarded.

Meanwhile Herbert's speaker faces, in the final stanza, the grim prospect that his 'heart, / Though press'd, runs thin' (ll. 37–8). Yet once again, distress is an opportunity for advantage. In the final lines of the poem the speaker prays for a calling that is at once evangelical and entrepreneurial:

O that I might some other hearts convert,
    And so take up at use good store:
That to thy chest there might be coming in
    Both all my praise, and more!   (ll. 39–42)

In this figure to become a priest is to become a spiritual venture capitalist, borrowing 'at use' (that is, at interest) others' hearts, as the 'store' from which he will spin praise to further enrich God's 'chest.' In terms of the material analogy the speaker prays to be transformed from an old-style 'market spinner' (solitary and dependent on middlemen) to a new-style capitalist market spinner (one of those opportunistic, risk-taking, prosperous middlemen). Only by breaking out of the mode of domestic production of praise (private devotion) and moving into a capitalist mode will the speaker be able to produce 'more' and 'more' praise.

Power, Patriarchy, and Priesthood

In chapter 5 I argued that *The Country Parson* straddles the divide between an idealized traditional, patriarchal, and authoritarian conception of social order and a more modern contractual one in which the mechanisms of power are increasingly diffused and obscured by a rhetoric of individual autonomy. Even as it clings to reassuring patriarchal and familial metaphors, *The Country Parson* describes a world in which the relationships to which those terms are applied fail to conform to traditional paradigms of deference and authority. This ambiguity is less clear in Herbert's poems than in *The Country Parson*, but it is clearer there than many critics have acknowledged. A case in point is 'Clasping of Hands,' a poem not included in the Williams manuscript, and a poem that revels in the bewildering complexity and instability of hierarchical relationships, rather than attributing to them a false simplicity. On the surface, 'Clasping of Hands' seems a perfect example of the poem as self-consuming artefact. Its corrective close – 'Or rather, make no mine and thine' – seems to assure readers that it is unnecessary to attempt to follow the logic of the poem, with its careful yet shifting distinctions between 'mine' and 'thine,' because the ultimate aim is to abolish such distinctions.[57] Nevertheless this abolition is the subject of a prayer, not necessarily the achievement of the poem. We need to look closely at the body of the poem before judging its concluding couplet. In particular we need to ask what the poem means by 'mine' and 'thine.' My what? Thy what? What sort of earthly relations of possession are its analogues for the relationship between God and the believer? William V. Nestrick, the poem's most careful reader, begins from the assumption that the terms 'mine' and 'thine' refer to the relationship between equal idealized lovers: 'Love as a state expressed in the formula ("to be" plus personal possessive pronoun) involves the gift of one's being and an increased sense of that being because one has been made more than oneself by the gift of the other's being.'[58] 'Mine' and 'thine,' in Nestrick's view, mean 'my beloved' and 'thy beloved,' but this reading seems to presuppose the perfect union for which the speaker pleads in the last line. It also supposes, on the level of the worldly vehicle, an equality as remote from the reality of early modern gender relations as it is from the other situations in which Herbert's contemporaries might have referred to another person as 'mine' and to themselves as 'thine.' I would suggest, on the contrary, that the poem is concerned throughout with hierarchical relationships and that it is, in part, a meditation on Paul's exhortation to humility in Philippians 2 and the concept of Christ's *kenosis* (self-emptying) derived from that passage. The terms 'mine' and 'thine,' at least initially, define the God/man relationship as one of patriarchal subordination, analogous to the relations of husband and wife, parent and child, and, especially, master and servant. The poem explores the paradoxes in Christ's taking 'the form of a servant' and being 'made in the likeness of men' (Philippians 2.7). Beginning from this assumption, I would offer the following rather stilted prose paraphrase, as a way of untangling the poem's deliberately playful and subtle repetitions and distinctions:

> Lord, you are my master, and if I am my own man, it is because I am your servant first: indeed I am your servant much more than I either ought or can be my own man. Yet being your servant restores me; so that I become my own man again, and I am the one who profits from the relationship, since this sort of individuality (this way of being my own man), partakes of your dignity, and you become yourself again in restoring me to myself.
>
> Should I attempt to be an utterly autonomous individual (without thee) I would be neither myself nor your servant.
>
> Lord, I am your master, and you are my servant: so much so that I may presume to say you belong to me even more than you belong to yourself. Because you suffered to restore, not yourself, but me, and you suffered to serve me, and I am the one who profits, because by dying you ceased to be yourself (ceased to be God – became human?), yet as my servant (my surrogate?) you restored me.
>
> O continue to be mine (my servant, my master, my surrogate), continue to make me your servant (your lord?). Or rather, abolish the distinctions altogether.

The first stanza is a fairly straightforward defence of the ideology of deferential hierarchy. Both master and servant derive their social identities from the hierarchical relationship. Crucially, in this argument, subordination is an 'advantage' to the subordinate, and not merely to the superior.[59] The servant partakes of his master's dignity (hence Gloucester's and then Lear's outrage over the stocking of Caius/Kent in *King Lear*); and a masterless man (that is, a vagrant) is the lowest and most dangerous sort, a man with no social identity.

The second stanza, however, complicates the situation, pressing the argument about reciprocity to its limits by reversing the terms. As readers we may hesitate, initially, to supply the word 'master' after 'I am thine' and 'servant' after 'thou art mine' (l. 11), but the next two lines, echoing the corresponding lines in stanza 1, seem to demand such a reading. In both cases the servant (the speaker in stanza 1; God in stanza 2) belongs more fully to the master (God in stanza 1; the speaker in stanza 2), than he does to himself. At this point things get truly complicated, as the poem maintains its structural symmetry while emphatically abandoning its logical symmetry to make a new point: 'thou didst suffer to restore / Not thee, but me' (ll. 14–15). In stanza 1, with God in the role of master, man gains the 'advantage'; in stanza 2, with man in the role of master, man *still* gains the 'advantage.' Indeed, Christ's power to restore, in stanza 2, seems directly proportional to his humiliation. His total abandonment of divinity – 'since thou in death wast none of thine' (l. 17) – is the guarantee of his omnipotence. Theologically there is nothing especially remarkable here. The paradox of mighty weakness is a Biblical topos that echoes throughout Christian literature. But Herbert's poem hints at the political utility of this doctrine in orchestrating an ideological shift from coercive tactics of power to productive ones, from the top-down paradigm of social control associated with (if not always practiced in) traditional hierarchies, to the bottom-up and sideways paradigm explored more fully in *The Country Parson*. The human reader can clearly identify with the servant who profits from servitude in stanza one, but his identification in the second stanza is much less clear and stable. As a human he is invited to conceive of himself as a master, served by the humbled Christ. As a servant, and as the 'Outlandish Proverb' asserts, 'everyone is a master and servant' (*Works*, 355), he is 'empowered' to conceive of his status as Godlike. The best example of this humble yet Godlike power is that of the pastor, Christ's 'Deputy ... for the reducing of man to the Obedience of God,' who 'knows well, that both for the generall ignominy which is cast upon the profession, and much more for those rules ... hee hath resolved to observe ... he must be despised; because this hath been the portion of God his Master' (*Country Parson*, 225, 268). This is a power that is magnified rather than diminished when the pastor deigns 'to enter into the poorest Cottage, though he even creep into it, and though it smell never so lothsomely.' According to Herbert, 'Nothing is little in Gods service: If it once have the honour of that Name, it grows great instantly' (249). By compressing these ideas into verse and generalizing them at the same time, 'Clasping of Hands,' moves beyond a traditional defence of subordination on the grounds of its advantages to the subordinate and towards a glorification (and a mystification) of subordination and humiliation as *loci* of true power. In this context, the closing line, 'Or rather, make no mine and thine' is less emphatically corrective and more continuous with the body of the poem than a superficial reading would suggest. The diffusion of human identity through both roles, dependent master and Godlike servant, is a prelude to the eschatological vision of an absolute abandonment of master/servant distinctions.

This diffusion of identity and distribution of authority transforms authoritarian discipline into self-discipline.[60] We can see this in the vision of domestic/spiritual order in 'The Familie.' Here, the speaker complains of a 'noise of thoughts within my heart,' figuring his own 'loud complaints and puling fears' as unruly children and servants (ll. 1, 3). In the second stanza, however, the speaker resigns his paternal authority to God, suddenly representing himself as the house and God as the householder. Yet even as he declines to play the authoritarian patriarch himself, he urges God to disown or dismiss the insubordinate children and servants: 'Turn out these wranglers, which defile thy seat: / For where thou dwellest all is neat' (ll. 7–8). The following stanza seems, at first, to begin with more imperatives: 'First Peace and Silence all disputes control' (l. 9). But if this *is* an imperative, it modulates imperceptibly into a present tense account of the workings of a self-regulating godly household. There is no indication that God *has* intervened, and yet it turns out that some of the subordinate members of the household are able to 'control' disputes, without the heavy hand of paternal authority. The result of such self-discipline, as Herbert will urge more emphatically in *The Country Parson*, is a whole set of improvements to the moral landscape:

> Then Order plaies the soul;
> And giving all things their set forms and houres,
> Makes of wilde woods sweet walks and bowres.   (ll. 10–12)

The heart is divided and subdivided into an increasing number of subordinate parts, each with its own regulated and regulatory function to perform:

> Humble Obedience near the doore doth stand,
>> Expecting a command:
> Then whom in waiting nothing seems more slow,
>> Nothing more quick when she doth go.   (ll. 13–16)

It is surely no accident that the figure of Obedience is gendered female. Yet the most lowly servant in the household is, in a sense, the most important, for she epitomizes the blend of passivity and activity that constitutes self-discipline. 'They also serve who only stand and wait,' to quote Milton's later and more famous formulation of the point.

If 'Clasping of Hands' invites readers to assume a posture of Godlike humility, powerful by virtue of its submissiveness, and 'The Familie' offers an allegory of mutual self-discipline among domestic subordinates, 'Obedience' charts the social extension of mighty weakness, as the submissive Christian seeks to exercise power by drawing others into like submission.[61] The means for this extension is not hierarchical authority, but legalistic contract, probably modelled on contemporary enclosure agreements. The first three stanzas figure devotional poetry as a deed of gift, conveying 'Lordship' over the speaker's heart to God. The next three stanzas seem, as Richard Strier points out, to renounce 'the language of willing and contracting,' language which, unfortunately for Strier's argument, reappears in the last three stanzas. If we are not to follow Strier's lead and dismiss the conclusion as 'an afterthought,' we need to reconsider the function of the middle stanzas, and the transformation of the poem's legalistic framework that they bring about.[62] The poem does indeed shift from a contractual mode into a prayerful one in these middle stanzas, but the latter need not imply a repudiation of the former. After all, oaths and promises are frequently sealed with the formulaic expression 'so help me God.' Stanzas four through six of 'Obedience' constitute a careful elaboration on that formulaic phrase:

> O let thy sacred will
>> All thy delight in me fulfill!
> Let me not think an action mine own way,
>> But as thy love shall sway,
> Resigning up the rudder to thy skill.   (ll. 16–20)

Saying 'so help me God' and *meaning* it involves reconsidering the role of the human will in 'voluntary' transactions, but the result of that reconsideration is not so much a rejection of voluntarism as a recognition that voluntary acts are enabled, constrained, and determined by God's providential oversight and by his prior actions:

> Yet since thou canst not choose but see my actions;
> So great are thy perfections,
> Thou mayst as well my actions guide, as see.
>
> Besides, thy death and blood
> Show'd a strange love to all our good:
> Thy sorrows were in earnest, no faint proffer,
> Or superficial offer
> Of what we might not take, or be withstood.   (ll. 23–30)

Voluntarism and constraint are not, in this view of things, mutually exclusive: a contract or covenant is the paradigm case of a relationship that is simultaneously voluntary and constrained.

The clearest evidence of the persistence of legal and contractual discourse in the middle part of the poem is the expression 'in earnest' (l. 28), which refers not merely to God's sincerity, but also to his payment in advance 'for the purpose of securing a bargain or contract' (*OED*). The speaker's recognition, registered in an amendment to the contract in stanza seven, is not that there is no contract, but that what he first saw as a deed of gift is actually a deed of sale finalizing the transfer of some land that was, as Herbert writes in 'Redemption,' 'dearly bought / Long since' (ll. 5–6):

> Where in the Deed there was an intimation
> Of a gift or donation,
> Lord, let it now by way of purchase go.   (ll. 33–5)

Here though, unlike in 'Redemption,' the contractual and legalistic conceit persists to the very end of the poem. Once he understands that the Lord's side of the contract has been fulfilled in advance, and contemplates the Lord's generosity, the nature of the speaker's obligation becomes clearer. In a conclusion that anticipates the evangelical thrust of 'Praise' [III], the speaker resolves not merely to convey his own land/ heart to God, but to become God's agent in recruiting his neighbour to sign on, so that the agreement might be 'in heav'ns Court of Rolls ... entred for both' (ll. 43–5).

The reference to 'heavn's Court of Rolls' and the peculiar nature of the land transaction described in the poem make it clear that the last stanzas are not an afterthought, but an integral part of the poem's definition of obedience. Hutchinson glosses 'Court of Rolls' as an allusion to the 'court of the Master of Rolls for the custody of records,' but this is slightly misleading.[63] The Master of Rolls was a Chancery official, custodian of the records of the court of Chancery, and the Lord Chancellor's senior deputy, so Herbert seems to have in mind a heavenly equivalent of Chancery. This is particularly appropriate, theologically, since Chancery was not a court of law, but a 'court of equity' whose function, in the words of Lord Ellesmere, was to 'mollify the extremity of the law.'[64] The Chancery was also preoccupied with matters of property. The speaker's situation in the poem is the same one faced by the consenting parties in seventeenth-century enclosure agreements.[65] Unless all tenants with common rights could be persuaded to accept enclosure, the agreement would not be legally binding. Those who wished to surrender their common rights to the lord in return for compensation had to persuade their neighbours to do the same. Increasingly, enclosure agreements were legitimated through suits in the courts of Chancery and Exchequer. These suits sometimes served merely to record agreements already achieved, but occasionally they served to intimidate reluctant neighbours into acquiescence.[66] Herbert is not, of course, urging such coercive tactics. As *The Country Parson* insists, gentle persuasion is preferable to adversarial procedure among Christian neighbours. Nevertheless the evangelical imperative is conceived here in emphatically worldly and legalistic terms, and it is represented, through the conceit of an enclosure agreement, as a necessary element of Christian obedience. Christian ministry becomes the answer offered most consistently in Herbert's later poems to the succession of questions posed by 'The Thanksgiving': 'how shall I grieve for thee, / Who in all grief preventest me?' (ll. 3–4). The appropriate response to Christ's sacrifice is neither the vainglorious contest of love with God rejected in 'The Thanksgiving,' and throughout 'The Church,' nor an eschatological quietism, but rather, a reorientation of the flow of love, power, and duty from the vertical axis (divine/ human) to the horizontal (human/human). The duty of the minister is, in the words of 'The Water-course,' to 'turn the pipe' and redirect the flow of 'soveraign tears' onto heretofore barren soil.[67]

Central to this redirection is the evolution of Herbert's internal dialogues, apostrophic poems (the latter, often, a one-sided version of the former), and other poems representing a divided subject between the

Williams manuscript and the later poems. As Rosalie Osmond has pointed out, these poems owe a great deal to the medieval body and soul dialogues, which express the dualistic 'preoccupations of an age obsessed by death, and viewing life primarily as a preparation for it.' 'In the early body and soul literature,' Osmond writes, 'it is the emphasis on death, its physical and mental torments, and the consequent vanity of earthly possessions and pleasures that is dominant.'[68] Several of Herbert's divided-self poems, particularly the earlier ones included in the Williams manuscript, fit neatly into this medieval *contemptus mundi* mold. Perhaps the most obvious example is 'Church Monuments,' which employs an allegory of hierarchical domestic order and religious instruction to drive home its cryptically stated but conventional theological point:

> That flesh is but the glasse, which holds the dust
> That measures all our time; which also shall
> Be crumbled into dust. (ll. 20–2)

In the narrative that forms the poem's conceit, the 'I' of the poem initially assumes a paternal role, entrusting his younger and less responsible child, 'My bodie to this school' (the grave), while the eldest child (the soul) 'repairs to her devotions' unsupervised. As the poem progresses, however, this family drama becomes increasingly complicated. The familial relationships implied in the opening lines dissolve like the flesh in the grave. In the second part of the poem the paternal speaker addresses his flesh/child directly, using the gentlest of tones in an effort to soften a devastating message: 'Deare flesh, while I do pray, learn here thy stemme / And true descent' (ll. 17–18).[69] You are not my real child. You are a foster-child whom I have so far raised as my own; but we must now be separated. You will have to endure the fate dictated by your 'birth'; your duty now is to 'fit thyself against thy fall' (l. 24). To add insult to injury, the father seems, in keeping with the English custom of primogeniture, to have merged with the elder sibling. When the flesh is relegated to the grave, the 'I' who oversaw both body and soul, because he was identical with neither, becomes indistinguishable from the soul who 'repairs to her devotions.'[70] Still, there is no sense of injustice in the poem, no challenge to the merciless stratification of the imaginary family within the individual. Indeed, the assumed rightness of the speaker's procedure in disowning the 'wanton' foster child and preferring the natural one (who also happens, like *King Lear*'s Edgar, to be the virtuous one) is what makes this difficult bit of doctrine 'slip the more easily into the hearts' of readers (*Country Parson*, 261).

Yet, as I argued in the previous chapter, the notion of a soul divided against itself need not merely reinforce deferential hierarchy and a renunciation of the world. It can easily be adapted as a productive instrument of social control, creating a paradoxical blend of reconciliation with and disorientation in the material and social world. Herbert increasingly employs the divided subject this way, in poems not included in the Williams manuscript. A prime example is 'Conscience,' the first of the large group of added poems, which upsets the stable social and theological dynamic of 'Church Monuments' by apparently celebrating insubordination rather than authoritarian self-discipline. The poem opens with what appears to be a revolt against the scrupulous conscience on behalf of the deprived senses:

> Peace pratler, do not lowre:
> Not a fair look, but thou dost call it foul:
> Not a sweet dish, but thou dost call it sowre:
> Musick to thee doth howl.
> By listning to thy chatting fears
> I have both lost mine eyes and eares. (ll. 1–6)

The conscience is conventionally assigned a position of supreme moral authority in the hierarchy of the faculties, as 'a thing placed of God in the middest betweene him and man, as an arbitrator to give sentence.'[71] When the poem's speaker rebukes his own conscience, therefore, he appears to violate the internal hierarchy that supposedly reflects a celestial model, and yet there is no suggestion of a transgression here. Herbert is, I think, grappling with a significant 'theoretical dilemma' built into hierarchical moral theology, the problem of the 'erring conscience.' Seventeenth-century casuists agreed that 'a man must always follow his conscience, even if it judges falsely ... [b]ut the man who follows his erring conscience into evil is also guilty.'[72] The poem's solution to the problem of the erring conscience (a microcosm of the political problem of the unjust ruler) involves a reconsideration of the hierarchical model of conscience in which moral authority is distributed among subordinates. On reflection it does not seem entirely clear that the 'conscience' of the title *is* the 'pratler' addressed by the poem's speaker. If the speaking voice is resisting authoritarian discipline, he is also, in a sense, administering it, and in the process, asserting a claim to the name of 'conscience' as well. Indeed, despite his complaint about the restrictions under which he suffers, his manner is every bit as superior as the posture he attributes to his adversary. The attack on conscience here is at the same time another manifestation of the scrupulous conscience. Recalling the injunctions to silence that appear in so many Herbert poems, we might say that this speaker attempts to silence the voice that urges silence. The poem thus works not to resolve moral uncertainties but to generate them. Which voice is the true voice of 'conscience'? Is it better to subscribe to an ethic of renunciation or one of moderate indulgence? The opposing positions are set up simultaneously as targets of moral outrage and platforms of moral superiority. All the faculties and senses, regardless of rank and degree, are simultaneously cast as instruments and objects of discipline and control.

'Conscience,' then, offers a model for poems of corrective self-address, which depart significantly from the medieval ethos of renunciation and deferential submission. In its place they substitute a view of human affairs and human psychology that is at once liberating and confining: liberating because it dismantles a host of traditional constraints, and confining because it replaces a single chain of hierarchical authority with a bewildering, contradictory, and inescapable network of surveillance and correction, much of it in the form of friendly council. Michael Schoenfeldt demonstrates how Herbert's poems repeatedly explore God's mastery of the technology of pain, the means by which 'the instrument of punishment is converted into the sign of royal [and divine] power.'[73] But a case can also be made that many of the poems describe an alternative technology of control in which the speaker takes upon himself elements of the disciplinary function, relieving God of the necessity to exercise violent correction. As often as Herbert's God plays the torturer, exercising his power from above and without, he plays the friend, guiding from within, beside, and below (as in 'A True Hymn,' 'Love Unknown,' and 'Artillerie').

Several poems of corrective self-address follow 'Conscience' in quick succession (none of which appear in the Williams manuscript). In these poems a chorus of interior voices urges, by turns, boldness and reserve, assurance and doubt, action and stasis, sadness and joy. In 'Vanitie' [II] the grave speaker chides his own 'Poore silly soul' for dwelling on earth's 'flat delights,' warning 'lest what you now do measure / And write for sweet, prove a most sowre displeasure.' (ll. 1, 2, 5–6). In 'The Dawning' the tone shifts, as a new voice, or the same voice in a different mood, attempts to awaken his 'sad heart' to the joys of the resurrection.

In 'Business' the speaker advocates a sturdy devotional work ethic: 'Canst be idle? canst thou play, / Foolish soul who sinn'd today?' (ll. 1–2). Common to all these poems is an insistence on submission. Yet in offering such a complex interplay of definitions of submission, they enact and promote the 'repining restlessnesse' celebrated in 'The Pulley.' In a traditional deferential hierarchy, order is largely a matter of knowing one's place and staying in it. In Herbert's poems, especially the later ones, order, spiritual and social, seems to be a matter of searching for a properly submissive place in a world where even the most strenuous gestures of submission may be read as assertive (as in 'The Holdfast') and the most meager ones may be deemed acceptable (as in 'A True Hymn'). As appealing as asceticism might be, in the face of such confusion, it is not an option. The world is the place where the search for God takes place (and the inner world in which Herbert searches resembles the material and social world in striking ways), and 'My searches are my daily bread' ('The Search,' l. 3).

chapter seven

Modernity, Teleology, and
The Country Parson

136. Old wine, and an old friend, are good provisions.

1117. New Things are fair.

1121. We must recoile a little, to the end we may leap the better.

George Herbert

Outlandish Proverbs

How modern was early modern England? To some extent, even posing the question presumes a '"discontinuist" interpretation of ... social development ... [in which] modern social institutions are [understood as] ... unique-distinct in form from all types of traditional order.'[1] Such interpretations are more in favour among social scientists and literary critics than historians these days. For many, such 'discontinuist' readings of early modern English history have become less and less tenable, as the consensus among historians has shifted away from accounts of the English Civil War as a bourgeois revolution and the early Stuart period as a pre-revolutionary era. At the same time we all know that the past was different from the present, and that change has taken place. The problem facing historians of early Stuart England is a particular instance of the most general and vexing historiographic problem: how to account for change, for the difference of the past from the present, and how to define what constitutes historical difference.

The most serious charge a historian can bring against an account of the past or an argument or analysis about the past is that it is 'ahistorical.' This, it seems to me, can mean one of two things. The first is that the account or analysis is simply inaccurate, historically speaking, that it represents as fact events that did not take place. Such ahistoricism is comparatively rare, though certainly not unheard of, in published scholarship. The second sort of ahistoricism is more subtle. It has to do with anachronism, getting the emphasis wrong, or failing to understand or even denying context and sequence. Hence, Conrad Russell accuses his predecessors of reading the history of the English Civil War 'back to front':

> some of the supposed 'effects' for which we have tried to find causes were imaginary: we deduced the effects from the supposed causes ... For example, it has become painfully clear that it is impossible to interpret the Civil War as the clash of two clearly differentiated social groups or classes: the fullest possible knowledge of men's social and economic background, if it leaves out the preaching available in their home parishes, tells us nothing about their likely allegiance in the Civil War.[2]

In the revisionist view championed by Russell, commentators who see the Civil War as a consequence of social change are simply imposing a nineteenth-century schema on seventeenth-century events, reading earlier events and situations teleologically, as preparation for subsequent events, and in the process, denying the pastness of the past.

This is a potent criticism. But there is a risk of a slightly different sort of ahistoricism in the strict refusal of teleology. Arguments against social change as a significant cause of the Civil War tend to emphasize social and ideological continuity, and sometimes drift, almost imperceptibly, into straightforward denials of social change. The insistence that the social and political vagaries of a period once thought of as pre-revolutionary were simply the normal ups and downs of a stable functioning polity can also amount to a denial of historical difference, a suggestion that the past, however different it may be from the present, is itself a coherent, undifferentiated whole. Historians seldom make such claims explicitly, of course, but they frequently say, in effect, 'no, this was not the watershed; significant change did indeed come, but only later.' To say this often enough is to create the impression of a static past, different from the present, yet paradoxically changeless. This approach, taken to an extreme, is as ahistorical in its way as 'Whig' teleology. As R. Malcolm Smuts summarizes the problem, in his recent book, *Culture and Power in England*, 'Turning ... [the Civil War] into the climactic moment of a much longer historical transition will ... inevitably generate highly teleological interpretations or – if the teleology is removed – a static picture of the pre-war period, devoid of any real dynamic until political events intervene in the reign of Charles I.'[3] The challenge, then, is to account for the dynamic quality of history, for the interplay of continuity and change, in a way that does a disservice to neither.

One approach to the problem, popular especially in literary-historical studies, is to de-emphasize chronological discontinuity, the revolutionary moment, and concentrate on formal discontinuities, linking the insights of structural anthropology and linguistics to a materialist sense of contradiction as both the essence of a social formation and the engine of change. This is the strategy employed by Charles Whitney, in grappling with the 'modernity' of Francis Bacon's thought. Whitney challenges Hans Blumenberg's metaphorical argument that a 'husk' of religious tradition surrounds a 'kernel' of secular innovation in Francis Bacon's thought, arguing that 'the discontinuities or contradictions grouped around tradition and innovation characterize Bacon's writing so deeply that to distinguish husk and kernel is meaningless; nor can the parts of Bacon's discontinuous vision be called valid and invalid, nor without oversimplification modern and medieval.'[4] In this view, the early modern mind is, itself, discontinuous. But we are left with a crucial question. How might such an insight help us to account for change? If discontinuity is to be understood synchronically rather than diachronically, what does that understanding allow us to say about diachrony? Through my analysis of Herbert's *Country Parson* I have sought to offer an account of the interplay of traditional and rationalist discourses that does address diachrony, to show how traditionalist rhetoric, the rhetoric of continuity, participates in and facilitates social and ideological change. If Blumenberg's husk and kernel metaphor oversimplifies, attributing too little to the traditionalist elements in Bacon's thought, Whitney's deconstructive approach risks indeterminacy in its effort to avoid over-simplification. In Herbert's synthesis, as in Bacon's, the traditional and the rationalist are profoundly interdependent, but not so profoundly as to make distinctions meaningless. Tradition, in *The Country Parson*, is more like the Trojan horse, or the flesh of a piece of fruit, than the husk on a kernel of grain. The horse or the fruit it is not merely protective; it is essential to the transportation of the seed or the invading army, and its utility depends on the fact that it is appealing, even nourishing, in and of itself. Yet for all its immediate utility it is still, ultimately, disposable. Eventually it must be abandoned, used up, or allowed to decay. Traditional practices, similarly, coexist with the practices that will eventually displace them, though the traditions gradually fade.

To the question, how modern was early modern England? historians continue to advance all three of the obvious answers: the once ortho-dox 'Whig' or Marxist answer, 'not yet modern but modernizing'; the revisionist answer, 'still profoundly traditional'; and the idiosyncratic 'already very modern' offered by Alan Macfarlane. The first two views have perhaps been adequately summarized in the preceding pages, but the third is suggestive in several respects, and deserves slightly fuller treatment here. Macfarlane's groundbreaking and controversial book, *The Origins of English Individualism*, argued that the economic, cultural, and social-structural foundations of modernity, including the absence of a true peasantry bound to the land, the prevalence of wage labour, alienable real property, and a nuclear family structure with loose kin-ship ties, had been established in England from the middle of the four-teenth century. Looking back on the critical responses to *Origins* in a later volume, Macfarlane aligns his early findings with the historical demography of Peter Laslett, and with the views of key revisionists 'Conrad Russell, Anthony Fletcher and John Morrill, among others, [who] were questioning the whole thesis of the political revolution of the seventeenth century.'[5] But Macfarlane fits uneasily into this group. In *Origins*, he had criticized Laslett for clinging to 'a picture of a society based on the household, on patriarchal power, a world very different from our own.'[6] This is the picture shared, for the most part, by Russell, Fletcher, Morrill, and other revisionists. However much Macfarlane might want to attenuate his earlier criticism in order to claim member-ship in a historical movement, the differences he pointed out are real and profound. To be sure, Macfarlane joins Laslett and the revisionists in stressing continuity, and denying the revolutionary character of sixteenth- and seventeenth-century England, but his is an account of early modern continuity with the modern world, theirs with the *Ancien Régime*. Though he aligns himself with the revisionists, Macfarlane's insights about the presence of crucial elements of modernity in seven-teenth-century England must be understood as challenging both 'Whig' and revisionist views, complicating, rather than simplifying, the historio-graphic problem. Even discounting the views of those who continue to defend versions of the 'Whig' or Marxist hypothesis, we would be left with a contradiction to explore. Paradoxically, any attempt to synthesize the views of the advocates of continuity yields, once again, a discontinu-ous seventeenth century, simultaneously (though in different respects) modern and medieval, traditional and rationalist.

In another attempt to construct a 'new synthesis,' R. Malcolm Smuts surveys recent treatments of the concept of honour, stressing the co-existence and interplay of medieval, chivalric honour code with newer humanist ideas: 'Many historians have seen a gradual but ultimately decisive shift ... as the violent chivalric ethos of the Middle Ages was domesticated by Tudor monarchs and ultimately supplanted by newer humanist and Protestant values.'[7] Nevertheless, he insists, this entailed no 'simple process of displacement ... [but] much more complicated interactions ... between ancient honour ideals and newer values.' Yet to speak, as Smuts does, of a 'symbiosis between medieval and modern aristocratic cultures' may be misleading, for the biological metaphor of symbiosis implies mutual benefit and sustenance, an indefinitely sustainable relationship. We must acknowledge, as Smuts does with the terms 'ancient' and 'newer,' that the coexistence is transitional, while insisting that transition is far from simple. After all, the chivalric honour code does, eventually, become more or less confined to the realm of fiction and folklore, always available as a cultural ideal, but less and less embodied in specific cultural practices. Despite periodic resurgences, duelling, the early modern version of trial by combat, eventually does go out of fashion.[8] We certainly cannot specify with any precision the onset of the modern, but we can surely say that at some point, at least in this sphere, the modern era arrived, with litigation and public prosecution displacing private satisfaction for injury, and with the state monopoly on violence more or less secured. It is not excessively teleological to suggest that the complex interplay of older and newer ideas of honour served to facilitate the containment and eventual erosion of chivalric practices. The coexistence of civic humanism with chivalric honour can thus be said to enable the displacement of the chivalric by rendering civic and legalistic ideologies 'safe' and comparatively unthreatening to chivalric ones, at least temporarily. Displacement of older ideas and practices by newer ones depends, paradoxically, on an initial and often protracted demonstration of their compatibility.

George Herbert's role in the process of cultural modernization must be regarded as symptomatic, rather than decisive. *The Country Parson* is not, like Bacon's *Essays* or *Advancement of Learning*, a canonical text in the history of modern thought. Nevertheless, it is an important instance for two reasons: first, because it illustrates that what Smuts sees as an ideological symbiosis is, rather, dynamic and purposeful, and second, because it ranges so widely, offering illustrations of the various processes of innovation through temporary symbiosis in the realms of theology, health, law, social regulation, and agriculture. In each of the areas under discussion in the preceding chapters, we can see tradition and traditionalist rhetoric helping to introduce and disseminate elements of modernity and rationalization. Moreover, in each case, the interaction is noticeably different.

The sphere of religion and theology is at once the best illustration of modernization and the one in which the issues of tradition and innovation are most vexed. Here, despite the centrality of Protestantism to Weber's account of rationalization, one might make a compelling case that 'traditional' is a meaningless, or at least an unhelpful, antonym. The Reformation precept, *sola scriptura*, was, after all, an explicit rejection of Church tradition as a justification for theological propositions and ecclesiastical arrangements. In this realm, it is impossible to construct a simple opposition between tradition and rationalist innovation, since early reformers attacked the sacraments, traditions, and customs of the Catholic Church as corrupt innovations, and argued for the restoration of allegedly purer, scripturally sanctioned beliefs and practices. They used 'tradition' and 'innovation' as synonyms! But by representing change as a restoration, the Reformation also offered a powerful model for the rhetoric of innovation. Moreover, the Protestant Church of England, had, by Herbert's day, spent a couple of generations creating its own distinctive traditions of worship and habits of thought, against which Hooker's legalism and Laud's ceremonialism could be constructed as dangerous innovations. Of course the same strategies were available to Laud and his allies. They could claim that the Reformation, with its iconoclasm and its anti-sacramentalism, had undermined the traditional majesty and mystery of the Church and insist that the program of beautification, ceremonialism, and attenuation of anti-Catholic rhetoric amounted to a restoration of the 'true' Church of England. In the turmoil of the English Reformation, all sides pointed to cherished traditions abolished or undermined by pernicious innovation, and insisted that going forward meant going back.

This confused situation obscures an area of innovation common to otherwise hostile ecclesiastical factions: what Patrick Collinson has called the 'neo-clerical ideology,' an attempt to make the clergy the instrument of Weber's 'rationalized methodical direction of the entire pattern of life.'[9] Common to Puritans and Laudian formalists was a desire, differently expressed by various groups, to extend the influence of the clergy in English life at every level, from the domestic and parochial to the national. How that new influence, often represented as a renewed influence, might best be achieved – through prayer or preaching, grandeur or studied humility – remained a matter of intense debate. Yet in a certain sense the debate can be seen as diversionary, rendering an otherwise contentious proposition (that the church and its agents should enjoy increased influence), as an area of common ground that might be taken for granted. Religious controversy, anxiety, and scrutiny probably made it difficult to be lukewarm about religion, even if that was one's inclination: to cultivate partisanship was to cultivate commitment. Herbert's careful equivocation on the question of kneeling for the sacrament and Bishop Davenant's willingness to endure restrictions on preaching can be understood in this context, as can Davenant's prosecution of Henry Sherfield, and Herbert's insistence on boldness in the face of contempt for the clergy from social superiors. Each of these gestures, whether conciliatory or confrontational, shares an overriding concern to defend, and if possible to advance, the status of church and clergy in the face of threats from above and below. If, as Karl Marx argued, the period is marked by the primitive accumulation of agrarian capital, then Herbert and Davenant are engaged, along with Laud, in a struggle to accumulate social and cultural capital for the church, even as the precise character of that church is profoundly in doubt.

This accumulation was not uncontested, however. The prestige and influence sought by the clergy was also coveted by members of the other learned professions, each of which sought to engross and enclose its own professional field. Through the creation of the College of Physicians, and through the College's prosecution of unlicenced practitioners, the early modern medical profession sought to regulate medical services at a time when its training and expertise were, in many respects, hard to distinguish from those of the more generally educated. Herbert's *Country Parson* responds in kind on behalf of the clergy. Even as it defends traditions of healing that the emerging medical profession sought to suppress, it does so by appropriating and emulating medical discourse in an effort to transform itself from a medieval estate into a professional elite. In the legal sphere, similarly, *The Country Parson* participates in a broad movement to counter the explosion of litigation, and the increasing complexity of law in early modern England, by cultivating traditions of local conciliation.[10] In this sense Herbert's text shares and perpetuates popular suspicion of law, lawyers, and courts. Yet it is only by extolling and emulating the impartiality and precision attributed to English law by its defenders that Herbert can set up clerical mediation as an alternative to litigation. Much like the equitable jurisdiction of the Court of Chancery, Herbert's ideal of neighbourly dispute resolution, facilitated by the pastor, promises an alternative to litigation, yet seems to offer another arena for litigation, extending the legalism it seemed to contest.

In these spheres Herbert comes closest to what Smuts describes, in his treatment of early modern honour, as a symbiosis of tradition and rationality. Elements of traditionalist and rationalist thought and practice are interspersed in a manner that seems calculated only to enhance the prestige and influence of the clergy, rather than advancing either a coherently rationalist or traditionalist agenda. Yet this is where a measure of hindsight and teleology become essential for a clear understanding. In light of the church's subsequent failure to secure a place as a premier instrument of social control in the emerging bureaucratic state, the concessions made to rationalism and professionalism loom much larger than the attempts to cling to tradition. To deploy a synthesis of traditionalist and legal-rationalist arguments in a losing cause, in a struggle that would eventually be won by less ambiguously rationalist arguments may be, however inadvertently, to discredit the traditional elements of the synthesis. It is in this sense that Herbert's synthesis of traditional and legal-rational discourses can be understood as facilitating the eventual ascendancy of the latter, and the marginalization of the former.

The Country Parson also suggests that the straightforward 'displacement' model is not always such a gross oversimplification. On what was already, in his day, a long-standing question concerning the ethics of enclosure and agricultural 'improvement,' Herbert seems, in a relatively short time, simply to have changed his mind. Yet even here the change does not entail a straightforward repudiation of a 'traditionalist' ethos, but rather, an attempt to assimilate the ideology of 'improvement' into that ethos. Moreover, this is as true of Rowland Vaughan's *Water-Workes*, a book explicitly dedicated to the causes of 'improvement' and innovation, as it is of *The Country Parson*. In both cases, and in the discourse of early modern agriculture as a whole, the principles of deference and local affiliation associated with a traditional hierarchical order seem to have been crucial to even the most innovative schemes. Herbert's rhetorical vacillation between subsistence and commerce, contentment and ambition, the familiar and the outlandish, the local and the national, serves to manufacture anxiety, a sense of dependence, which functions to secure compliance in a society that had few means to compel it. Herbert's treatment of rural life also offers another slightly different illustration of the continuity/discontinuity problem. It may well be that even observed differences in rural character, manners, and temperament, grounded in different economic and geographic conditions, are represented as aspects of continuity in a book like *The Country Parson*. If so, the book shows the strength of the habitual rhetoric of continuity. It is at least possible that the coherence some revisionists see in the early modern world view results from a blend of decorum and strenuous literary effort, a fiction of continuity grounded in powerful convictions about how things ought to be, and how they ought to be described.

The power of such fictions is nowhere more evident than in the discourse of domestic patriarchy. There, despite the poverty of the patriarchal analogy as a description of the English social order, Herbert and his contemporaries clung to that analogy with tenacity. In this case, it is not merely that a familiar, familial discourse provided a secure backdrop for social and economic change. It is also that the family serves as a testing ground for the transition from an ethos of obedience to an ethos of voluntarism, from surveillance to privacy and autonomy, regulated by careful self-scrutiny. Without ever relinquishing the claim that he is describing an established order, Herbert shifts the emphasis of household discipline from overt exercise of patriarchal authority to covert procedures of social control, and in so doing provides a model for the extension of similar procedures of control throughout the community.

Herbert's later poems echo and confirm these insights, in their drift from ascetic inwardness towards evangelical, pastoral, liturgical, and homiletic modes, and in their reconciliation with the material world and the materiality of the poetic conceit. Poems like 'The Water-course' and 'The Glimpse' share an emphasis on the homely and familiar found throughout Herbert's work, but they also embody a movement from a residually medieval *contemptus mundi* to a protomodern covenant mentality, embracing concrete human endeavour as a manifestation of the devotional spirit. The soul in these poems remains, as in *contemptus mundi*, divided against itself, disoriented in the world it embraces. As both the instrument and the object of evangelism, Herbert's poetic speaker keeps himself off balance. If his world is still, in important respects, the traditional one of deference and subordination, the traditional option of renouncing that world is largely gone. The country parson may fear to 'goe into the world,' but in the end it is his only option, so he must go 'full of all knowledg' (241, 228).

Notes

1 Introduction

1 *The Works of George Herbert*, 225. Subsequent references to Herbert's poetry and prose in the text and notes are to this edition and appear parenthetically. Parenthetical citations refer to prose works by page numbers and to poems by line numbers. Unless otherwise indicated, italics in quotations are in the original sources. I refer to the book by its short title, *The Country Parson*, accepting the arguments of Joseph Summers and Cristina Malcolmson that 'A Priest to the Temple' was added by Barnabus Oley for his posthumous publication of *Herbert's Remaines*. See Joseph Summers, *George Herbert: His Religion and Art*, 13, and Cristina Malcolmson, *Heart-Work*, 231 n1.

2 Articles dedicated primarily to *The Country Parson* are few. They include Harold H. Kollmeier, '*The Country Parson* in Its Time'; Daniel W. Doerksen, '"Too Good for Those Times": Politics and the Publication of George Herbert's *The Country Parson*'; Kristine Wolberg, 'All Possible Art: George Herbert's *The Country Parson* and Courtesy'; Douglas J. Swartz, 'Discourse and Direction: *A Priest to the Temple, or, The Country Parson* and the Elaboration of Sovereign Rule'; and Cristina Malcolmson, 'George Herbert's *Country Parson* and the Character of Social Identity,' the last included, with some revision, in *Heart-Work: George Herbert and the Protestant Ethic*. In the other book-length studies devoted to Herbert's poetry, *The Country Parson* receives the fullest treatment in Michael C. Schoenfeldt, *Prayer and Power: George Herbert and Renaissance Courtship*, and Christopher Hodgkins, *Authority, Church and Society in George Herbert: Return to the Middle Way*. See also Jeffrey Powers-Beck's discussion of the critical neglect of Herbert's didactic poem 'The Church-Porch' in *Writing the Flesh: The Herbert Family Dialogue*, 60–3.

3 John Dryden, 'Mac Flecknoe,' l. 208.

4 In this sense it is a crucial supplement to, though by no means a substitute for, the concrete documentary information available from sources such as *The Diary of Ralph Josselin.*

5 See Keith Wrightson, 'The Social Order of Early Modern England,' 179, and Peter Laslett, *The World We Have Lost,* 40–1.

6 Sharpe, *Remapping Early Modern England,* 4.

7 Powers-Beck, *Writing the Flesh,* 66.

8 Veith, 'The Religious Wars in George Herbert Criticism: Reinterpreting Seventeenth-Century Anglicanism.'

9 Ilona Bell, 'Setting Foot into Divinity'; Barbara K. Lewalski, *Protestant Poetics and the Seventeenth Century Religious Lyric*; Richard Strier, *Love Known: Theology and Experience in George Herbert's Poetry.* These, and indeed all Herbert critics, owe a profound debt to Joseph H. Summers's pioneering study, *George Herbert: His Religion and Art.*

10 Herbert had, of course, written *Musae Responsoriae,* a series of satirical Latin verses directed at the Scots Puritan Andrew Melville (*Works,* 384–403).

11 The culmination of these efforts is Doerksen's *Conforming to the Word: Herbert, Donne and the English Church before Laud,* but his articles from 1980 onward have consistently explored these issues.

12 Anthony Milton, *Catholic and Reformed: The Roman and Protestant Churches in English Protestant Thought 1600–1640*; Kenneth Fincham, *Prelate as Pastor: The Episcopate of James I;* Nicholas Tyacke, *Anti-Calvinists: The Rise of English Arminianism c.1590–1640*; Patrick Collinson, *The Religion of Protestants: The Church in English Society 1559–1625.*

13 See the discussion of Herbert and Herbert scholarship in Kevin Sharpe, *Remapping Early-Modern England,* 359–64.

14 Hodgkins, *Authority, Church and Society,* 2–3, 33.

15 Cressy, 'Foucault, Stone, Shakespeare and Social History,' 124; 'Conflict, Consensus,' 133.

16 Weber, *The Theory of Social and Economic Organization,* 328 ff. See also 'Social Psychology of the World Religions.' In her recent book, *Heart-Work: George Herbert and the Protestant Ethic,* Cristina Malcolmson draws heavily on Weber's most famous work, *The Protestant Ethic and the Spirit of Capitalism.* While I agree with many of Malcolmson's conclusions, I seek to place Herbert's work, and especially *The Country Parson,* in the larger theoretical framework of which *The Protestant Ethic* is a single component.

17 The classic exposition is Sir John Fortescue's fifteenth-century treatise *In Praise of the Laws of England,* and the chief seventeenth-century spokesman, Sir Edward Coke. For a modern scholarly account of these theories, see J.G.A. Pocock, *The Ancient Constitution and the Feudal Law.*

18 Cressy, 'Foucault, Stone, Shakespeare and Social History,' 126–7.
19 See, for example, Conrad Russell, *The Causes of the English Civil War*, and *Unrevolutionary England, 1603–1642*; John Morrill, *The Nature of the English Revolution*; and Kevin Sharpe, *Sir Robert Cotton, 1586–1631: History and Politics in Early Modern England*.
20 Morrill, *The Nature of the English Revolution*, 6–7.
21 Cust and Hughes, 'After Revisionism,' 17. See also Marjorie Kenniston McIntosh, *A Community Transformed*; David Underdown, *Fire from Heaven*; and David Harris Sacks, *The Widening Gate*.
22 See, for example, Ann Jennalie Cook, *Making a Match: Courtship in Shakespeare and His Society*; Michael Schoenfeldt, *Bodies and Selves in Early Modern England*; Achsah Guibbory, *Ceremony and Community from Herbert to Milton*; and Garrett A. Sullivan, *The Drama of Landscape*.
23 Foucault, 'Truth and Power,' 118–19; *History of Sexuality*, 1: 15–50. On the tension between Foucaultian and Materialist approaches see Mark Poster, 'Foucault and History,' and Barry Smart, *Foucault, Marxism and Critique*.
24 Neale, *Writing Marxist History*, 255–79. See also R.H. Hilton, introduction to *The Brenner Debate*.
25 See, for example, the articles in T.H. Aston and C.H.E. Philpin, eds., *The Brenner Debate*; John E. Martin, *Feudalism to Capitalism*, 103–12 and 140–50; Nicos Poulantzas, *State, Power, Socialism*, 157–67.
26 Indeed many would accept Peter Laslett's contention that pre-industrial England was a 'one-class society' (*The World We Have Lost*, 22–52).
27 Angenot, 'The Concept of Social Discourse,' 4.
28 Hughes, *The Causes of the English Civil War*, 3.
29 Fowler, 'Georgic and Pastoral,' 82.
30 As Amy Charles has pointed out, the book opens with seven chapters that 'define, limit and classify,' but thereafter, 'the chapters take up whatever subject comes to mind' (*Life of George Herbert*, 159–60).
31 Hagedorn, 'Received Wisdom: The Reception History of Alfred's Preface to the *Pastoral Care*,' 89. Hagedorn also refers to Foxe's and Camden's use of Parker's translation.
32 Gregory I, *Pastoral Care*, 32, 78, 96, 134.
33 See Erich Auerbach, *Mimesis*, 72.
34 The fullest discussion of English Protestant pastoral literature is Patrick Collinson, 'Shepherds, Sheepdogs, and Hirelings: The Pastoral Ministry in Post-Reformation England.' See also Neal Enssle, 'Patterns of Godly Life: The Ideal Parish Minister in Sixteenth and Seventeenth-Century English Thought.'
35 Donne, *Sermons*, 6: 81–113.

36 Bernard, *The Faithful Shepherd*, title page, 1, 12–13.
37 Ibid., 98, 98–109.
38 Charles, *A Life of George Herbert*, 157.
39 Malcolmson, *Heart-Work*, 29.
40 Ibid., 31, 45.
41 Aldington, ed., *A Book of 'Characters.'*
42 J.W. Smeed, *The Theophrastan 'Character,'* 24–5; William Harrison, *The Description of England*, 94–123. For discussion of renaissance 'chorography' see Richard Helgerson, *Forms of Nationhood*, 105–48. Important works in this tradition include Camden's *Brittania*, Drayton's *Poly-Olbion*, and local works like Lambarde's *Perambulation of Kent*, Stow's *Survey of London*, and Somner's *Antiquities of Canterbury*.
43 Brennan, *Literary Patronage in the English Renaissance*, 184.
44 Earle, *Micro-Cosmographie*, 23, 24.
45 Helgerson, *Forms of Nationhood*, 147.
46 See the lengthy chapters 'The Variety of Books' in H.S. Bennett, *English Books and Readers*, vols. 2–3. Herbert specifically recommends one such book in *The Country Parson*, Michael Dalton's *Countrey Justice.*
47 Wyn Ford suggests that 'manuals and other literature from the sixteenth century onwards offer evidence of a widespread ability to read and comprehend print among tradesmen and craftsmen' ('The Problem of Literacy in Early Modern England,' 29). For the connections between *The Country Parson* and Tudor courtesy literature, see Kristine Wolberg, 'All Possible Art.'
48 Bennett, *English Books and Readers*, 3: 149–55. See also F.N.L. Poynter, *A Bibliography of Gervase Markham.*
49 Bennett, *English Books and Readers*, 2: 180.
50 Eamon, *Science and the Secrets of Nature*, 5. See also the discussion of medicine and sorcery in Keith Thomas, *Religion and the Decline of Magic*, 209–334.
51 Hence, Arnold Stein, no inexpert reader, quotes *The Country Parson* 'by way of balance,' to counteract a misapprehension readers might derive from 'The Altar' (*George Herbert's Lyrics*, 20–1).
52 Charles, Introduction to *The Williams Manuscript of George Herbert's Poems*, xvii, xviii.
53 Walton, *Lives*, 286.
54 Palmer, *The English Works of George Herbert*, 34.
55 Charles, *Life of George Herbert*, 87 n63.
56 Schoenfeldt, for example, shows 'how fully Herbert's purported turn from the world is involved in the discourse of this world' (*Prayer and Power*, 22.). Other important contributions include Sidney Gottlieb, 'From "Content" to "Affliction" [III]: Herbert's Anti-Court Sequence,' 'Herbert's Case of "Con-

science": Public or Private Poem?,' 'Herbert's Political Allegory of "Humilitie,"' and 'The Social and Political Backgrounds of George Herbert's
Poetry'; Claude J. Summers and Ted-Larry Pebworth, 'Herbert, Vaughan,
and Public Concerns in Private Modes,' and 'The Politics of *The Temple*: "The
British Church" and "The Familie"'; Marion White Singleton, *God's Courtier;
Configuring a Different Grace in George Herbert's Temple*; and Diana Benet, 'Herbert's Experience of Politics and Patronage in 1624.'

57 Charles, *Life of George Herbert*, 158; see also Margaret Bottrall, *George Herbert*,
   80. Even Christopher Hodgkins's 'regenerative nostalgia' thesis has a faintly
   Waltonian air.
58 See, for example, William Jerdan's introduction to his 1853 edition, reproduced in C.A. Patrides, ed., *George Herbert: The Critical Heritage*, 195–207.
59 Swartz, 'Discourse and Direction,' 191, 195.
60 For a fuller discussion of this 'double object' commonplace see chapter 2 of
   this volume.
61 There are several instances of this technique: 'The Countrey Parson values
   Catechizing highly' (255); 'The Countrey Parson desires to be all to his Parish' (259); 'The Countrey Parson knows well, that ... he must be despised'
   (268); 'The Countrey Parson is a Lover of old Customes' (238).
62 Collinson describes Herbert's parson as a clerical 'entrepreneur, setting to
   work on a Sunday like a market man on market-day' (*Religion of Protestants*,
   98). Like Charles's portrait, this is an incomplete picture, but one that supplies needed balance.
63 Angenot, 'The Concept of Social Discourse,' 4.

2 *The Country Parson* and the Early Stuart Church

1 For details on *The Country Parson*'s early publication history see Daniel W.
  Doerksen, '"Too Good for Those Times."' That it was not, in fact, published
  until 1652 should not distract us from the conclusions prompted by its date
  of composition.
2 See Collinson, *Religion of Protestants*, 109. For a detailed account of the issues
  surrounding painted scripture texts, see Margaret Aston, *England's Iconoclasts*, 1: 361–8.
3 John Davenant, *A Treatise on Justification ... Together with Translations of the
  Determinationes of the Same Prelate*, 2: 330. As Daniel Doerksen points out, even
  Calvin held that 'within each church situation orderliness and charity call on
  the individual to conform' ('Things Fundamental or Indifferent,' 16). Bernard Verkamp distinguishes two streams of adiaphorism among early English
  Protestant divines; a negative view, which held traditional ceremonies to be

'neither good, nor commanded,' and a positive view, which held ceremonies to be 'neither evil nor forbidden' and hence subject to considerations of unity and authority (*Indifferent Mean*, 36–85). Among Elizabethan and Jacobean conformists, including Herbert, the latter view clearly prevailed.

4 The note 'The Authour to the Reader' is dated 1632 (224). Since Herbert was not ordained Priest until 1630, most readers have assumed the book was composed in this two-year period.

5 Other seventeenth-century English pastoral handbooks, such as Richard Bernard's *Faithful Shepherd*, are narrower in scope, treating chiefly homiletics.

6 These include William Halewood, *The Poetry of Grace: Reformation Themes and Structures in English Seventeenth-Century Poetry*; Barbara Lewalski, *Protestant Poetics and the Seventeeth-Century Religious Lyric*; Richard Strier, *Love Known: Theology and Experience in George Herbert's Poetry*, Gene Edward Veith Jr., *Reformation Spirituality: The Religion of George Herbert*; Christopher Hodgkins, *Authority, Church and Society in George Herbert: Return to the Middle Way*. Significant exceptions to this trend are Daniel W. Doerksen, *Conforming to the Word: Herbert, Donne and the English Church before Laud*, and Cristina Malcolmson, *Heart-Work: George Herbert and the Protestant Ethic*.

7 See, for example, Rosemond Tuve, *A Reading of George Herbert;* Louis L. Martz, *The Poetry of Meditation: A Study in English Religious Literature of the Seventeenth Century*; Stanley Stewart, *George Herbert.*

8 Strier, *Love Known*, 85–6. For a counterpoint see Jeanne Clayton Hunter, 'Salvation under Covenant: Herbert's Poetry and Puritan Sermons'; Daniel W. Doerksen, 'Show and Tell,' and chapter 6 of this volume.

9 Hodgkins, *Authority, Church and Society*, 1, 85, 147.

10 The most important of these works are Patrick Collinson, *Religion of Protestants*; Rosemary O'Day, *The English Clergy*; Nicholas Tyacke, *Anti-Calvinists*; and Kenneth Fincham, *Prelate as Pastor.*

11 Hodgkins is an exception. He argues that 'Herbert chose the Bemerton ministry ... to revive publicly the fading Tudor social vision' (*Authority, Church and Society*, 182–3), but as I argue in this volume, especially in chapter 4, there are important differences between Herbert's vision of the godly commonwealth and that of the Tudor humanists.

12 James VI and I, *Minor Prose Works*, 61.

13 For a complementary discussion of Herbert's situation in light of the careers of Sir Robert Naunton, Sir Francis Nethersole, and Bishop John Williams, see Diana Benet, 'Herbert's Experience of Politics and Patronage in 1624.'

14 Amy Charles argues that Letter V, with its reference to entering 'into a Benefice,' may date from 1615 rather than 1618 as Hutchinson conjectures. See *Life of George Herbert*, 88; cf. *Works*, 366–7, 579. Moreover, Herbert held several

official university posts while studying divinity, becoming praelector in rhetoric in 1618 and public orator in 1620. It seems likely, therefore, that Herbert would have known Davenant in several capacities, even before the latter left Cambridge for Salisbury.

15 Davenant, *A Treatise on Justification*, 2: 334, 275, 437.

16 Collinson, 'Jacobean Religious Settlement,' 46.

17 Fincham and Lake, 'Ecclesiastical Policy,' 171–2, 175.

18 Ibid., 180.

19 Shriver, 'Hampton Court Revisited,' 62–3.

20 In Charles's view, Herbert's acquisition of an income from his share of the Ribbesford Manor may have been an important factor in his decision to leave Cambridge, and eventually, to be ordained (*Life of George Herbert*, 134–5). Malcolmson suggests that the grant of property but not patronage was Herbert's 'definitive answer from the crown' on the question of preferment (*Heart-Work*, 24).

21 For discussion of the significant role played by lecturers in churches Herbert attended in his youth, see Doerksen, *Conforming to the Word*, chapters 4–5.

22 Collinson, 'Lectures by Combination,' 472–4.

23 Church of England, *Constitutions and Canons Ecclesiastical*, Canon 72; see also Collinson, 'Lectures by Combination,' 476; and Fincham and Lake, 'Ecclesiastical Policy,' 180.

24 Collinson, 'Lectures by Combination,' 483–5.

25 Lake, 'Calvinism and the English Church,' 39.

26 Collinson, *Birthpangs of Protestant England*, 20–1.

27 The distinction is drawn from R.T. Kendall's *Calvin and English Calvinism to 1649*, and figures prominently in the work of Peter Lake and Nicholas Tyacke. The English 'covenant theologians,' Perkins, Preston, Sibbes, and Ames, fall within the 'experimental' tradition.

28 Lake, 'Calvinism and the English Church,' 39.

29 See Paul Slack, 'Poverty and Politics in Salisbury 1597–1666'; Keith Wrightson and David Levine, *Poverty and Piety in an English Village: Terling, 1525–1700*; and David Underdown, *Fire from Heaven: The Life of an English Town in the Seventeenth Century*. The link between 'Puritanism' and social control has been questioned by Margaret Spufford in 'Puritanism and Social Control?' and by Margo Todd in *Christian Humanism and the Puritan Social Order*.

30 Fincham and Lake, 'Ecclesiastical Policy,' 169.

31 Walter Balcanqual to Sir Dudley Carlton, 9 February 1619, in John Hales, *Golden Remaines of the Ever Memorable Mr. John Hales*, 101.

32 *Judgement of the Synod Holden at Dort*, F2v.–F3r.

33 Lake, 'Calvinism and the English Church,' 58.

34 Davenant, *A Treatise on Justification*, 1:1.

35 O'Day, *The English Clergy*, 2–3; see also O'Day, 'Anatomy of a Profession'; Ian Green, 'Career Prospects and Clerical Conformity'; Patrick Collinson, 'Shepherds, Sheepdogs, and Hirelings'; and Neal Ennsle, 'Patterns of Godly Life.' For qualifications to O'Day's views on professionalization, see Collinson, *Religion of Protestants*, 95–100; for patterns of regional variation in clerical recruitment see Fincham, *Prelate as Pastor*, 181–2.

36 O'Day, *English Clergy*, 49–74; Collinson, *Elizabethan Puritan Movement*, 171.

37 O'Day, *English Clergy*, 74.

38 Fincham, *Prelate as Pastor*, 32, 6, 5. See also Kenneth Fincham and Peter Lake, 'Ecclesiastical Policy of James I.' Administratively these developments anticipate Laudian 'thorough,' though the ideals of pastoral ministry involved are far from Laudian.

39 O'Day, *English Clergy*, 74. For a more pessimistic account of this process see Mark Curtis, 'Alienated Intellectuals.'

40 Hodgkins, *Authority, Church and Society*, 128; Clarke, *Lives*, 95.

41 O'Day, *English Clergy*, 143.

42 Earle, *Micro-Cosmographie*, 22.

43 O'Day, *English Clergy*, 142.

44 Green, 'Career Prospects,' 105–6; Curtis, 'Alienated Intellectuals.'

45 Tom Webster, *Godly Clergy in Early Stuart England*, 25, 28, 34.

46 For the strategy of criticism through flattery, see Frank Wigham, *Ambition and Privilege*, and Michael Schoenfeldt, *Prayer and Power*. Collinson argues that Herbert's idealizations mean *The Country Parson* is 'not an instruction manual of any kind' ('Shepherds, Sheepdogs, and Hirelings,' 197).

47 For discussions of Herbert's rhetorical strategy in the 1623 oration, see Michael Schoenfeldt, *Prayer and Power*, 33–6, and Jeffrey Powers-Beck, 'Conquering Laurels.'

48 Collinson, *Religion of Protestants*, 113–14.

49 O'Day, *English Clergy*, 211.

50 Collinson, *Religion of Protestants*, 111. Peter Lake agrees that this tendency is not uniquely formalist. Presbyterians were equally susceptible to portrayal as a 'self-seeking clericalist interest group, motivated primarily by envy [of the bishops] ... and by pride in their own learning and importance' (*Anglicans and Puritans?* 109).

51 Collinson, *Religion of Protestants*, 104–5.

52 Such a transitional posture is not unique to Herbert's *Country Parson*. Quoting a 1608 sermon of George Downame, Collinson remarks on the 'transition from the Calvinist emphasis on the minister as God's instrument of

Salvation to the stress later associated with Arminianism on the uniquely exalted status and privilege of the priesthood' (ibid., 112).

53 *Dictionary of National Biography*, s.v. 'Davenant, John'; Clausen, *Calvinism in the Anglican Hierarchy*, 114–16; Gardiner, *History of England*, 7: 132.

54 Ward to Ussher, 25 May 1630, *Whole Works*, 15: 500. See also Tyacke, *Anti-Calvinists*, 138.

55 Davenant, *A Treatise on Justification*, 2: 354.

56 Todd, '"An Act of Discretion,"' 584.

57 Prest, *Rise of the Barristers*, 30–4; Slack, 'Religious Protest,' 299. See also the account in Samuel Gardiner, *History*, 7: 254–8. Sidney Gottlieb uses the Sherfield case to illuminate Herbert's Wiltshire years in 'Herbert's Case of "Conscience": Public or Private Poem?'

58 For further discussion of these initiatives see chapter 3 of this volume.

59 Slack, 'Religious Protest,' 296.

60 Gardiner, *History*, 7: 257.

61 McGee, 'William Laud,' 323.

62 Lake, 'Calvinism and the English Church,' 68.

63 Gardiner, *History*, 7: 255.

64 Slack, 'Public Conscience,' 168.

65 Hodgkins, *Authority, Church and Society*, 88.

66 Malcolmson, *Heart-Work*, 32, 44–5.

67 Green, 'Career Prospects,' 88.

68 As Amy Charles explains, it may well have been William Herbert, the third Earl, who urged the King to bestow the living on George Herbert, though by the time of Herbert's induction, William had died and his younger brother Philip had become the fourth Earl of Pembroke (Charles, *Life of George Herbert*, 145–6).

69 Kevin Sharpe, 'Faction at the Early Stuart Court,' 44.

70 Charles, *Life of George Herbert*, 145.

71 Tyacke suggests that Pembroke may have helped Joseph Hall secure the bishopric of Exeter in 1627 (*Anti-Calvinists*, 168).

72 Stewart, *George Herbert*, 40.

73 Doerksen, '"Too Good for Those Times,"' 10–11.

74 Davies, *Worship and Theology*, 2: 207.

75 See also Daniel W. Doerksen, *Conforming to the Word*, pp. 68–9. The practice was begun by Bishop Neile and other members of the Durham house group as early as 1617, though it did not become compulsory until 1633. See also Tyacke, *Anti-Calvinism*, 116–18, 202–9; and Yates, *Buildings, Faith, and Worship*, 30–3.

76 This is similar to the argument for conformity in Herbert's poem 'Lent.' See

Hodgkins, *Authority, Church and Society*, 64–86. Hodgkins also offers a very helpful account of Herbert's Eucharistic theology, 24–32.

77 Church of England, *Canon* 27, my italics.

78 Davies misreads the passage, taking *The Country Parson*'s publication date (1652) as its composition date, and claiming that 'at this time it was the independents and the Fifth Monarchists (apart from the few remaining Separatists) who ... [insisted on sitting] at communion' (*Worship and Theology*, 2: 207). In 1632, when the book was composed, the situation was less polarized, though Herbert still applies the term 'Schismatick' to puritan nonconformists.

79 Herbert's discussion of kneeling suggests that he shared Samuel Ward's view that the need for godly ministers to retain their positions in the church was a powerful argument for conformity. See Todd, '"An Act of Discretion,"' 593–4.

80 Doerksen, 'Things Fundamental or Indifferent,' 17, quoting *The Country Parson*, 263.

81 As Hutchinson points out, 'scandall' is used in the New Testament sense '... of a cause of offence or stumbling' (*Works*, 561).

82 For a comprehensive account of the way anti-Roman rhetoric gradually ceases to be a central feature in 'Anglican' self-definition see Anthony Milton, *Catholic and Reformed*.

83 See, for instance, Helen Vendler, *The Poetry of George Herbert*, 25–56; Stanley Fish, *Self-Consuming Artifacts*, 156–223; and Achsah Guibbory, *Ceremony and Community*, 44–78.

84 Slights, *The Casuistical Tradition*, 7–8.

85 See 'The Parson in Liberty,' 'The Parson's Library,' and 'Concerning Detraction.'

86 Herbert's 'double object' is a version of the traditional division of the Decalogue into two tables, expressing man's duties to God and to other men. See J. Sears McGee, *The Godly Man*, ix–x.

87 Hooker, *Lawes of Ecclesiastical Politie*, in *Works*, 2: 413–14.

88 Archbishop Grindal had cited the same chapter in his 1576 letter to Elizabeth 'Concerning Suppression of the Prophecies and Restraining the Number of Preachers' *Remains*, 376, 383.

89 Hooker, *Lawes of Ecclesiastical Politie*, in *Works*, 2: 425.

90 Compare the similar agricultural imagery in *The Temple*, where the poet is a gardener in 'The Dedication,' only to become a fruit tree pruned by God in 'Paradise.' For a broader discussion of Herbert's appropriation of agricultural discourse see Malcolmson, *Heart-Work*, 179–204 and chapter 4 of this volume.

91 Sherwood, *Herbert's Prayerful Art*, 18–19.
92 See Joseph Summers, *George Herbert: His Religion and Art*, 141; 226–7 n28. Compare *Paradise Lost* 11. 22–5, where the Son, as 'Priest,' places Eve and Adam's penitent prayers before his Father.
93 Davies, *Worship and Theology*, 2: 191.
94 Jonathan M. Atkins links growing Arminian influence in the late 1620s and 1630s to the 'diligence with which Charles and Laud attempted to suppress teaching on predestination' and to the 'Calvinist bishops' desire for unity and their consensual approach to the church' ('Calvinist Bishops,' 419).
95 Cardwell, *Documentary Annals*, 2: 202.
96 Tyacke, *Anti-Calvinists*, 209.
97 Donne, *Sermons*, 4: 202; 6: 103.
98 Hooker, *Lawes of Ecclesiastical Politie*, in *Works*, 2: 113–17, 141, 135 (my italics).
99 Lake, *Anglicans and Puritans?* 170.
100 Cardwell, *Documentary Annals*, 2: 202.
101 This is particularly so given Herbert's Socratic model of catechism. See Stanley Fish, *The Living Temple*, 11–24.
102 Hooker, *Lawes of Ecclesiastical Politie*, in *Works*, 2: 122.
103 Charles, *Life of George Herbert*, 121.
104 Tyacke, *Anti-Calvinists*, 49.
105 Charles, *Life of George Herbert*, 100. Jeffrey Powers-Beck has challenged the view that Herbert extolled peace 'in full knowledge' of the Prince and the Duke's contrary inclinations ('Conquering Laurels'). Still, Buckingham's recollection of the Cambridge Orator, if he remembered him at all, would hardly have been favourable.
106 Charles, *Life of George Herbert*, 121.
107 See Malcolmson, *Heart-Work*, 23.

3 The *Country Parson* and the Enclosure of Professional Fields

1 Holmes, *Augustan England*, 3–4.
2 Addison refers to the 'three great Professions of Divinity, Law and Physick' (*Spectator* 21, 24 Mar. 1711; Bond ed. 1: 88). See also Prest, *Professions in Early Modern England*, 8.
3 Friedson, *Professional Powers*, 34–5. The definition of professions is, of course, a matter of considerable debate among sociologists.
4 Hicks, *Profit, Piety, and the Professions*, xiv.
5 For good discussions of early modern child-rearing literature and practice see Susan Dwyer Amussen, *An Ordered Society*, 34–66; Deborah Kuller Shuger,

Habits of Thought in the English Renaissance, 218–50; and Linda Pollock, *Forgotten Children.*

6 In 'Ambiguity and Contradiction in "the Rise of Professionalism,"' Michael Hawkins helpfully distinguishes between the alleged rise of the clerical profession and the 'professionalization' of the clergy, arguing that the early modern clergy were 'falling,' in terms of influence and prestige, even as they were becoming increasingly 'professional.'

7 Cressy, 'Foucault, Stone, Shakespeare and Social History,' 125.

8 See Geoffrey Holmes, *Augustan England.*

9 See, for example, Rosemary O'Day, *The Professions in Early Modern England, 1450–1800*, and *The English Clergy*; Brian P. Levack, *The Civil Lawyers in England, 1603–1641*; C.W. Brooks, *Pettyfoggers and Vipers of the Commonwealth: The 'Lower Branch' of the Legal Profession in Early Modern England*; Wilfred Prest, *The Rise of the Barristers*; Harold J. Cook, *The Decline of the Old Medical Regime in Stuart London*; and the essays in Wilfred Prest, ed., *The Professions in Early Modern England.*

10 Prest, *Professions in Early Modern England*, 8.

11 Stone, 'Social Mobility in England.'

12 Herbert's concern for 'the necessity of a vocation' and the shaping influence of vocational literature is most evident in chapter XXXII, 'The Parson's Surveys,' which begins as an account of the 'great and national sin of ... Idlenesse' and evolves into an essay on secular callings (274–8). This chapter has many echoes of contemporary works like William Perkins's *Treatise of the Vocations or Callings of Men* in *Works of William Perkins*, 441–76. Important discussions of vocation in Herbert's work include Cristina Malcolmson, *Heart-Work*; Donald M. Friedman, 'Donne, Herbert and Vocation'; Diana Benet, *Secretary of Praise*; and Robert B. Shaw, *The Call of God.*

13 See, for example, Psalm 103:2–3, Mark 2:17, Matthew 9:12, Luke 4:23 and 5:31, and Colossians 4:14.

14 Herbert suffered major illnesses in 1616–17, in 1622, in 1626, and before his death in 1633. See Amy Charles, *Life of George Herbert*, pp. 86–8, 73, 93, 128–31.

15 'Synodal Statutes of Bishop William of Bitton I for the Diocese of Bath and Wells' (1258?), in Powicke and Cheney, eds., *Councils and Synods with Other Documents Relating to the English Church*, 615. Lewis and Short list the most common classical signification as 'to take charge of, to manage, guide, administer, execute, accomplish, do, perform etc.' (s.v. *administro* II), as well as the more literal, 'to be near as an aid, to attend upon, to serve' (I).

16 The obsolete sense of to *be administered* as to *receive* the sacrament is a little earlier, in 1495 (4a).

17 The charter grants to the apothecaries an exclusive right 'to make, mix, compound, prepare, give, apply or administer any medicines' (C.R.B. Barret, *The History of the Society of Apothecaries*, xxxi).

18 Cartwright, *Social History of Medicine*, 43–4. The 1512 statute granting that authority to the Bishops was not repealed when the College was created (Harold J. Cook, *Decline*, 79–80).

19 Cartwright, *Social History of Medicine*, 23–4, 32–6.

20 Charles Webster, *Great Instauration*, 255.

21 Pelling and Webster, 'Medical Practitioners,' 199.

22 Harold J. Cook, *Decline*, 70–93, and 'Policing'; Slack, 'Books of Orders,' 'Dearth and Social Policy,' and *Impact of Plague*, 199–226.

23 Charles Webster, *Great Instauration*, 253.

24 Harold J. Cook, *Decline*, 79, and 'Against Common Right.'

25 Harold J. Cook, 'Institutional Structures,' 99.

26 Charles Webster, *Great Instauration*, 254.

27 Slack, 'Books of Orders,' 3–4.

28 Pocock, *Machiavellian Moment*, 353–60.

29 Slack, 'Books of Orders,' 8–9; Harold J. Cook, 'Policing,' 25.

30 Slack, 'Books of Orders,' 9–10.

31 Hart, *KΛINIKH or The Diet of the Diseased*, 12–13; see also John Cotta, *A Short Discoverie of the Unobserved Dangers of Several Sorts of Ignorant and Unconsiderate Practisers of Physicke in England*. For a discussion of these works see Peter Elmer, 'Medicine, Religion and the Puritan Revolution.' On clerical practice and the physicians' complaints see Harold J. Cook, *Decline*, 32.

32 Burton, *Anatomy of Melancholy*, 21, 23.

33 Harold J. Cook, *Decline*, 73–4. Charles Webster takes a much more sceptical view of the standards of medical education in *Great Instauration*, 121.

34 Hart, *KΛINIKH*, 12.

35 Harold J. Cook, 'Good Advice and Little Medicine.'

36 Brownlow and Goldesborough, *Reports*, 260–1.

37 Clark, *Working Life of Women in the Seventeenth Century*, 254–8. For an account of one such lady see Linda Pollock, *With Faith and Physic: The Life of a Tudor Gentlewoman*.

38 Porter, 'The Patient in England,' 97.

39 Charles Webster, *Great Instauration*, 125–6; Batey, *Oxford Gardens*, 30–3. See also Cristina Malcomson's discussion of the ambitious gardens of Sir John Danvers and Philip Herbert in *Heart-Work*, 179–204.

40 Porter, 'The Patient in England,' 97.

41 This process, like the formation of the professions, is often seen as a later phenomenon, but as Monica Green has observed, licensing and regulation

of medical practitioners, usually the first steps towards exclusion of women, began in the late middle ages and early modern period ('Women's Medical Practice,' 51–2).

42 This view accords with sociologist Anne Witz's hypothesis that the exclusion of women from medical practice must be seen in terms of the shift from a pre- and early modern social system in which the patriarchal family 'regulated as well as facilitated' women's medical practice, to the 'occupational professionalism' of industrial capitalist society (*Professions and Patriarchy*, 79).

43 For an account of the ideology of English common law, see J.G.A. Pocock, *The Ancient Constitution and the Feudal Law*, and Glenn Burgess, *The Politics of the Ancient Constitution.*

44 Burgess, *Politics*, 130–8, 200–3, 179.

45 Ibid., 179; Brooks, *Pettyfoggers and Vipers*, 12.

46 Baker, *An Introduction to English Legal History*, 35–6, 45, 37–41, 89, 92–4.

47 Brooks, *Pettyfoggers and Vipers*, 13–14.

48 Baker, *Introduction*, 112–13, 114.

49 Burgess, *Politics*, 121–30.

50 Baker, *Introduction*, 23–4. Officials served multiple, competing functions even in the superior courts, especially in King's Bench, where the attorneys who represented clients in lawsuits often served simultaneously as clerks to court officials (Brooks, *Pettyfoggers and Vipers*, 21–2).

51 Wrightson, 'Two Concepts of Order.'

52 David Underdown, *Fire From Heaven*, 164.

53 *OED* s.v. 'lawyer,' 1a. See also Prest, 'Lawyers,' in *The Professions in Early Modern England*, 67.

54 For an account of the importance of counsel in the practice of the learned physicians, see Harold J. Cook, 'Good Advice.'

55 Brewer and Styles, *An Ungovernable People*,' 14.

56 Hill, *Liberty against the Law*, 234.

57 Ingram, 'Communities and Courts,' 110–34.

58 Wrightson, 'Two Concepts of Order,' 24.

59 Prest, *Rise of the Barristers*, 224–5. See also the discussion of clerical and popular attitudes towards litigation in Richard L. Greaves, *Society and Religion in Elizabethan England*, 258–9, 649–57.

60 Earle, *Micro-cosmographie*, 24.

61 Coincidentally, this is just the contradiction into which the equitable jurisdiction of the Court of Chancery was forced. To serve as a viable alternative to the Common Law it increasingly had to emulate Common Law procedures.

62 Ingram, *Church Courts, Sex and Marriage*, 27–69, 43–6.

63 Keith Wrightson addresses this issue in 'Two Concepts of Order.'

64 See the note in *Works of George Herbert*, 563, and David Underdown, *Revel, Riot and Rebellion*, 47. Much has been written on the complex ideological character of such festive customs, which both disrupt and reinscribe the *status quo*. See, for example, Leah S. Marcus, *The Politics of Mirth*.

65 Underdown, *Revel Riot and Rebellion*, 66, 47, and *Fire from Heaven*; Slack, 'Poverty and Politics in Salisbury.'

66 Douglas Swartz addresses the issue of charity as social control in 'Discourse and Direction.' Swartz's reading of *The Country Parson* differs from my own in presenting Herbert's book as an unambiguously absolutist document. For a broad discussion of the connection between charity and hospitality in early modern England and the role of the clergy in this system see Felicity Heal, *Hospitality in Early Modern England*.

67 Slack, 'Poverty and Politics.' Sidney Gottlieb discusses the social tensions in Herbert's Wiltshire in 'Herbert's Case of "Conscience,"' 120–3.

68 Sharp, *In Contempt of All Authority*, 82–125. See also Martin Ingram, 'Religion, Communities and Moral Discipline,' 184–5, for an account of the social and economic distress in the Wiltshire parish of Keevil.

69 Slack, 'Poverty and Politics,' 164.

70 Sherfield's civic reforms and his act of iconoclasm in 1633 were intimately connected as manifestations of lay assertiveness. See Slack, 'Religious Protest and Urban Authority,' 295–302, and 'The Public Conscience of Henry Sherfield.'

71 See the account of the Poor Law of 1601 in Paul Slack, 'Poverty and Social Regulation in Elizabethan England,' 221–41.

72 In doing so he seems, if we can trust the hyperbole of a funeral sermon, to follow the example of his mother, who 'never turned her face from those who, in a strict inquisition, might be call'd idle, and vagrant Beggers, yet she ever look't first, upon them, who *labour'd*' (*The Sermons of John Donne*, 8: 89).

73 See Christopher Hodgins, *Authority, Church and Society*, 84–5.

4 *The Country Parson* and the Parson's Country

1 Laslett, *The World We Have Lost*, 7. Herbert offers corroboration for this sense of impermanence in *The Country Parson* when he urges catechism according to set forms on the grounds that 'many remove from Parish to Parish' (255).

2 Laslett, *The World We Have Lost*, 4.

3 Marx, *Capital*, 787.

4 Beier, *Masterless Men*, 9. On the absence of a peasantry in early modern England, see Alan Macfarlane, *The Origins of English Individualism*, and *The Culture of Capitalism*, 1–24.

5 Foucault, *Discipline and Punish*, 138.
6 For cautions about the application of Foucault's observations to seventeenth-century England see David Cressy, 'Foucault, Stone, Shakespeare and Social History.' and Susan Dwyer Amussen, 'Punishment, Discipline, and Power.' The classic expression of the paradox of freedom in bondage is, of course, Luther's *Freedom of a Christian*.
7 Walton, *Lives*, 286.
8 Works setting out the characteristics of early modern deferential hierarchy are too numerous to list. Some examples include Susan Dwyer Amussen, *An Ordered Society*, 34–66 and 134–179; Mervyn James, *The Family, Lineage, and Civil Society*; Peter Laslett, *The World We Have Lost*; Harold Perkin, *The Origins of Modern English Society 1780–1880*; and Keith Wrightson, *English Society, 1580–1680*, and 'Social Order.'
9 See Herbert's poems 'Matt 3.3' and 'The Collar'; and Leah Sinanoglou Marcus, *Childhood and Cultural Despair*, 97–120. Every Herbert critic must contend with his biblicism, but the crowning achievement in the study of Herbert's biblical poetics is Chana Bloch, *Spelling the Word: George Herbert and the Bible*. For specific discussion of Herbert's parabolic technique see Bloch, 214–30, and Esther Gilman Richey, '"Wrapt in Nights Mantle."'
10 Herbert translated Luigi Cornaro's treatise on the subject, and everywhere *The Country Parson* advocates a spare diet and frugality in dress and lifestyle.
11 For a discussion of 'Avarice' in terms of early modern theories of money and value see Jeffrey Powers-Beck, '"Whence Com'st Thou."' This and other passages in *The Country Parson*, very different in tone from 'Avarice,' suggest the complexity of Herbert's attitude towards money.
12 See Cristina Malcolmson's discussion of Herbert's pastoral imagery in the context of enclosure and agricultural improvement in *Heart-Work*, 145–204.
13 Marx, *Capital*, 784–805.
14 See James R. Siemon, 'Landlord Not King,' and William C. Carroll, '"The Nursery of Beggary."'
15 More, *Utopia*, 18–19.
16 4 Henry VII, c. 19.
17 Beresford, 'Habitation Versus Improvement,' 40. A few years later (if we accept Charles's argument for the early date of 'The Church Porch'), Herbert, as Cambridge University Orator, wrote a series of official letters that formed part of the university's campaign to protect the flow of the rivers Cam and Ouse, in anticipation of a controversial scheme to drain the Bedford Levels. While Herbert had no initiative or special influence in this debate, the matter raised a considerable stir, and the threat to the University's interests may well have shaped his early view of 'improvement' schemes.

See *Epistolae* II, IV–VII; Hutchinson's notes, *Works*, 457, 460–2, 604–5; and H.C. Darby, *The Draining of the Fens*, 52–3.

18 Smith, *A Discourse of the Commonweal*, 17.
19 See Geoffrey Elton, *Reform and Renewal*, 98–128; Joan Thirsk, *Agrarian History*, 213–40; and for a contemporary voice, Sir Thomas Smith, *A Discourse of the Commonweal*, 49–53.
20 Thirsk, *Agrarian History*, 206.
21 According to Cristina Malcolmson, 'Herbert imagines ... incorrectly ... that enclosure and other agrarian improvements can take place to the best advantage of one's neighbour as well as the capitalist farmer' (*Heart-Work*, 151), but given his awareness of Tudor antienclosure discourse and his reversal on the subject it is hard to account for Herbert's later pro-improvement position in terms of naive optimism.
22 Thirsk, *Agrarian History*, 211.
23 Blith, *The English Improver*, A4v.
24 Anthony Low touches briefly and dismissively on these books in 'New Science and the Georgic Revolution,' 244–6. Joan Thirsk's 'Plough and Pen' and Andrew McRae's 'Husbandry Manuals' offer fairer and more thorough surveys.
25 Tusser, *Five Hundred Points*, 'A Comparison,' st. 1, 17. See also John Fitzherbert's *Boke of Husbandrie*, 76–81.
26 Smith, *A Discourse of the Commonweal*, 50.
27 Norden, *Surveiors Dialogue*, 4.
28 Ibid., 27.
29 Thirsk, *Agrarian History*, 236. She adds that 'the 1607 commission turned out to be the last large-scale enquiry' into the evils of enclosure and rural depopulation, and Maurice Beresford describes 'the revival of anti-depopulation Commissions during Charles I's period of non-Parliamentary government [as] a familiar mixture of paternalism and pickpocketry' rather than a serious effort to inhibit enclosure by agreement ('Habitation Versus Improvement,' 50).
30 McRae, 'Husbandry Manuals,' 38–9.
31 As Andrew McRae has pointed out, Tusser's defence of enclosure in his *Five Hundred Points of Good Husbandry* involves a similar ideological inversion ('Husbandry Manuals,' 49–50).
32 Economic historian Joyce Oldham Appleby suggests that the arguments for and against enclosure in seventeenth-century polemic embody two irreconcilable social visions (*Economic Thought and Ideology*, 58–63), but the coexistence of these two contradictory visions is significant. As Raymond Williams points out, 'the mystified feudal order [is] replaced by a mystified agrarian

capitalist order, with just enough continuity, in titles and in symbols of authority, in successive conceptions of a "natural order" to confuse and control' (*The Country and the City*, 39). A similarly confusing continuity is evident in Herbert's appropriation of gerontocratic authority in his attack on Andrew Melville (*Works*, 386; see Schoenfeldt's discussion in *Prayer and Power*, 30).

33 My analysis is broadly consistent with Cristina Malcolmson's position that 'Herbert's poetry displays an attitude toward labour and the economy characteristic of the transitional period between feudalism and capitalism,' but in Malcolmson's view, 'individual achievement is [for Herbert] justified only when the "fruits" of such labour are dedicated to the "common good" rather than used to increase "private benefit"' (*Heart-Work*, 145). I would argue that *The Country Parson* is engaged in the collective early capitalist enterprise of recasting 'private benefit' *as* 'common good.'

34 See Alastair Fowler, 'Georgic and Pastoral,' and Anthony Low, *Georgic Revolution*, 3–34. For an assessment of Herbert's georgic qualities, see Anthony Low, *Georgic Revolution*, 88–98.

35 Herbert uses the word 'pastor' about as often as he uses the term 'priest,' and 'parson' far more often than either, but 'pastor' is the word he uses to head chapter I, 'Of a Pastor.'

36 Cristina Malcolmson suggests, however, that the playful, formal, and artificial structure of the poem evokes the formal renaissance garden (*Heart-Work*, 179–84).

37 Bacon, *Novum Organum*, in *Works*, 4: 50. For Bacon's connections with and influence on Herbert, see Joseph Summers, *George Herbert*, 195–7; Andrew M. Cooper, 'The Collapse of the Religious Hieroglyph'; and Kenneth Alan Hovey, 'Divinitie and Poesie, Met.'

38 Herbert was intimately familiar with Bacon's ideas on method, having translated portions of *Advancement of Learning* into Latin. See F.E. Hutchinson's introduction to Herbert's *Works*, xl.

39 'Wallow' and its forms are extremely rare in the authorized Bible: it appears only twice in the New Testament, and of the five Old Testament uses, three have penitential associations at odds with Herbert's usage here.

40 Brennan, *Literary Patronage*, 183. Markham farmed for a time at Leighton Bromswold, where George Herbert was later to be prebendary. His many books, some of which he merely translated, published, or republished under his own name, include *The English Husbandman* (1613), *Cheap and Good Husbandry* (1623), and *Markham's Farewell to Husbandry* (1625).

41 Charles, *Life of George Herbert*, 171–3. For an account of Lady Anne's frustration in her attempt, as a woman, to exercise the prerogatives and fulfil the

duties of a landlord, see Mary Ellen Lamb, 'The Agency of the Split Subject;' Barbara K. Lewalski, 'Writing Women and Reading the Renaissance'; and George C. Williamson, *Lady Anne Clifford.*

42 Charles, *Life of George Herbert,* 22
43 Thirsk, *Agrarian History,* 133, 163–6.
44 Charles, *Life of George Herbert,* 31–5.
45 Ibid., 27.
46 The first view follows the lead of agricultural historian Eric Kerridge in *The Agricultural Revolution;* the second, Marxist commentaries like Richard Lachmann's *From Manor to Market;* the third, local historians such as Joan Thirsk and Alan Everitt.
47 Charles, *Life of George Herbert,* 136, 145.
48 Underdown, *Revel, Riot and Rebellion,* 7; see also Eric Kerridge, 'Agriculture 1500–1793.'
49 For a picture of this sort of work see Peter Laslett, *The World We Have Lost,* 14–16, and Ann Kussmaul, *Servants in Husbandry.* For details of weaving and the cloth trade see G.D. Ramsay, *Wiltshire Woolen Industry,* 65–84, and chapter 6 of this volume.
50 For disafforestation and its consequences, see R. Grant, 'Forests' 4: 412–14; and Buchanon Sharp, *In Contempt of All Authority* and 'Rural Discontents.' It is important to note that disafforestation refers to the transfer of a forest from crown to private control. While this permitted commercial exploitation, it did not imply wholesale clearing of forests.
51 See Eric Kerridge, 'Agriculture 1500–1763,' 4: 43–6.
52 Underdown, *Revel, Riot and Rebellion.* For the 'reformation of manners' see also Peter Burke, *Popular Culture;* Keith Wrightson and David Levine, *Poverty and Piety in an English Village;* and Robert von Friedeberg, 'Reformation of Manners.'
53 Underdown, *Revel, Riot and Rebellion,* 40–1; see also Underdown's 'Chalk and Cheese.'
54 Underdown's distinctions have been criticized as overly schematic. See Buchanan Sharp, 'Rural Discontents,' and my discussion later in this chapter.
55 On Herbert and georgic see Anthony Low, *Georgic Revolution,* 88–98. Low also notes the contrary elements in Herbert's depiction of rural life and manners.
56 See Christopher Hodgkins, *Authority Church and Society,* 98–9.
57 Heresbach, *Foure Bookes of Husbandry,* 5r.
58 Underdown, *Revel, Riot and Rebellion,* 77–88, 93.
59 Ibid., 82.

60 As Laura Stevenson O'Connell has argued in 'Anti-Entrepreneurial Attitudes,' the entrepreneurial spirit was not deeply entrenched in most early
seventeenth-century English minds. Rather, acquisitiveness and social mobility seemed to many a threat to the social order. See also Malcolmson, *Heart-
Work*, 4–6.

61 See chapter 6 of this volume.

62 A few years later, John Aubrey would be more explicit about linking differences in temperament to soil and agricultural practice in his *Natural History
of Wiltshire*, 11.

63 See Kerridge, 'Note Book,' 420.

64 The divergent associations of 'idleness' show just how far Herbert has come
from the antienclosure rhetoric of 'The Church Porch.' In the poem, agricultural 'improvement' is evidence of 'sloth' among the gentry; in *The Country Parson*, it is the solution to 'idleness' among the poorer sort.

65 Ignoring Herbert's remarks on agricultural matters, David Underdown uses
Herbert's defence of Rogationtide processions to present him as an advo-
cate of the traditional social order prevalent in south Wiltshire. See also
Janice Lull, *The Poem in Time*, 123–4 and Jeffrey Powers-Beck, 'Not onely a
Pastour.'

66 A similar point can be made about religious and political culture in and
around Salisbury. Sidney Gottlieb, in 'Herbert's Case of "Conscience,"' and
Claude J. Summers and Ted-Larry Pebworth, in 'Politics of *The Temple*,' suggest a traditionalist consensus by noting the disruptive activities of Wiltshire
Puritans and implicitly placing Herbert at the opposite, 'high-church'
extreme. As I argue in chapter 2, Herbert's position was probably closer to
that of his own bishop, John Davenant: too high-church for iconoclasts like
Henry Sherfield, who destroyed the 'idolatrous' church window in 1632, and
too Calvinist for Laud. Given Sherfield's prominence before the church window incident, there is reason to see him as a mainstream figure, not a mar-
ginal extremist.

67 Sharp, 'Rural Discontents,' 263.

68 Kerridge, 'Note Book,' 417.

69 Kerridge, 'Agriculture 1500–1763,' 49.

70 Kerridge, *Agricultural Revolution*, 257, 263. See also Cristina Malcolmson,
Heart-Work, 193.

71 A century earlier, Tusser had urged the necessity to 'provide ... of meadow
for hay' in April. Before artificial floating and drainage, a rich spring
meadow would be found only 'if fennes be undrowned' ('April's Husbandrie,' st. 4, in *Five Hundred Points*).

72 Kerridge, 'Sheepfold,' 289.

73 For a full discussion of 'The Water-course' in the context of these innovations see chapter 6 of this volume.

74 Herbert is not quite, as Sidney Gottlieb suggests, threatening the destruction of those who break through boundaries ('Social and Political Backgrounds,' 112). Rather, he represents grazing 'without bounds' as a self-destructive transgression, and proposes an alternative.

75 Since George Herbert's sister married a John Vaughan, and the poet eventually became guardian of their daughters, it is possible that Rowland Vaughan's links to the minor branch of the Herberts are even stronger than his links to the more powerful Earls of Pembroke and Montgomery.

76 The relative importance of technological and political factors in this transition is the subject of a controversy among Marxist historians that has become known as the 'Brenner Debate.' As the example of Rowland Vaughan shows, the two elements are so profoundly intertwined that it is difficult to assign priority to either with much confidence.

77 Thirsk, *Agrarian History*, 108–9.

78 Vaughan, *Most Approved and Long Experienced Water-Workes*, E2v.

79 Laslett, *The World We Have Lost*, 4.

80 Vaughan, *Water-Workes*, E2r, E4v.

81 Ibid., G–G2, K2r. In *Economic Policy and Projects*, Joan Thirsk suggests that the abstract rhetoric of commonweal gives way, in the early seventeenth century, to an enthusiasm for concrete economic 'projects.' Like *The Country Parson*, Vaughan's *Water-Workes* shows the strategic coexistence of these seemingly distinct discourses.

82 Vaughan, *Water-Workes*, G3v, H4r, F4r.

83 Compare Herbert's 1618 letter to his brother Henry in Paris: 'Bee covetous ... of all good which you see in Frenchmen ... [and] when you meet with a witty French speech, try to speak the like in English: so shall you play a good marchant, by transporting French commodities to your own country' (*Works*, 366).

84 Thirsk, *Economic Policy*, 2.

85 Compare the Williams manuscript's text of 'The Church Porch': 'Leave not thine own deere-cuntry cleenlines/ ffor this ffrench sluttery' (*Works*, 367–70).

86 Foucault, *Discipline and Punish*, 135–69, 143.

87 Helgerson, *Forms of Nationhood*, 133, 138.

5 Pastor as Patriarch

1 Marcus, *Childhood and Cultural Despair*, 44; Powers-Beck, *Writing the Flesh*, 1–32.

2 Marcus, *Childhood and Cultural Despair*, 104.

3 Examples include Ralph Houlebrooke, *The English Family, 1450–1700*, 13–15; Margaret Ezell, *The Patriarch's Wife: Literary Evidence and the History of the Family*, 4–7; John R. Gillis, *For Better, For Worse: British Marriages, 1600 to the Present*, 3–4; and Alan Macfarlane, *Marriage and Love in England: Modes of Reproduction, 1300–1840*, 44 n29.
4 Laslett, 'Mean Household Size in England since the Sixteenth Century.'
5 Pollock, *Forgotten Children*; Shuger, *Habits of Thought*, 218–49; Macfarlane, *Marriage and Love*, 51–78, 103–16.
6 Houlbrooke, *English Family*, 63–4.
7 Stone, *The Causes of the English Revolution, 1529–1642*; Cressy, 'Foucault, Stone, Shakespeare,' 126. See also Kevin Sharpe, *Remapping Early Modern England*, 7.
8 Mendelson, 'Review,' 851.
9 Shuger, *Habits of Thought*, 220.
10 See, for example, Mervyn James, *Family, Lineage and Civil Society*. To be sure, Stone subscribes to this model as well, but for him patriarchy is a fundamentally unstable structure, 'surviving only so long as it is not questioned and challenged' (*Family*, 150).
11 Gataker, *Marriage Duties*, 7–8; William Gouge, *Of Domesticall Duties*, 260.
12 Gataker, *Marriage Duties*, 5. Other contemporary examples include John Dod and Robert Clever, *A Godly Forme of Household Government*; Matthew Griffith, *Bethel: or a Forme for Families*; Edmund Tilney, *A Brief and Pleasant Discourse of Duties in Marriage, Called the Flower of Friendshippe*.
13 Gataker, *Marriage Duties*, 19.
14 Amussen, *An Ordered Society*, 66. See also Linda Pollock's 'Rethinking Patriarchy and Family,' which argues against 'a simple hierarchy of principles that would dictate behaviour' (20).
15 Gouge, *Of Domesticall Duties*, 23, 175; italics in orig.
16 Ibid., 275, 290.
17 According to Anthony Fletcher and John Stevenson, early modern England experienced 'a whole series of developing polarities – of speech, dress, manners, living conditions, leisure pursuits and literary interests ... [a] withdrawal by the Gentry and middling groups from a common heritage of assumptions about social integration' (*Order and Disorder in Early Modern England*, 10).
18 The dating of *Patriarcha* is controversial, but Johann P. Sommerville argues convincingly that it was composed, like *The Country Parson*, in the late 1620s or early 1630s, and published posthumously (Filmer, *Patriarcha*, xxxii–xxxiv).
19 Bodleian Tanner 233, cited in Laslett, 'Sir Robert Filmer,' 527.
20 Schochet, *Patriarchalism in Political Thought*, 7, 136–68; Daly, *Sir Robert Filmer and English Political Thought*, 57–81.
21 Filmer, *Patriarcha*, 7.

22 Schochet, *Patriarchalism in Political Thought*, 57.

23 Marcus, *Childhood and Cultural Despair*, 95.

24 Schochet, *Patriarchalism in Political Thought*, 56.

25 Shuger, *Habits of Thought*, 218–49.

26 Ibid., 236.

27 Dod and Clever, *A Godly Forme of Household Government*, A8v; see also Amussen, *Ordered Society*, 38–41, and Laslett, *World We Have Lost*, 2.

28 Houlbrooke, *English Family*, 96.

29 Laslett, *World We Have Lost*, 12; Schochet, 'Patriarchalism, Politics and Mass Attitudes,' 422–3.

30 For detailed comparisons, and discussion of the many variables involved, see Ann Kussmaul, *Servants in Husbandry*, 143–4.

31 Macfarlane, *Family Life*, 17.

32 Schoenfeldt, *Prayer and Power*, 253.

33 For the general European 'reform of popular culture' see Peter Burke, *Popular Culture*, 207–86.

34 Ingram, 'Reform of Popular Culture?' 157.

35 Wrightson and Levine, *Poverty and Piety in an English Village*, 110–85.

36 Slack, 'Poverty and Politics'; Ingram, 'Reform of Popular Culture?' 157–9.

37 Compare William Gouge's remark from the *Epistle Dedicatory* to his *Of Domesticall Duties*: the husband 'ought to make her a joynt Governour of the family with himself, and referre the ordering of many things to her discretion.'

38 Macfarlane, *Marriage and Love*, 119–47.

39 Wrigley, 'Family Limitation.'

40 Instances of the civil/contractual thinking that underlies Herbert's notion of pastoral authority are especially prevalent in the opening chapters: 'A Pastor is the Deputy of Christ for the reducing of Man to the Obedience of God' (225); Chaplains 'are Parsons of the families they live in, and are entertained to that end, either by an open, or implicite covenant' (226).

41 This movement is consistent with both the contractual metaphors of covenant theology and the particularist thinking associated with casuistry and the Baconian method.

42 Thirsk, 'Younger Sons,' 363.

43 Ibid., 361; examples include John Ap Robert's *Apology for a Younger Brother*, and Leveller tracts like William Sprigge's *A Modest Plea for an Equal Commonwealth*.

44 Charles, *Life of George Herbert*, 29, 48.

45 Alan Macfarlane stresses the link between 'primogeniture and complete individual property in real estate' in *The Origins of English Individualism*, 87. It is not necessary to accept the whole of Macfarlane's controversial thesis to see that primogeniture is an aspect of English 'tradition' essential to the transition to agrarian capitalism.

202 Notes to pages 126–36

46 For a discussion of the friction between the patriarchal authority of the clergy and that of other householders see Patricia Crawford, *Women and Religion,* 51.

47 Schochet, *Patriarchalism in Political Thought,* 66, my emphasis.

48 Even here the problem of contumacy (failure to appear or cooperate) diminished the effectiveness of ecclesiastical justice to a considerable extent. See Ingram, *Church Courts,* 340–63.

49 Macfarlane, *Family Life,* 55.

50 Amussen, *Ordered Society,* 66.

51 Hodgkins, *Authority, Church and Society,* 99, 95.

52 Foucault, *The History of Sexuality,* 1: 92–3.

53 Without making this distinction explicitly, Schochet hints at this view in discussing the family as a site of 'political socialization' in 'Patriarchy, Politics and Mass Attitudes,' 413–15.

54 See Philip Stewart, 'This is not a Book Review,' 525.

55 For humiliation as manipulation see Schoenfeldt, *Prayer and Power,* ch. 1, and Frank Wigham, *Ambition and Privilege: The Social Tropes of Elizabethan Courtesy Theory.* Schoenfeldt cites an instance of the parson's humiliation in performing his parish duties, but fails to note that the same techniques of securing position through humiliation apply to inferiors as well as superiors. On festivity, see Peter Stallybrass and Allon White, *Politics and Poetics of Transgression,* and Leah Marcus, *Politics of Mirth.*

56 See Amussen, 'Punishment, Discipline, and Power,' 4 n11, and Foucault, *Discipline and Punish,* 170.

57 This represents a significant departure from the inward-looking traditional patriarchy in which 'the patriarchal head alone represented the family community in relation to the wider, formal structures of society and politics' (James, *Family, Lineage and Civil Society,* 27).

58 Underdown, 'Taming of the Scold.'

59 Ingram, 'Ridings,' 178–86; see also Burke, *Popular Culture,* ch. 8–9.

60 Ingram, 'Ridings,' 188.

61 Ibid., 187.

62 See chapter 4 of this volume. Herbert's strategy here is also reminiscent of James's ecclesiastical policy of seeking to harness the evangelical zeal of the godly by offering ecclesiastical preferment in exchange for conformity.

6 *The Country Parson* and *The Temple*

1 Michael Schoenfeldt describes this posture as 'tactical, [and] opportunistic' (*Prayer and Power,* 183).

2 Rickey, *Utmost Art,* 103–47.

3 Charles and DiCesare, introduction to *Bodleian Manuscript*, xix.

4 One clear instance is 'The Crosse,' which Amy Charles links to Herbert's installation as prebendary of Leighton Bromswold, and to his resolution to re-edify the decrepit parish church. According to Charles, 'among the three churches Herbert undertook to rebuild, [this is] the only cruciform church' (*Life of George Herbert*, 128).

5 Ibid., 81–7.

6 As Charles and DiCesare explain, the sheets on which the wills of Herbert and his niece, Dorothy Vaughan, are written bear the blind impression of lengthy lists, which, though illegible, may well be lists of poems. Charles conjectures that these were the under-sheets used on Herbert's writing desk, picked up as the nearest blank paper to hand when the time came for the customary deathbed composition of wills. This would imply that Herbert finalized the plan of his book in the last months, weeks, or even days of his life (introduction to *Bodleian Manuscript*, xvii–xviii).

7 Charles, *Life of George Herbert*, 138.

8 Gottlieb, 'Two Endings,' 71–2.

9 Lull, *The Poem in Time*, 74.

10 Malcolmson, *Heart-Work*, 97–8.

11 Helen Vendler suggests that 'the habit of preaching perhaps caused Herbert to write some of his verses addressing himself as he would a congregation' (*Poetry of George Herbert*, 163). While it seems unlikely that Herbert had developed a 'habit of preaching' at the time he wrote most of this poetry, there *is* reason to see him practicing a homiletic voice, especially in the later poems.

12 Terry Sherwood cites and endorses Douglas Thorpe's estimate of 'a little more than half' (*Herbert's Prayerful Art*, 3). My own count is more conservative because I have excluded poems that modulate between prayer and other discursive modes. These seem to me, on the whole, more liturgical and less 'private' than poems entirely addressed to God. For specific discussion of these modulations, see Bruce A. Johnson, 'The Audience Shift in Herbert's Poetry.'

13 Rickey was the first to point out that 'in his last years Herbert not only addressed an estimable group of poems to a second person; he also conducted dialogues of one with some aspect of his own personality' (*Utmost Art*, 127). I explore both of these tendencies in this chapter.

14 Strier, *Love Known*, 85–6. For overviews of covenant theology, see Michael McGiffert, 'Covenant Crown and Commons in Elizabethan Puritanism,' and 'Grace and Works: The Rise and Division of Covenant Divinity among Elizabethan Puritans'; and Perry Miller, *The New England Mind in the Seventeenth Century*, 432–62, the key source for Strier's characterization of covenant

divinity. For studies linking Herbert to covenant theology, see Jeanne Clayton Hunter, 'George Herbert and Puritan Piety,' and 'Salvation under Covenant: Herbert's Poetry and Puritan Sermons,' and Daniel W. Doerksen, 'Show and Tell: George Herbert, Richard Sibbes, and Communings with God.' Terry Sherwood has also noted that Preston and Sibbes were Herbert's 'Cambridge contemporaries,' and has compared their theologies of prayer (*Herbert's Prayerful Art*, 38).

15 Preston, *The Breastplate of Faith and Love*, 'Of Effectuall Faith,' 31.

16 Gottlieb, 'Two Endings,' 65, 68.

17 Strier, *Love Known*, 85; see also Joseph Summers, *George Herbert*, 58; Barbara K. Lewalski, *Protestant Poetics*, 286; and Gene Edward Veith, *Reformation Spirituality*, 90–1.

18 Gottlieb, 'Two Endings,' 71.

19 Hesiod, *Works and Days*, 53.

20 See Bernard Knieger, 'The Purchase-Sale.'

21 Preston, *The Breastplate of Faith and Love*, 'Of Faith,' 40.

22 For a contrasting view, see Richard Strier, 'George Herbert and the World.'

23 Perry Miller, *The New England Mind*, 387.

24 Preston, *The Breastplate of Faith and Love*, 'Of Effectual Faith,' 38, 40.

25 Preston, *The New Covenant*, 217.

26 McGiffert, 'Grace and Works,' 481.

27 Veith, *Reformation Spirituality*, 91.

28 Strier argues that 'Conscience' is 'one of the few poems in *The Temple* that shares Luther's antiasceticism' (*Love Known*, 116). I would argue, on the contrary, that this is a recurrent note in the non-Williams poems.

29 Jean Calvin, *Institutes of the Christian Religion*, 3.24.3 and 4.17.9. See Gene Edward Veith, *Reformation Spirituality*, 91, and Jeanne Clayton Hunter, 'Herbert's "The Water Course."'

30 Veith, *Reformation Spirituality*, 91.

31 Jeanne Clayton Hunter points out the passage in 2 Chronicles, though not the one in Job, in 'Herbert's "The Water Course."' Without a recognition of the way scriptural images resonate with contemporary agricultural practice, Herbert's emphasis on irrigation and fruitfulness in the poem is nearly lost.

32 Dickson, *The Fountain of Living Waters*, 120.

33 Vendler, *Poetry of George Herbert*, 187.

34 Lull, *Poem in Time*, 74.

35 Slights, *Casuistical Tradition*, 184 n4; Stein, *George Herbert's Lyrics*, 120. See also Claud J. Summers and Ted-Larry Pebworth, 'Public Concerns in Private Modes'; and Sidney Gottlieb, 'Herbert's Case of "Conscience": Public or Private Poem?'

36 Strier, *Love Known*, 57, 58.

37 For a contrary view, see Michael Schoenfeldt, *Prayer and Power*, 81.

38 Fish, *Self-Consuming Artifacts*, 156. It is worth noting that the poems Fish treats in *Self-Consuming Artifacts* are predominantly poems included in the Williams manuscript.

39 Gottlieb, 'From "Content" to "Affliction" [III]: Herbert's Anti-Court Sequence,' 474, 473. James Boyd White defines the sequence slightly differently, including 'The Starre' in the group, and describing the unifying subject as 'the appeal of the things of this world' (*This Book of Starres*, 174–83).

40 To some extent this is implicit in Sidney Gottlieb's argument that the poems construct 'a Neostoic ideal of accommodation' ('Herbert's Anti-Court Sequence,' 475).

41 Ibid., 480.

42 Ibid., 483, 481, 482; see also 'Herbert's Political Allegory of "Humilitie."'

43 Gottlieb, 'Herbert's Anti-Court Sequence,' 486.

44 Compare *The Country Parson*'s treatment of charity, 244–5, and the discussion in chapter 3 of this volume.

45 Compare Herbert's presentation of the 'true Pastour' as 'a mark to aim at' in the authorial preface to *The Country Parson*, 224.

46 See Michael C. Schoenfeldt, *Prayer and Power*, 83, and Elizabeth Stambler, 'The Unity of Herbert's *Temple*,' 259.

47 A distinguished tradition in Herbert scholarship stresses Herbert's affinity for the worldly, the ordinary, and the material, his 'exact observations drawn from actual experience' (Stein, *George Herbert's Lyrics*, 120). See, for instance, Jeffrey Powers-Beck's discussion of the sensuality of 'The Banquet' in *Writing the Flesh*, 49–52.

48 Tellingly, Diana Benet links 'The Glimpse' thematically to 'Man's Medley' and 'Joseph's Coat,' without referring to their shared imagery (*Secretary of Praise*, 74–5).

49 Vendler, *Poetry of George Herbert*, 258.

50 Benet, *Secretary of Praise*, 76.

51 Ramsay, *The Wiltshire Woolen Industry*, 76, 77, 82.

52 This interference by the state was far from welcome; on one occasion Wither was flung into a river on an inspection tour.

53 Ramsay, *The Wiltshire Woolen Industry*, 90–1. These 'yarn badgers' came to be called 'market spinners,' a name they seem to have appropriated from the small independent spinners who had once sold their product in local markets, and were now dependent on middlemen.

54 Ramsay, *The Wiltshire Woolen Industry*, 9.

55 Vendler, *Poetry of George Herbert*, 195.

56 For an account of the scriptural intertexts here, see Chana Bloch, *Spelling the Word*, 85–6.

57 Stanley Fish quotes the final lines as if they were entirely self-explanatory, without so much as mentioning the rest of the poem (*Self-Consuming Artifacts*, 173). William V. Nestrick argues that at the end, 'The spatial world with its time dimension expressed as the giving and receiving of the self is annihilated' ('Mine and Thine,' 121).

58 Nestrick, 'Mine and Thine,' 120. Insofar as this view is persuasive, it undermines Anthony Low's claim, in 'The Best Love,' that Herbert studiously avoids the biblical metaphor of Christ as bridegroom, which has so much appeal for poets like Donne and Crashaw; see also Janel Mueller, 'Women among the Metaphysicals,' on this subject.

59 Compare William Fleetwood's discussion of the advantages of servitude in *The Relative Duties of Parents, Husbands, Masters*, 385–6.

60 A similar ideological shift might be detected in 'Discipline' where the speaker urges God to 'Throw away thy rod' in favour of the productive power of love. In his account of the poem, Michael Schoenfeldt emphasizes God's mastery of the technology of pain (*Prayer and Power*, 131). But a case can also be made that in proposing to God an alternative technology of control the speaker takes upon himself elements of the disciplinary function, relieving God of the necessity to exercise violent correction.

61 Significantly, 'Obedience' marks a structural turning point in 'The Church,' the point at which Herbert inserted a block of seventy-six new poems into the sequence reflected in the Williams manuscript. Among the Williams manuscript poems, 'Obedience' is perhaps the one that most closely approximates the evangelical and metaphorical pragmatism of many of these later poems.

62 Strier, *Love Known*, 93, 96.

63 *Works of George Herbert*, 514.

64 Earl of Oxford's case, 1615, qtd. in J.H. Baker, *Introduction to English Legal History*, 90. Over the course of the seventeenth century, as Chancery developed its own body of precedents, 'equity hardened into law' (94).

65 For a general account of the process of 'enclosure by agreement,' see E.C.K. Gonner, *Common Land and Inclosure*, 51–6. During the period between the sixteenth-century antienclosure statutes and the enabling legislation of the eighteenth century, enclosure agreements replaced unilateral enclosure of commons by landlords as the most common method of enclosure. See also R.A. Butlin, 'The Enclosure of Open Fields' and *The Transformation of Rural England*.

66 See Maurice Beresford, 'Habitation Versus Improvement,' 60–3.

67 It is worth noting that the speaker of 'Obedience,' in signing over his land to the lord, has disinherited his child, 'Pleasure,' exchanging the role of patriarch for the role of good neighbour.

68 Rosalie Osmond, *Mutual Accusation*, 69, 61.

69 Though Hutchinson follows the 1633 text in printing the poem in six-line stanzas, both manuscripts omit stanzaic divisions and indent line 17, presenting the apostrophe to the flesh in a new paragraph.

70 The pathos of this story may owe something to the fact that George Herbert's father died when the poet was three, leaving the eldest brother, Edward Herbert, as the bearer of the family name and fortune.

71 Perkins, *A Discourse of Conscience* in *Works* 1:517. For a general discussion of seventeenth-century theories of conscience see Camille Wells Slights, *Casuistical Tradition*, 10–34.

72 Slights, *Casuistical Tradition*, 13.

73 Schoenfeldt, *Prayer and Power*, 131.

7 Modernity, Teleology, and *The Country Parson*

1 Anthony Giddens, *The Consequences of Modernity*, 3. Definitions of modernity are themselves contentious, of course. Capitalism, urbanization, and industrialization are obviously crucial aspects of the modern, but I am persuaded by sociologist Derek Sayer's view, influenced strongly by Weber, that these developments rest on 'a radical transformation of the character of social relationships and the nature of social power' in which 'the ethical becomes ... a question of *character*, a core constituent of personal identity,' and the ethical character is achieved through 'a rationalized methodical direction of the entire pattern of life' (*Capitalism and Modernity*, 2, 121–2).

2 Russell, *The Causes of the English Civil War*, 2.

3 R. Malcolm Smuts, *Culture and Power in England, 1585–1685*, 4–5.

4 Charles Whitney, *Francis Bacon and Modernity*, 4; Hans Blumenberg, *The Legitimacy of the Modern Age*.

5 Macfarlane, *The Culture of Capitalism*, ix.

6 Macfarlane, *Origins*, 60.

7 Smuts, *Culture and Power*, 11–12; see also Reta A. Terry, '"Vows to the Blackest Devil."'

8 See A. Mark Liddle, 'State, Masculinities and Law.'

9 Collinson, *Religion of Protestants*, 111; Weber, *On Charisma and Institution Building*, 272.

10 See Craig Muldrew, 'The Culture Of Reconciliation.'

Bibliography

Addison, Joseph, and Sir Richard Steele. *The Spectator.* Edited by Donald F. Bond. 5 vols. Oxford: Clarendon Press, 1965.

Aldington, Richard, ed. *A Book of 'Characters.'* London: Routledge, 1924.

Amussen, Susan Dwyer. *An Ordered Society: Gender and Class in Early Modern England.* Oxford: Basil Blackwell, 1988.

– 'Punishment, Discipline, and Power: The Social Meanings of Violence in Early Modern England.' *Journal of British Studies* 34 (1995): 1–34.

Angenot, Marc. 'The Concept of Social Discourse.' *English Studies in Canada* 21 (1995): 1–19.

Ap Robert, John. *An Apology for a Younger Brother.* Oxford: 1641.

Appleby, Joyce Oldham. *Economic Thought and Ideology in Seventeenth-Century England.* Princeton: Princeton University Press, 1978.

Asals, Heather A.R. *Equivocal Predication: George Herbert's Way to God.* Toronto: University of Toronto Press, 1981.

Aston, Margaret. *England's Iconoclasts*, vol. I, *Laws against Images.* Oxford: Clarendon Press, 1988.

Aston, T.H., and C.H.E. Philpin, eds. *The Brenner Debate: Agrarian Class Structure and Economic Development in Pre-industrial Europe.* New York : Cambridge University Press, 1985.

Atkins, Jonathan M. 'Calvinist Bishops, Church Unity, and the Rise of Arminianism.' *Albion* 18 (1986): 411–27.

Aubrey, John. *Natural History of Wiltshire.* Edited by John Britton. 1847.

Auerbach, Erich. *Mimesis: The Representation of Reality in Western Literature.* Translated by Willard R. Trask. Garden City, NY: Doubleday, 1957.

Bacon, Francis. *The Works of Francis Bacon.* Edited by James Spedding, Robert Leslie Ellis and Douglas Denon Heath. 7 Vols. London: Longmans, 1870.

Baker, J.H. *An Introduction to English Legal History,* 2nd ed. London: Butterworths, 1979.

Barret, C.R.B. *The History of the Society of Apothecaries of London.* 1905. Reprint, New York: AMS, 1977.

Batey, Mavis. *Oxford Gardens: The University's Influence on Garden History.* Aldershot, England: Scolar Press, 1986.

Beier, A.L. *Masterless Men: The Vagrancy Problem in England, 1560-1640.* London: Methuen, 1985.

Bell, Ilona. '"Setting Foot into Divinity": George Herbert and the English Reformation.' *Modern Language Quarterly* 38 (1977): 219–44.

Benet, Diana. 'Herbert's Experience of Politics and Patronage in 1624.' *George Herbert Journal* 10 (1986): 33–45.

– *Secretary of Praise; The Poetic Vocation of George Herbert.* Columbia: University of Missouri Press, 1984.

Bennett, H.S. *English Books and Readers, 1558–1603: Being a Study in the History of the Book Trade in the Reign of Elizabeth I.* Cambridge: Cambridge University Press, 1965.

– *English Books and Readers, 1603–1640: Being a Study in the History of the Book Trade in the Reigns of James I and Charles I.* Cambridge: Cambridge University Press, 1970.

Beresford, Maurice. 'Habitation Versus Improvement: The Debate on Enclosure by Agreement.' In *Essays in the Economic and Social History of Tudor and Stuart England,* edited by F.J. Fisher. Cambridge: Cambridge University Press, 1961.

Bernard, Richard. *The Faithful Shepherd.* London, 1621.

Blith, Walter. *The English Improver.* London, 1649.

Bloch, Chana. *Spelling the Word: George Herbert and the Bible.* Berkeley: University of California Press, 1985.

Blumenberg, Hans. *The Legitimacy of the Modern Age.* Translated by Robert Wallace. Cambridge MA.: MIT Press, 1983.

Bottrall, Margaret. *George Herbert.* London: Murray, 1954.

Brennan, Michael G. *Literary Patronage in the English Renaissance: The Pembroke Family.* London: Routledge, 1988.

Brewer, John, and John Styles, eds. *An Ungovernable People: The English and Their Law in the Seventeenth and Eighteenth Centuries.* New Brunswick, N.J.: Rutgers University Press, 1980.

Brooks, C.W. *Pettyfoggers and Vipers of the Commonwealth: The 'Lower Branch' of the Legal Profession in Early Modern England.* Cambridge: Cambridge University Press, 1986.

Brownlow, Richard, and John Goldesborough. *Reports of Diverse Choice Cases in Law, Taken by those Late and Most Judicious Prothonotaries ...* 2nd ed. London, 1654.

Burgess, Glenn. *The Politics of the Ancient Constitution: An Introduction to English Political Thought, 1603–1642.* London: Macmillan, 1992.

Burke, Peter. *History and Social Theory.* Ithaca: Cornell University Press, 1992.

– *Popular Culture in Early Modern Europe.* New York: Harper and Row, 1978.

Burton, Robert. *The Anatomy of Melancholy.* Edited by Thomas C. Faulkner, Nicholas K. Keissling, and Rhonda A. Blair. 5 vols. Oxford: Clarendon Press, 1989.

Butlin, R.A. 'The Enclosure of Open Fields and Extinction of Common Rights in England, *circa* 1600–1750: A Review.' In *Change in the Countryside: Essays on Rural England, 1500–1900,* edited by H.S.A. Fox and R.A. Butlin, 65–82. London: Institute of British Geographers, 1979.

– *The Transformation of Rural England, c. 1580–1800: A Study in Historical Geography.* Oxford: Oxford University Press, 1982.

Calvin, Jean. *Institutio Christianae Religionis [Institutes of the Christian Religion].* Edited by John T. McNeill. Translated by Ford Lewis Battles et al. 2 vols. Philadelphia: Westminster Press, 1960.

Camden, William. *Brittania.* London, 1607.

Cardwell, Edward, ed. *Documentary Annals of the Reformed Church of England, Being a Collection of Injunctions, Declarations Orders, Articles of Inquiry etc.* 2 vols. Oxford: Oxford University Press, 1844.

Carroll, William C. '"The Nursery of Beggary": Enclosure, Vagrancy, and Sedition in the Tudor-Stuart Period.' In *Enclosure Acts: Sexuality, Property, and Culture in Early Modern England,* edited by Richard Burt and John Michael Archer, 35–47. Ithaca: Cornell University Press, 1994.

Cartwright, Frederick F. *A Social History of Medicine.* London: Longman, 1977.

Charles, Amy M. *A Life of George Herbert.* Ithaca: Cornell University Press, 1977.

– Introduction to *The Williams Manuscript of George Herbert's Poems.* Delmar, N.Y.: Scholars' Facsimiles and Reprints, 1977.

– Charles, Amy M., and Mario Di Cesare. Introduction to *The Bodleian Manuscript of George Herbert's Poem: A Facsimile of Tanner 307.* Delmar, N.Y.: Scholars' Facsimiles and Reprints, 1984.

Chartres, John, and David Hey, eds. *English Rural Society, 1500–1800: Essays in Honour of Joan Thirsk.* Cambridge: Cambridge University Press, 1990.

Church of England. *Constitutions and Canons Ecclesiastical.* London, 1604.

Clark, Alice. *Working Life of Women in the Seventeenth Century.* London: Frank Cass, 1919.

Clarke, Samuel. *Lives of Sundry Eminent Persons in this Later Age.* London, 1683.

Clausen, Sara Jean. *Calvinism in the Anglican Hierarchy, 1603–1643: Four Episcopal Examples.* Ann Arbor: UMI, 1989.

Collinson, Patrick. *The Birthpangs of Protestant England: Religious and Cultural Change in the Sixteenth and Seventeenth Centuries.* Basingstoke: Macmillan, 1988.

- *The Elizabethan Puritan Movement.* Berkeley: University of California Press, 1967.
- 'The Jacobean Religious Settlement: The Hampton Court Conference.' In *Before the English Civil War: Essays on Early Stuart Politics and Government,* edited by Howard Tomlinson, 27–51. New York: St Martin's, 1983.
- 'Lectures by Combination: Structures and Characteristics of Church Life in 17th-Century England.' In *Godly People: Essays on English Protestantism and Puritanism,* 467–98. London: Hambleton, 1983.
- *The Religion of Protestants: The Church in English Society, 1559–1625.* Oxford: Clarendon Press, 1982.
- 'Shepherds, Sheepdogs, and Hirelings: The Pastoral Ministry in Post-Reformation England.' In *The Ministry: Clerical and Lay,* edited by W.J. Sheils and Diana Wood, 185–220, Studies in Church History 26. Oxford: Basil Blackwell, 1989.
Cook, Ann Jennalie. *Making a Match: Courtship in Shakespeare and His Society.* Princeton: Princeton University Press, 1991.
Cook, Harold J. '"Against Common Right and Reason": The College of Physicians versus Dr. Thomas Bonham.' *American Journal of Legal History* 29 (1985): 301–22.
- *The Decline of the Old Medical Regime in Stuart London.* Ithaca: Cornell University Press, 1986.
- 'Good Advice and Little Medicine: The Professional Authority of Early Modern Physicians.' *Journal of British Studies* 3 (1994): 1–31.
- 'Institutional Structures and Personal Belief in the London College of Physicians.' In *Religio Medici: Medicine and Religion in Seventeenth-Century England,* edited by Ole Peter Grell and Andrew Cunningham, 91–114. Aldershot: Scolar Press, 1996.
- 'Policing the Health of London: The College of Physicians and the Early Stuart Monarchy.' *Social History of Medicine* 2 (1989): 1–33.
Cooley, Ronald W. '"Untill the Book Grow to a Compleat Pastorall": Re-reading *The Country Parson.' English Studies in Canada* 18 (1992): 247–60.
Cooper, Andrew M. 'The Collapse of the Religious Hieroglyph: Typology and Natural Language in Bacon and Herbert.' *Renaissance Quarterly* 45 (1992): 96–118.
Cotta, John. *A Short Discoverie of the Unobserved Dangers of Several Sorts of Ignorant and Unconsiderate Practisers of Physicke in England.* London, 1612.
Crawford, Patricia. *Women and Religion in England, 1500–1700.* London: Routledge, 1993.
Cressy, David. 'Conflict, Consensus, and the Willingness to Wink: The Erosion of Community in Charles I's England.' *Huntington Library Quarterly* 61 (2000): 131–49.

- 'Foucault, Stone, Shakespeare and Social History.' *English Literary Renaissance* 21 (1991): 121–33.

Crooke, Samuel. *The ministeriall husbandry and building.* London, 1618.

Curtis, Mark. 'The Alienated Intellectuals of Early Stuart England.' *Past and Present* 23 (1962): 25–43.

- 'The Hampton Court Conference and Its Aftermath.' *History* 46 (1961): 1–16.

Cust, Richard, and Ann Hughes. 'After Revisionism.' Introduction to *Conflict in Early Stuart England: Studies in Religion and Politics, 1603–1642*, edited by Richard Cust and Ann Hughes. London: Longman, 1989.

Dalton, Michael. *The Countrey Justice.* London, 1619.

Daly, James W. *Sir Robert Filmer and English Political Thought.* Toronto: University of Toronto Press, 1979.

Darby, H.C. *The Draining of the Fens.* Cambridge: Cambridge University Press, 1956.

Davenant, John. *A Treatise on Justification ... Together with Translations of the Determinationes of the Same Prelate.* Translated by Josiah Allport. 2 vols. London: Hamilton, Adams, 1844.

Davies, Horton W. *Worship and Theology in England.* 5 vols. Princeton: Princeton University Press, 1961–75.

Delorme, Mary. 'A Watery Paradise: Rowland Vaughan and Hereford's "Golden Vale."' *History Today* 39 (July 1989): 38–43.

Dickson, Donald R. 'Between Transubstantiation and Memorialism: Herbert's Eucharistic Celebration.' *George Herbert Journal* 11.1 (1987): 1–14.

- *The Fountain of Living Waters: The Typology of the Waters of Life in Herbert, Vaughan and Traherne.* Columbia: University of Missouri Press, 1987.

Dod, John, and Robert Clever. *A Godly Forme of Household Government.* London, 1612.

Doerksen, Daniel W. *Conforming to the Word: Herbert, Donne and the English Church before Laud.* Lewisburg: Bucknell University Press, 1997.

- 'Magdalen Herbert's London Church.' *Notes and Queries* n.s. 34 (1987): 302–5.

- 'Nicholas Ferrar, Arthur Woodnoth, and the Publication of George Herbert's *The Temple*, 1633.' *George Herbert Journal* 3 (1980): 22–44.

- 'Preaching Pastor versus Custodian of Order: Donne Andrewes and the Jacobean Church.' *Philological Quarterly* 73 (1994): 417–29.

- 'Recharting the *Via Media* of Spenser and Herbert.' *Renaissance and Reformation* n.s. 8 (1984): 215–25.

- 'Show and Tell: George Herbert, Richard Sibbes, and Communings with God.' *Christianity and Literature* 51 (2002): 175–90.

- 'Things Fundamental or Indifferent: Adiaphorism and Herbert's Church Attitudes.' *George Herbert Journal* 11.1 (1987): 15–22.

- '"Too Good for Those Times": Politics and the Publication of George Herbert's *The Country Parson.*' *Seventeenth-Century News* (Spring/Summer 1991): 10–13.

Donne, John. *The Sermons of John Donne.* Edited by Evelyn M. Simpson and George R. Potter. 10 vols. Berkeley: University of California Press, 1953.

Dort, Synod of. See *The Judgement of the Synode Holden at Dort.*

Drayton, Michael. *The Works of Michael Drayton.* Edited by J. William Hebel. 5 vols. Oxford: Shakespeare Head Press, 1961.

Eamon, William. *The Science and the Secrets of Nature: Books of Secrets in Medieval and Early Modern Culture.* Princeton: Princeton University Press, 1994.

Earle, John. *Micro-cosmographie.* Editio Princeps, 1628. With Additional Characters from the Fifth Edition of 1629; and the Sixth Edition of 1633. Edited by Edward Arber. English Reprints. West Orange, N.J.: Albert Saifer, n.d.

Elmer, Peter. 'Medicine, Religion and the Puritan Revolution.' In *The Medical Revolution of the Seventeenth Century,* edited by Roger French and Andrew Wear, 10–45. Cambridge: Cambridge University Press, 1989.

Elton, Geoffrey. *Reform and Renewal: Thomas Cromwell and the Common Weal.* Cambridge: Cambridge University Press, 1973.

Enssle, Neal. 'Patterns of Godly Life: The Ideal Parish Minister in Sixteenth and Seventeenth-Century English Thought.' *Sixteenth Century Journal* 28 (1997): 3–28.

Ezell, Margaret J.M. *The Patriarch's Wife: Literary Evidence and the History of the Family.* Chapel Hill: University of North Carolina Press, 1987.

Filmer, Sir Robert. *Patriarcha and Other Writings.* Edited by Johann P. Sommerville. Cambridge: Cambridge University Press, 1991.

Fincham, Kenneth. *Prelate as Pastor: The Episcopate of James I.* Oxford: Clarendon Press, 1990.

Fincham, Kenneth, and Peter Lake. 'The Ecclesiastical Policy of James I.' *Journal of British Studies* 24 (1985): 169–207.

Fish, Stanley. *The Living Temple: George Herbert and Catechizing.* Berkeley: University of California Press, 1978.

- *Self-Consuming Artifacts: The Experience of Seventeenth-Century Literature.* Berkeley: University of California Press, 1972.

Fitzherbert, John. *Boke of Husbandry.* London, [1530?].

Fleetwood, William. *The Relative Duties of Parents, Husbands, Masters.* London, 1705.

Fletcher, Anthony, and John Stevenson, eds. *Order and Disorder in Early Modern England.* Cambridge: Cambridge University Press, 1985.

Ford, Wyn. 'The Problem of Literacy in Early Modern England.' *History* 78 (1993): 22–37.

Fortescue, Sir John. *De Landibus Legum Angliae.* Edited by Shelley Lockwood. Cambridge: Cambridge University Press, 1997.

Foucault, Michel. *The History of Sexuality.* Translated by Robert Hurley. 3 vols. New York: Random House, 1978–86.

– 'Truth and Power.' In *Discipline and Punish: The Birth of the Prison,* translated by Alan Sheridan, 109–33. New York: Random House, 1979.

Fowler, Alastair. 'Georgic and Pastoral: Laws of Genre in the Seventeenth-Century.' In *Culture and Cultivation in Early Modern England: Writing and the Land,* edited by Michael Leslie and Timothy Raylor, 81–8. Leicester: Leicester University Press, 1992.

Friedman, Donald M. 'Donne, Herbert and Vocation.' *George Herbert Journal* 18 (1994–5): 135–58.

Freidson, Eliot. *Professional Powers: A Study of the Institutionalization of Formal Knowledge.* Chicago: University of Chicago Press, 1986.

Frye, Northrop. *The Great Code: the Bible and Literature.* New York: Harcourt Brace Jovanovich, 1982.

Fussell, G.E. *The Old English Farming Books from Fitzherbert to Tull.* London: Lockwood, 1947.

Gardiner, Samuel R. *History of England from the Accession of James I to the Outbreak of the Civil War, 1603–1642.* 10 vols. London: Longman, 1884.

Gataker, Thomas. *Marriage Duties Briefly Couched Togither.* London, 1620.

Giddens, Anthony. *The Consequences of Modernity.* Stanford: Stanford University Press, 1990.

Gifford, George. *A Brief Discourse of Certaine Points of the Religion, Whiche is Among the Common Sort of Christians: Which may be Termed the Country Divinitie: With a Plaine and Manifest Confutation of the Same, After the Order of a Dialogue.* London, 1592.

Gillis, John R. *For Better, For Worse: British Marriages, 1600 to the Present.* New York: Oxford University Press, 1985.

Glassock, Robin, ed. *Historic Landscapes of Britain from the Air.* Cambridge: Cambridge University Press, 1992.

Gonner, E.C.K. *Common Land and Inclosure.* London: MacMillan, 1912.

Gottlieb, Sidney. 'From "Content" to "Affliction" [III]: Herbert's Anti-Court Sequence.' *English Literary Renaissance* 23 (1993): 472–89.

– 'Herbert's Case of "Conscience": Public or Private Poem?' *Studies in English Literature, 1500–1900* 25 (1985): 109–26.

– 'Herbert's Political Allegory of "Humilitie."' *Huntington Library Quarterly* 52 (1989): 469–80.

– 'The Social and Political Backgrounds of George Herbert's Poetry.' In *The Muses Common-Weale: Poetry and Politics in the Seventeenth Century,* edited by

Claude J. Summers and Ted-Larry Pebworth, 107–18. Columbia: University of Missouri Press, 1988.

– 'The Two Endings of George Herbert's "The Church."' In *A Fine Tuning: Studies of the Religious Poetry of Herbert and Milton*, edited by Mary A. Maleski, 57–76. Medieval and Renaissance Texts and Studies 64. Binghamton: Medieval and Renaissance Texts and Studies, 1989.

Gouge, William. *Of Domesticall Duties: Eight Treatises.* 3rd ed. London, 1634.

Grant, R. 'Forests.' In *A History of Wiltshire*, edited by Elizabeth Crittall, 4: 391–457. 16 vols. The Victoria History of the Counties of England. London: Oxford University Press, 1953–99.

Greaves, Richard L. *Society and Religion in Elizabethan England.* Minneapolis: University of Minnesota Press, 1981.

Green, Ian. 'Career Prospects and Clerical Conformity in the Early Stuart Church.' *Past and Present* 90 (1981): 71–115.

Green, Monica. 'Women's Medical Practice and Health Care in Medieval Europe.' In *Sisters and Workers in the Middle Ages*, edited by Judith M. Bennett et al., 39–78. Chicago: University of Chicago Press, 1989.

Gregory I. *Pastoral Care.* Translated by Henry Davis, S.J. Westminster, MD: Newman Press, 1950.

Grindal, Edmund. *The Remains of Edmund Grindal, Successively Bishop of London and Archbishop of York and Canterbury.* Edited by William Nicholson. Cambridge: Cambridge University Press, 1843.

Griffith, Matthew. *Bethel: or, a Forme for Families.* London, 1633.

Guibbory, Achsah. *Ceremony and Community from Herbert to Milton.* Cambridge: Cambridge University Press, 1998.

Hagedorn, Suzanne C. 'Received Wisdom: The Reception History of Alfred's Preface to the *Pastoral Care*.' In *Anglo-Saxonism and the Construction of Social Identity*, edited by Allen J. Frantzen and John D. Niles, 86–110. Gainesville: University Press of Florida, 1997.

Hales, John. *Golden Remaines of the Ever Memorable Mr. John Hales.* London, 1673.

Halewood, William H. *The Poetry of Grace: Reformation Themes and Structures in English Seventeenth-Century Poetry.* New Haven: Yale University Press, 1970.

Harnack, Andrew. 'Both Protestant and Catholic: George Herbert's "To all Angels and Saints."' *George Herbert Journal* 11.1 (1987): 23–40.

Harrison, William. *The Description of England*, edited by Georges Edelen. Ithaca: Cornell University Press, 1968.

Hart, James. *KAINIKH or The Diet of the Diseased.* London, 1633.

Hawkins, Michael. 'Ambiguity and Contradiction in "the Rise of Professionalism": The English Clergy, 1570–1730.' In *The First Modern Society: Essays in English History in Honour of Lawrence Stone*, edited by A.L. Beier, David Cannadine, and James M. Rosenheim, 241–70. Cambridge: Cambridge University Press, 1989.

Heal, Felicity. *Hospitality in Early Modern England*. Oxford: Clarendon Press, 1990.

Helgerson, Richard. *Forms of Nationhood: The Elizabethan Writing of England*. Chicago: University of Chicago Press, 1992.

Herbert, George. *The Bodleian Manuscript of George Herbert's Poems: A Facsimile of Tanner 307*. Intro. Amy M. Charles and Mario Di Cesare. Delmar, N.Y.: Scholars' Facsimiles and Reprints, 1984.

– *The Complete Works in Verse and Prose of George Herbert*, edited by Alexander B. Grosart. Fuller Worthies' Library. Vol. 3. London: Robson, 1874.

– *The Latin Poems of George Herbert: A Bilingual Edition*. Translated by Mark McClosky and Paul R. Murphy. Athens: Ohio University Press, 1965.

– *The Williams Manuscript of George Herbert's Poems*. Intro. Amy M. Charles. Delmar, New York: Scholars' Facsmiles and Reprints, 1977.

– *The Works of George Herbert*, edited by F.E. Hutchinson. Oxford: Clarendon Press, 1941.

Heresbach, Konrad. *Foure Bookes of Husbandry*. Translated by Barnaby Googe. London, 1596.

Hesiod. *Works and Days*. Translated by David W. Tandy and Walter C. Neale. Berkeley: University of California Press, 1996.

Hicks, Michael, A. ed. *Profit, Piety, and the Professions in Later Medieval England*. Gloucester: Alan Sutton, 1990.

Hieron, Samuel. *The Spirituall fishing. A Sermon preached in Cambridge*. London, 1618.

Higbie, Robert. 'Images of Enclosure in George Herbert's *The Temple*.' *Texas Studies in Language and Literature* 15 (1974): 627–38.

Hill, Christopher. *Liberty against the Law: Some Seventeenth-Century Controversies*. London: Penguin, 1996.

– *Society and Puritanism in Pre-Revolutionary England*. 2nd ed. New York: Schocken, 1967.

Hilton, R.H. Introduction to *The Brenner Debate: Agrarian Class Structure and Economi: Development in Pre-industrial Europe*, edited by T.H. Aston and C.H.E. Philpin. New York: Cambridge University Press, 1985

Hodgkins, Christopher. *Authority, Church and Society in George Herbert: Return to the Middle Way*. Columbia: University of Missouri Press, 1993.

Holmes, Geoffrey. *Augustan England: Professions, State and Society, 1680–1730*. London: George Allen and Unwin, 1982.

Hooker, Richard. *The Folger Library Edition of the Works of Richard Hooker*. 4 vols. Cambridge, MA: Belknap-Harvard University Press, 1977.

Houlbrooke, Ralph. *The English Family, 1450–1700.* London: Longman, 1984.

Hovey, Kenneth Alan. 'Church History in "The Church."' *George Herbert Journal* 6 (1982): 1–14.

– '"Divinitie and Poesie, Met": The Baconian Context of George Herbert's Divinity.' *English Language Notes* 22:3 (1985): 30–9.

Hughes, Ann. *The Causes of The English Civil War.* 2nd ed. New York: St Martin's Press, 1998.

– 'Local History and the Origins of the Civil War.' In *Conflict in Early Stuart England: Studies in Religion and Politics, 1603–1642,* edited by Richard Cust and Ann Hughes, 224–53. London: Longman, 1989.

Hunter, Jeanne Clayton. 'George Herbert and Puritan Piety.' *Journal of Religion* 68 (1988): 226–41.

– 'Herbert's "The Water Course": Notorious and Neglected.' *Notes and Queries* n.s. 34 (1987): 310–12.

– 'Salvation under Covenant: Herbert's Poetry and Puritan Sermons.' In *Praise Disjoined: Changing Patterns of Salvation in 17th-Century English Literature,* edited by William P. Shaw, 201–20. New York: Peter Lang, 1991.

Ingram, Martin. *Church Courts, Sex and Marriage in England, 1570–1640.* Cambridge: Cambridge University Press, 1987.

– 'Communities and Courts: Law and Disorder in Early Seventeenth-Century Wiltshire.' In *Crime in England, 1550–1800,* edited by J.S. Cockburn, 110–34. Princeton: Princeton University Press, 1977.

– 'The Reform of Popular Culture? Sex and Marriage in Early Modern England.' In *Popular Culture in Seventeenth-Century England,* edited by Barry Reay, 129–65. London: Croom Helm, 1985.

– 'Religion, Communities and Moral Discipline in Late Sixteenth and Early-Seventeenth-Century England: Case Studies.' In *Religion and Society in Early Modern Europe, 1500–1800,* edited by Kaspar von Greyerz, 177–93. London: Allen and Unwin, 1984.

– 'Ridings, Rough Music and Mocking Rhymes in Early Modern England.' In *Popular Culture in Seventeenth-Century England,* edited by Barry Reay, 166–97. London: Croom Helm, 1985.

James VI and I. *Minor Prose Works of James VI and I,* edited by James Craigie. Edinburgh: Scottish Text Society, 1982.

James, Mervyn. *The Family, Lineage and Civil Society: A Study of Society, Politics and Mentality in the Durham Region, 1500–1640.* Oxford: Clarendon Press, 1974.

Johnson, Bruce A. 'The Audience Shift in George Herbert's Poetry.' *Studies in English Literature, 1500–1900* 35 (1995): 89–103.

Jones, Whitney R.D. *The Tudor Commonwealth 1529–1559.* London: Athlone, 1970.

Josselin, Ralph. *The Diary of Ralph Josselin, 1616–1683.* Edited by Alan Macfarlane. London: Oxford University Press, 1976.

The Judgement of the Synode Holden at Dort, Concerning the Five Articles. London, 1619.

Kendall, R.T. *Calvin and English Calvinism to 1649.* Oxford: Oxford University Press, 1979.

Kerridge, Eric. *The Agricultural Revolution.* London: George Allen and Unwin, 1967.

– 'Agriculture 1500–1793.' In *A History of Wiltshire,* edited by Elizabeth Crittall, 4:43–64. 16 Vols. The Victoria History of the Counties of England. London: Oxford University Press, 1953–99.

– 'The Note Book of a Wiltshire Farmer in the Early Seventeenth Century.' *Wiltshire Archeological and Natural History Magazine* 5 (1952): 416–28.

– 'The Sheepfold in Wiltshire and the Floating of the Watermeadows.' *Economic History Review,* 2nd ser. 6 (1954): 282–9.

– *Textile Manufactures in Early Modern England.* Manchester: Manchester University Press, 1985.

Keynes, Geoffrey. *Dr. Timothie Bright, 1550–1615: A Survey of His Life with a Bibliography of His Writings.* London: Wellcome Historical Medical Library, 1962.

Knieger, Bernard. 'The Purchase-Sale: Patterns of Business Imagery in the Poetry of George Herbert.' *Studies in English Literature, 1500–1900* 6 (1966): 111–24.

Kollmeier, Harold H. '*The Country Parson* in Its Time.' In *Like Season'd Timber: New Essays on George Herbert,* edited by Edmund Miller and Robert Di Yanni, 191–206. New York: Peter Lang, 1987.

Kussmaul, Ann. *Servants in Husbandry in Early Modern England.* Cambridge: Cambridge University Press, 1981.

Lachmann, Richard. *From Manor to Market: Structural Change in England, 1536–1640.* Madison: University of Wisconsin Press, 1987.

Lake, Peter. *Anglicans and Puritans? Presbyterianism and English Conformist Thought from Whitgift to Hooker.* London: Unwin Hyman, 1988.

– 'Calvinism and the English Church: 1570–1635.' *Past and Present* 114 (1987): 32–76.

Lamb, Mary Ellen. 'The Agency of the Split Subject: Lady Anne Clifford and the Uses of Reading.' *English Literary Renaissance* 22 (1992): 347–68.

Lambarde, William. *A Perambulation of Kent* [1570]. Bath: Adams and Dart, 1970.

Larkin, James F., and Paul L. Hughes eds. *Stuart Royal Proclamations.* 3 vols. Oxford: Clarendon Press, 1973.

Laslett, Peter. 'Mean Household Size in England since the Sixteenth Century.' In *Household and Family in Past Time,* edited by Peter Laslett and Richard Wall. Cambridge: Cambridge University Press, 1972.

- 'Sir Robert Filmer: The Man versus the Whig Myth.' *William and Mary Quarterly* ser. 3, no. 4, vol. 5 (1948): 523–46.
- *The World We Have Lost.* New York: Scribners, 1965.
- *The World We Have Lost Further Explored.* New York: Scribners, 1984.

Levack, Brian P. *The Civil Lawyers in England, 1603–1641.* Oxford: Oxford University Press, 1973.
- 'Law and Ideology: The Civil Law and Theories of Absolutism in Elizabethan and Jacobean England.' In *The Historical Renaissance: New Essays on Tudor and Stuart Literature and Culture,* edited by Heather Dubrow and Richard Strier, 220–41. Chicago: University of Chicago Press, 1988.

Lever, Tresham. *The Herberts of Wilton.* London: John Murray, 1967.

Lewalski, Barbara Kiefer. *Protestant Poetics and the Seventeenth-Century Religious Lyric.* Princeton: Princeton University Press, 1979.
- 'Writing Women and Reading the Renaissance.' *Renaissance Quarterly* 44 (1991): 792–821.

Liddle, A. Mark. 'State, Masculinities and Law: Some Comments on Gender and English State-Formation.' *The British Journal of Criminology* 36 (1996): 361–80.

Low, Anthony. 'George Herbert: The Best Love.' *Renascence* 45 (1993): 159–78.
- *The Georgic Revolution.* Princeton: Princeton University Press, 1985.
- 'New Science and the Georgic Revolution in Seventeenth-Century English Literature.' *English Literary Renaissance* 13 (1983): 231–59.

Lull, Janis. *The Poem in Time: Reading George Herbert's Revisions of The Church.* Newark: University of Delaware Press, 1990.

Luther, Martin. *Works,* edited by Jaroslav Pelikan. St Louis: Concordia, 1955–8.

Macfarlane, Alan. *The Culture of Capitalism.* Oxford: Basil Blackwell, 1987.
- *The Family Life of Ralph Josselin, A Seventeenth-Century Clergyman.* New York: Norton, 1970.
- *Marriage and Love in England: Modes of Reproduction, 1300–1840.* Oxford: Basil Blackwell, 1986.
- *The Origins of English Individualism: The Family, Property and Social Transition.* New York: Cambridge University Press, 1979.
- 'Review of *The Family, Sex and Marriage in England, 1500–1800,* by Lawrence Stone. *History and Theory* 18 (1979): 103–25.

Malcolmson, Cristina. 'George Herbert's *Country Parson* and the Character of Social Identity.' *Studies in Philology* 85 (1988): 245–66.
- *Heart-Work: George Herbert and the Protestant Ethic.* Stanford: Stanford University Press, 1999.

Marcus, Leah Sinanoglou. *Childhood and Cultural Despair: A Theme and Variations in Seventeenth-Century Literature.* Pittsburgh: University of Pittsburgh Press, 1978.

– *The Politics of Mirth: Jonson, Herrick, Marvell and the Defense of Old Holiday Pastimes.* Chicago: University of Chicago Press, 1986.

Markham, Gervase. *Cheap and Good Husbandry.* London, 1623.

– *The English Husbandman.* London, 1613.

– *Markham's Farewell to Husbandry.* London, 1625.

Martin, John E. *Feudalism to Capitalism: Peasant and Landlord in English Agrarian Development.* Atlantic Highlands, N.J.: Humanities Press, 1983.

Martz, Louis. *The Poetry of Meditation: A Study in English Religious Literature of the Seventeenth Century.* New Haven: Yale University Press, 1954.

Marx, Karl. *Capital: A Critique of Political Economy.* Translated by Samuel Moore and Edward Aveling. Edited by Frederick Engels. New York: Modern Library-Random House, 1906.

McGee, J. Sears. *The Godly Man in Stuart England: Anglicans, Puritans and the Two Tables, 1620–1670.* New Haven: Yale University Press, 1976.

– 'William Laud and the Outward Face of Religion.' In *Leaders of the Reformation,* edited by Richard L. DeMolen. Selinsgrove, Pa.: Susquehanna University Press, 1984.

McGiffert, Michael. 'Covenant Crown and Commons in Elizabethan Puritanism.' *Journal of British Studies* 20 (1980): 32–52.

– 'Grace and Works: The Rise and Division of Covenant Divinity among Elizabethan Puritans.' *Harvard Theological Review* 75 (1982): 464–502.

McIntosh, Marjorie Kenniston. *A Community Transformed: The Manor and Liberty of Havering, 1500–1620.* Cambridge: Cambridge University Press, 1991.

McRae, Andrew. *God Speed the Plough: The Representation of Agrarian England, 1500–1660.* New York: Cambridge University Press, 1996.

– 'Husbandry Manuals and the Language of Agrarian Improvement.' In *Culture and Cultivation in Early Modern England: Writing and the Land,* edited by Michael Leslie and Timothy Raylor, 35–62. Leicester: Leicester University Press, 1992.

Megill, Allan. 'The Reception of Foucault by Historians.' *Journal of the History of Ideas* 48 (1987): 117–41.

Mendelson, Sarah Heller. Review of *Marriage and Love in England, 1300–1840,* by Alan Macfarlane, and *The Patriarch's Wife: Literary Evidence and the History of the Family* by Margaret J.M. Ezell. *Renaissance Quarterly* 44 (1991): 850–3.

Miller, Edmund. *Drudgerie Divine: The Rhetoric of God and Man in George Herbert.* Salzburg Studies in English Literature. Elizabethan and Renaissance Studies 84. Salzburg: Institut fur Anglistik und Americanistik, 1979.

– *George Herbert's Kinships: An Ahnentafel with Annotations.* Bowie, MD: Heritage Books, 1993.

Miller, Perry. *The New England Mind in the Seventeenth Century.* Cambridge, MA: Belknap-Harvard University Press, 1939.

Milton, Anthony. *Catholic and Reformed: The Roman and Protestant Churches in English Protestant Thought, 1600–1640.* Cambridge: Cambridge University Press, 1995.

More, Paul Elmer, and Frank Leslie Cross, eds. *Anglicanism: The Thought and Practice of the Church of England, Illustrated from the Religious Literature of the Seventeenth Century.* London: S.P.C.K., 1962.

More, Thomas. *Utopia.* Edited by George M. Logan and Robert M. Adams. Cambridge: Cambridge University Press, 1988.

Morgan, John. *Godly Learning: Puritan Attitudes towards Reason, Learning and Education, 1560–1640.* Cambridge: Cambridge University Press, 1986.

Morrill, John. *The Nature of the English Revolution: Essays by John Morrill.* London: Longman, 1993.

Mueller, Janel. 'Women among the Metaphysicals: A Case, Mostly, of Being Donne For.' *Modern Philology* 87 (1989): 142–58.

Muldrew, Craig. 'The Culture of Reconciliation: Community and the Settlement of Economic Disputes in Early Modern England.' *Historical Journal* 39 (1996): 915–42.

Neale, R.S. *Writing Marxist History: British Society, Economy, & Culture Since 1700.* New York: Basil Blackwell, 1985.

Nestrick, William V. '"Mine and Thine" in *The Temple*.' In *'Too Riche to Clothe the Sun': Essays on George Herbert*, edited by Claude J. Summers and Ted-Larry Pebworth, 115–27. Pittsburg: University of Pittsburg Press, 1980.

Noiriel, Gerard. 'Foucault and History: The Lessons of a Disillusion.' *Journal of Modern History* 66 (1994): 547–68.

Norden, John. *The Surveiors Dialogue.* London, 1610.

Notestein, Wallace. *Four Worthies: John Chamberlain, Anne Clifford, John Taylor, Oliver Heywood.* London: Jonathan Cape, 1956.

O'Connell, Laura Stevenson. 'Anti-Entrepreneurial Attitudes in Elizabethan Sermons and Popular Literature.' *Journal of British Studies* 15:2 (1976): 1–20.

O'Day, Rosemary. 'Anatomy of a Profession: The Clergy of the Church of England.' In *The Professions in Early Modern England*, edited by Wilfred Prest, 25–63. London: Croom Helm, 1987.

– *The English Clergy: The Emergence and Consolidation of A Profession.* Leicester: Leicester University Press, 1979.

– 'The Professions in Early Modern England.' *History Today* 36 (June 1986): 52–5.

– *The Professions in Early Modern England, 1450–1800: Servants of the Commonweal.* London: Longmans, 2000.

Osmond, Rosalie. *Mutual Accusation: Seventeenth-Century Body and Soul Dialogues in Their Literary and Theological Context.* Toronto: University of Toronto Press, 1990.

Ozment, Steven E. *When Fathers Ruled: Family Life in Reformation Europe.* Cambridge, MA: Harvard University Press, 1983.

Palmer, George Herbert, ed. *The English Works of George Herbert, Newly Arranged and Annotated and Considered in Relation to His Life.* 3 vols. Boston: Houghton Mifflin, 1905.

Patrides, C.A., ed. *The English Poems of George Herbert.* London: Everyman-Dent, 1974.

– *George Herbert: The Critical Heritage.* London: Routledge and Kegan Paul, 1983.

Pelling, Margaret, and Charles Webster. 'Medical Practitioners.' In *Health, Medicine and Mortality in the Sixteenth Century,* edited by Charles Webster, 165–236. Cambridge: Cambridge University Press, 1979.

Perkin, Harold. *The Origins of Modern English Society, 1780–1880.* London: Routledge, 1969.

Perkins, William. *The Works of William Perkins,* edited by Ian Breward. Abingdon: Sutton Courtenay Press, 1970.

Pocock, J.G.A. *The Ancient Constitution and the Feudal Law.* Cambridge: Cambridge University Press, 1957.

– *The Machiavellian Moment: Florentine Political Thought and the Atlantic Republican Tradition.* Princeton: Princeton University Press, 1975.

Pollock, Linda. *Forgotten Children: Parent-Child Relations from 1500 to 1900.* Cambridge: Cambridge University Press, 1983.

– 'Rethinking Patriarchy and the Family in Seventeenth-Century England. *Journal of Family History* 23 (1998): 3–27.

– *With Faith and Physic: The Life of a Tudor Gentlewoman, Lady Grace Mildmay, 1552–1620.* London: Collins and Brown, 1993.

– 'Younger Sons in Tudor and Stuart England.' *History Today* 39 (June 1989): 23–9.

Ponting, Kenneth G. *The Woolen Industry of Southwest England.* Bath: Adams and Dart, 1971.

Porter, Roy. 'The Patient in England, c. 1660–1800.' In *Medicine in Society: Historical Essays,* edited by Andrew Wear, 91–118. Cambridge: Cambridge University Press, 1992.

Poster, Mark. 'Foucault and History.' *Social Research* 49 (1982): 116–42.

Poulantzas, Nicos Ar. *State, Power, Socialism.* Translated by Patrick Camiller. London: NLB, 1978.

Powers-Beck, Jeffrey. 'Conquering Laurels and Creeping Ivy: The Tangled Politics of Herbert's *Reditum Caroli.' George Herbert Journal* 17 (1993): 1–24.

– '"Not onely a Pastour, but a Lawyer also": George Herbert's Vision of Stuart Magistracy.' *Early Modern Literary Studies* 1:2 (1995) Article 3, ¶1–25. http://purl.oclc.org/emls/01-2/beckherb.html

- '"Whence Com'st Thou ... So Fresh and Fine": The King's Stamp and the Origins of Value in Herbert's "Avarice."' *English Language Notes* (1993): 14–23.
- *Writing the Flesh: The Herbert Family Dialogue.* Pittsburgh: Duquesne University Press, 1998.
Powicke, F.M., and C.R. Cheney, eds. *Councils and Synods with Other Documents Relating to the English Church.* 2 vols. Oxford: Clarendon Press, 1964.
Poynter, F.N.L. *A Bibliography of Gervase Markham.* Oxford: Oxford Bibliographic Society, 1962.
Poynter, F.N.L., and K.D. Keele. *A Short History of Medicine.* London: Mills and Boon, 1961.
Prest, Wilfred R. *The Rise of the Barristers: A Social History of the English Bar, 1590–1640.* Oxford: Clarendon Press, 1986.
Prest, Wilfred R., ed. *The Professions in Early Modern England.* London: Croom Helm, 1987.
Preston, John. *The Breastplate of Faith and Love, in 18 Sermons.* London, 1630.
- *The New Covenant, or The Saints Portion. A Treatise unfolding the all-sufficiencie of God, and Man's Uprightness, and The Covenant of Grace.* London, 1629.
Ramsay, G.D. *The Wiltshire Woolen Industry in the Sixteenth and Seventeenth Centuries.* New York: Augustus M. Kelly, 1965.
Richey, Esther Gilman. 'The Political Design of Herbert's *Temple.*' *Studies in English Literature, 1500–1900* 37 (1997): 73–96.
- '"Wrapt in Nights Mantle": George Herbert's Parabolic Art.' *John Donne Journal*, 9 (1990): 157–72.
Rickey, Mary Ellen. *Utmost Art: Complexity in the Verse of George Herbert.* Lexington: University of Kentucky Press, 1966.
Russell, Conrad. *The Causes of the English Civil War.* Oxford: Clarendon Press, 1990.
- *Unrevolutionary England, 1603–1642.* London: Hambledon Press, 1990.
Sacks, David Harris. *The Widening Gate: Bristol and the Atlantic Economy, 1450–1700.* Berkeley: University of California Press, 1991.
Sayer, Derek. *Capitalism and Modernity: An Excursus on Marx and Weber.* London: Routledge, 1991.
Schochet, Gordon J. *Patriarchalism in Political Thought: The Authoritarian Family and Political Speculation and Attitudes Especially in Seventeenth-Century England.* Oxford: Basil Blackwell, 1975.
- 'Patriarchalism, Politics and Mass Attitudes in Stuart England.' *The Historical Journal* 12 (1969): 413–41.
Schoenfeldt, Michael C. *Bodies and Selves in Early Modern England: Physiology and Inwardness in Spenser, Shakespeare, Herbert and Milton.* Cambridge: Cambridge University Press, 1999.

– *Prayer and Power: George Herbert and Renaissance Courtship.* Chicago: University of Chicago Press, 1991.

Sharp, Buchanan. *In Contempt of all Authority: Rural Artisans and Riot in the West of England, 1586–1660.* Berkeley: University of California Press, 1980.

– 'Rural Discontents and the English Revolution.' In *Town and Countryside in the English Revolution,* edited by R.C. Richardson, 251–72. Manchester: Manchester University Press, 1992.

Sharpe, J.A. *Early Modern England: A Social History, 1550–1760.* London: Edward Arnold, 1987.

Sharpe, Kevin. 'Faction at the Early Stuart Court.' *History Today* 33 (October 1993): 39–46.

– *Remapping Early Modern England: The Culture of Seventeenth-Century Politics.* Cambridge, Cambridge University Press, 2000.

– *Sir Robert Cotton, 1586–1631: History and Politics in Early Modern England.* Oxford: Oxford University Press, 1979.

Shaw, Robert B. *The Call of God: The Theme of Vocation in the Poetry of Donne and Herbert.* Cambridge, MA: Cowley Publishers, 1981.

Sherwood, Terry G. *Herbert's Prayerful Art.* Toronto: University of Toronto Press, 1989.

Shriver, Frederick. 'Hampton Court Revisited: James I and the Puritans.' *Journal of Ecclesiastical History* 33 (1982): 48–71.

Shuger, Deborah Kuller. *Habits of Thought in the English Renaissance.* Berkeley: University of California Press, 1990.

Siemon, James R. 'Landlord Not King: Agrarian Change and Interarticulation.' In *Enclosure Acts: Sexuality, Property, and Culture in Early Modern England,* edited by Richard Burt and John Michael Archer, 18–34. Ithaca: Cornell University Press.

Singleton, Marion White. *God's Courtier: Configuring a Different Grace in George Herbert's Temple.* Cambridge: Cambridge University Press, 1987.

Skulsky, Harold. *Language Recreated: Seventeenth-Century Metaphorists and the Act of Metaphor.* Athens: University of Georgia Press, 1992.

Slack, Paul. 'Books of Orders: The Making of English Social Policy, 1577–1631.' *Transactions of the Royal Historical Society* 30 (1980): 1–22.

– 'Dearth and Social Policy in Early Modern England.' *Social History of Medicine* 5 (1992): 1–17.

– *The English Poor Law, 1531–82.* Basingstoke: Macmillan, 1990.

– *The Impact of Plague in Tudor and Stuart England.* London: Routledge, 1985.

– 'Poverty and Politics in Salisbury 1597–1666.' In *Crisis and Order in English Towns, 1500–1700,* edited by Peter Clark and Paul Slack, 164–203. Toronto: University of Toronto Press, 1972.

- 'Poverty and Social Regulation in Elizabethan England.' In *The Reign of Elizabeth I*, edited by Christopher Haigh, 221–42. London: Macmillan Education, 1984.
- 'The Public Conscience of Henry Sherfield.' In *Public Duty and Private Conscience in Seventeenth-Century England: Essays Presented to G.E. Aylmer*, edited by John Morrill, Paul Slack, and Daniel Woolf, 151–71. Oxford: Clarendon Press, 1993.
- 'Religious Protest and Urban Authority: The Case of Henry Sherfield, Iconoclast, 1633.' In *Schism, Heresy and Religious Protest*, edited by Derek Baker. Studies in Church History 9. Cambridge: Cambridge University Press, 1972.

Slights, Camille Wells. *The Casuistical Tradition in Shakespeare, Donne, Herbert and Milton.* Princeton: Princeton University Press, 1981.

Smart, Barry. *Foucault, Marxism and Critique.* London: Routledge, 1993.

Smeed, J.W. *The Theophrastan 'Character': The History of a Literary Genre.* Oxford: Clarendon Press, 1985.

[Smith, Sir Thomas?]. *A Discourse of the Commonweal in this Realm of England* [1581]. Edited by Mary Dewar. Charlottesville: University Press of Virginia, 1969.

Smuts, R. Malcolm. *Culture and Power in England, 1585–1685.* New York: St Martin's, 1999.

Somner, William. *The Antiquities of Canterbury, or, A Survey of that Ancient Citie, with the Suburbs, and Cathedrall.* London, 1640.

Sprigge, William. *A Modest Plea for an Equal Commonwealth Against Monarchy.* London, 1659.

Spufford, Margaret. 'Puritanism and Social Control?' In *Order and Disorder in Early Modern England*, edited by Anthony Fletcher and John Stevenson, 41–57. Cambridge: Cambridge University Press, 1985.

Stallybrass, Peter, and Allon White. *The Politics and Poetics of Transgression.* Ithaca: Cornell University Press, 1986.

Stambler, Elizabeth. 'The Unity of Herbert's *Temple*.' *Cross Currents* 10 (1960): 251–66.

Stein, Arnold. *George Herbert's Lyrics.* Baltimore: Johns Hopkins University Press, 1968.

Stewart, Philip. 'This is not a Book Review: On Historical Uses of Literature.' *Journal of Modern History* 66 (1994): 521–38.

Stewart, Stanley. *George Herbert.* Twayne's English Authors Series 428. Boston: Twayne–G.K. Hall, 1986.

Stone, Lawrence. *The Causes of the English Revolution, 1529–1642.* London: Routledge, 1972.

- *The Family, Sex and Marriage in England, 1500–1800.* London: Weidenfeld and Nicolson, 1977.
- 'Social Mobility in England, 1500–1700.' *Past and Present* 33 (1966): 16–55.

Stow, John, *A Survey of London: Written in the Year 1598*. Phoenix Mill, UK: A. Sutton, 1994.

Strier, Richard. 'George Herbert and the World.' *Journal of Medieval and Renaissance Studies* 12 (1981): 211–36.

– 'Getting Off the Map: Response to "George Herbert's Theology: Nearer Rome or Geneva?"' *George Herbert Journal* 11 (1987); 41–8.

– *Love Known: Theology and Experience in George Herbert's Poetry*. Chicago: University of Chicago Press, 1984.

Sullivan, Garrett A. *The Drama of Landscape: Land, Property, and Social Relations on the Early Modern Stage*. Stanford: Stanford University Press, 1998.

Summers, Claude J., and Ted-Larry Pebworth. 'Herbert, Vaughan, and Public Concerns in Private Modes.' *George Herbert Journal* 3 (1979): 1–21.

– 'The Politics of *The Temple*: "The British Church" and "The Familie."' *George Herbert Journal* 8 (1984): 1–15.

Summers, Joseph H. *George Herbert: His Religion and Art*. Cambridge MA: Harvard University Press, 1968.

Swartz, Douglas J. 'Discourse and Direction: *A Priest to the Temple, or, The Country Parson* and the Elaboration of Sovereign Rule.' *Criticism* 36 (1994): 189–212.

Taylor, Mark. *The Soul in Paraphrase: George Herbert's Poetics*. The Hague: Mouton, 1974.

Terry, Reta A. '"Vows to the Blackest Devil": *Hamlet* and the Evolving Code of Honor in Early Modern England.' *Renaissance Quarterly* 52 (1999): 1070–86.

Thirsk, Joan ed. *The Agrarian History of England and Wales, Volume IV, 1500–1640*. Cambridge: Cambridge University Press, 1967.

– *Economic Policy and Projects: The Development of a Consumer Society in Early Modern England*. Oxford: Clarendon–Oxford University Press, 1978.

– 'Plough and Pen: Agricultural Writers in the Seventeenth Century.' In *Social Relations and Ideas*, edited by T.H. Ashton et al., 295–318. Cambridge: Cambridge University Press, 1983.

– 'Younger Sons in the Seventeenth Century.' *History* 54 (1969): 358–77.

Thomas, Keith. *Religion and the Decline of Magic*. New York: Scribner's, 1971.

Tillyard, E.M.W. *The Elizabethan World Picture*. New York: Macmillan, 1944.

Tilney, Edmund. *The Flower of Friendship: A Renaissance Dialogue Contesting Marriage*, edited by Valerie Wayne. Ithaca: Cornell University Press, 1992.

Todd, Margo. '"An Act of Discretion": Evangelical Conformity and the Puritan Dons.' *Albion* 18 (1986): 581–99.

– *Christian Humanism and the Puritan Social Order*. Cambridge: Cambridge University Press, 1987.

Toliver, Harold. *George Herbert's Christian Narrative*. University Park: Pennsylvania State University Press, 1993.

Tomlinson, Howard, ed. *Before the English Civil War: Essays in Early Stuart Politics and Government.* New York: St Martin's, 1983.

Tusser, Thomas. *Five Hundred Points of Good Husbandry* [1573]. Oxford: Oxford University Press, 1984.

Tuve, Rosemond. *A Reading of George Herbert.* Chicago: University of Chicago Press, 1952.

Tyacke, Nicholas. *Anti-Calvinists: The Rise of English Arminianism, c. 1590–1640.* Oxford: Clarendon Press, 1987.

Underdown, David. 'The Chalk and the Cheese: Contrasts among the English Clubmen.' *Past and Present* 85 (1979). Rept. in *Rebellion, Popular Protest and the Social Order in Early Modern England,* edited by Paul Slack. Cambridge: Cambridge University Press, 1984.

– *Fire from Heaven: The Life of an English Town in the Seventeenth Century.* London: Harper Collins, 1992.

– *Revel, Riot and Rebellion: Popular Politics and Culture in England, 1603–1660.* Oxford: Oxford University Press, 1985.

– 'The Taming of the Scold: The Enforcement of Patriarchal Authority in Early Modern England.' In *Order and Disorder in Early Modern England,* edited by Anthony Fletcher and John Stevenson, 116–36. Cambridge: Cambridge University Press, 1985.

Ussher, James. *The Whole Works of the Most Reverend James Ussher,* edited by Charles Richard Elrington. 17 vols. Dublin: Hodges and Smith, 1847.

Vaughan, Rowland. *Most Approved and Long Experienced Water-Workes.* London: 1610. Facs. Rept. Norwood, N.J.: Walter J. Johnson, 1977.

Veith, Gene Edward, Jr. *Reformation Spirituality: The Religion of George Herbert.* Lewisburg; Bucknell University Press, 1985.

– 'The Religious Wars in George Herbert Criticism: Reinterpreting Seventeenth-Century Anglicanism.' *George Herbert Journal* 11.2 (1988): 19–35.

Vendler, Helen. *The Poetry of George Herbert.* Cambridge, MA: Harvard University Press, 1975.

Verkamp, Bernard J. *The Indifferent Mean: Adiaphorism in the English Reformation to 1554.* Athens: Ohio University Press, 1977.

Virgil. *Works.* Translated by H. Rushton Fairclough. Cambridge, MA: Harvard University Press, 1986.

von Friedeberg, Robert. 'Reformation of Manners and the Social Composition of Offenders in an East Anglian Cloth Village: Earls Colne, Essex, 1531–1642.' *Journal of British Studies* 29 (1990): 347–85.

Walton, Izaak. *The Lives of John Donne, Sir Henry Wotton, Richard Hooker, George Herbert and Robert Sanderson.* London: Oxford University Press–World's Classics, 1927.

Weber, Max. *The Protestant Ethic and the Spirit of Capitalism.* Translated by Talcott Parsons. New York: Scribners, 1958.
– *On Charisma and Institution Building,* edited by S.N. Eisenstadt. Chicago: University of Chicago Press, 1968
– 'Social Psychology of the World Religions.' In *From Max Weber,* edited by H.H. Gerth and C. Wright Mills, 267–95. New York: Oxford University Press, 1958.
– *The Theory of Social and Economic Organization.* Translated by A.M. Henderson and Talcott Parsons. Oxford: Oxford University Press, 1947.
Webster, Charles. *The Great Instauration: Science, Medicine and Reform, 1626–1660.* New York: Holmes and Meier, 1975
Webster, Tom. *Godly Clergy in Early Stuart England: The Caroline Puritan Movement, c. 1620–1643.* Cambridge: Cambridge University Press, 1997.
White, James Boyd. *'This Book of Starres': Learning to Read George Herbert.* Ann Arbor: University of Michigan Press, 1994.
Whitney, Charles. *Francis Bacon and Modernity.* New Haven: Yale University Press, 1986.
Wigham, Frank. *Ambition and Privilege: The Social Tropes of Elizabethan Courtesy Theory.* Berkeley: University of California Press, 1984.
Williams, Raymond. *The Country and the City.* New York: Oxford University Press, 1973.
Williamson, George C. *Lady Anne Clifford, Countess of Dorset, Pembroke and Montgomery.* 1922. Reprint, Wakefield, UK: SR Publishers, 1967.
Witz, Anne. *Professions and Patriarchy.* London: Routledge, 1992.
Wolberg, Kristine. 'All Possible Art: George Herbert's *The Country Parson* and Courtesy.' *John Donne Journal* 8 (1989): 167–89.
Wordie, J.R. 'The Chronology of English Enclosure, 1500–1914.' *Economic History Review* 2nd ser. 36 (1983): 483–505.
Wrightson, Keith. *English Society, 1580–1680.* New Brunswick, N.J.: Rutgers University Press, 1982.
– 'The Social Order of Early Modern England: Three Approaches.' In *The World We Have Gained: Histories of Population and Social Structure,* edited by Lloyd Bonfield, Richard M. Smith, and Keith Wrightson, 177–202. Oxford: Basil Blackwell, 1986.
– 'Two Concepts of Order: Justices, Constables and Jurymen in Seventeenth-Century England.' In *An Ungovernable People: The English and Their Law in the Seventeenth and Eighteenth Centuries,* edited by John Brewer and John Styles, 21–46. New Brunswick, N.J.: Rutgers University Press, 1980.
Wrightson, Keith, and David Levine. *Poverty and Piety in an English Village: Terling, 1525–1700.* New York: Academic Press, 1979.

Wrigley, E.A. 'Family Limitation in Pre-Industrial England.' *Economic History Review* 2nd ser. 19 (1966): 82–109.

Yates, Nigel. *Buildings, Faith, and Worship: The Liturgical Arrangements of Anglican Churches 1600–1900.* Oxford: Clarendon Press, 1991.

Yule, George. 'James VI and I: Furnishing the Churches in His Two Kingdoms.' In *Religion, Culture and Society in Early Modern Britain,* edited by Anthony Fletcher and Peter Roberts, 182–208. Cambridge: Cambridge University Press, 1994.

Index

Martz, Louis L., 184n7

Marx, Karl, and Marxism, 9, 10–11, 82–3, 85, 175

Macfarlane, Alan, 114, 172, 193n4, 200n3, 201n45

McGee, J. Sears, 39, 188n86

McGiffert, Michael, 143, 203n14

McIntosh, Marjorie Kenniston, 181n21

McRae, Andrew, 195n24

medicine, 58–68; gender and, 67–8, 191nn41, 42; regulation of, 60–3

Miller, Perry, 142, 202n14

Milton, Anthony, 7, 188n82

Milton, John, 162, 189n92

modernity, 5, 7, 169–77, 207n1

More, Sir Thomas, 86

Morrill, John, 172, 181n19

Mueller, Janel, 206n58

nationalism, 29, 107–11

Naunton, Sir Robert, 184n13

Neale, R.S., 10

Neile, Richard, Bishop, 50, 187n75

Nethersole, Sir Francis, 184n13

Nestrick, William V., 158

Norden, John, 89

new historicism, 57. *See also* historiography

O'Connell, Laura Stevenson, 198n60

O'Day, Rosemary, 34, 184n10, 186n35, 190n9

Osmond, Rosalie, 165

Overbury, Sir Thomas, 16, 17

Palmer, George Herbert, 20, 137

parable, 84, 87, 112, 113

Parker, Matthew, Archbishop of Canterbury, 12

pastoral, 12–15, 90–3, 194n12

patriarchy, domestic, 112–34, 158–68, 177; pastor/father analogy, 116, 118–20, 124–8; political theory and, 113–18. *See also* family, domestic advice books

Patrides, C.A., 183n58

Paul, Saint, 5, 78

Pebworth, Ted-Larry, 183n56, 198n66, 204n35

Perkins, William, 190n12

Physicians, College of, 19, 60–6, 175. *See also* medicine

Philpin, C.H.E., 181n25

Pocock, J.G.A., 180n17, 192n43

Pollock, Linda, 189n5, 191n37, 200n14

Porter, Roy, 66

Poster, Mark, 181n23

Poulantzas, Nicos, 181n25

poverty, 76–9, 105–6, 185n29, 193n67

Powers-Beck, Jeffrey, 6, 112, 179n2, 186n47, 189n105, 194n11, 198n65, 205n47

Poynter, F.N.L., 182n48

prayer(s), 22–3, 34, 47–51, 67–8, 79, 100, 121, 129–31, 135, 138–9, 158, 162, 174

preaching, sermons, and homiletics, 13–15, 17–18, 30–1, 34–5, 38–40, 46, 49–53, 92, 98–100, 131, 138–9, 157–8, 170

Prest, Wilfred, 57, 73, 187n57, 189n2, 190n9

Preston, John, 139, 142

professions, 55–8, 115–16, 175–6. *See also* clergy, law, medicine

puritan(ism), 6–8, 28, 30–1, 37–53, 75–7, 99, 101, 107, 113, 122, 139–42, 174

Ramsey, G.D., 197n49, 205n53
Ranters, 6
revisionism, 172, 177. *See also* historiography
Richey, Esther Gilman 194n9
Rickey, Mary Ellen, 136, 202n13
rogationtide processions, 75–6, 198n65
ruralism and nationalism, 107–11
Russell, Conrad, 115, 170, 172, 181n19, 207n2

Sacks, David Harris, 181n21
Sayer, Derek, 207n1
Schochet, Gordon, 118, 202n53
Schoenfeldt, Michael, 167, 179n2, 181n22, 182n56, 186nn46, 47, 196n32, 202nn55, 1, 205nn37, 46, 206n60
scripture. *See* Bible
sermons. *See* preaching, sermons, and homiletics
servants, treatment of, 120, 124
Sharp, Buchanan, 104, 197nn50, 54
Sharpe, Kevin, 5, 180n13, 181n19
Shaw, Robert B., 190n12
sheep and corn husbandry, 95–7, 103–4. *See also* water meadows
Sherfield, Henry, 38–40, 76–7, 175, 193n70, 198n66. *See also* Davenant, John, Bishop
Sherwood, Terry, 49, 203n12
Shuger, Deborah Kuller, 119, 189n5
Sibbes, Richard, 139
Singleton, Marion White, 183n56
Slack, Paul, 39, 61, 62, 185n29, 187n57, 193nn70, 71
Slights, Camille Wells, 44
Smart, Barry, 181n23
Smeed, J.W., 182n42

Smith, Sir Thomas, 86, 195n19
social order, traditional and legal-rational, 79–80, 85, 180n16, 207n1
social control, 8–9, 28, 32, 57, 76–9, 128–34, 160, 166, 176–7
Sommerville, Johann P., 200n18
spanish medleys, 155
Spufford, Margaret, 185n29
Stambler, Elizabeth, 205n46
Stallybrass, Peter, 202n55
Stein, Arnold, 182n51, 204n35
Stevenson, John, 200n17
Stewart, Stanley, 41, 184n7
Stone, Lawrence, 8, 9, 10, 57, 113–14, 200n10
Strier, Richard, 6, 27, 139, 140, 147, 162, 184n6, 203n14
Stubbes, Philip, 6
Sullivan, Garrett A., 181n22
Summers, Claude J., 198n66
Summers, Joseph, 140, 179n1, 180n9, 189n92, 196n37
Swartz, Douglas J., 179n2, 193n66

Tawney, R.H., 9
textile sequence. *See* cloth trade
theory, 10–12
Thirsk, Joan, 87, 125–6, 195nn19, 24, 29, 197n46, 199n81
Thomas, Keith, 182n50
Tilney, Edmund, 200n12
Todd, Margot, 38, 185n29, 188n79
tradition and traditionalism, 4–6, 9, 19, 37, 55, 60, 66–9, 75–6, 79–80, 85, 87, 90, 95–7, 99, 103, 106–11, 113–19, 123, 128–9, 133, 156, 158–61, 167, 169–77
Tuve, Rosemond, 7, 52, 184n10, 185n27, 187nn71, 75
Tusser, Thomas, 88, 93, 198n71

238   Index

Tyacke, Nicholas, 7, 52, 184n10,
185n27, 187nn71, 75

Underdown, David, 96, 181n21,
185n29, 193n64, 197n54, 198n65

Vaughan, Dorothy, 203n6
Vaughan, Rowland, 93, 105–8,
199nn75, 76, 81
Veith, Gene Edward, 6, 27, 140, 143,
184n6
Vendler, Helen, 145, 152, 157,
188n83, 203n11
vocational literature, 18–19, 190n12
Von Friedberg, Robert, 197n52

Walmsley, Justice, 66
Ward, Samuel, 52
water meadows, 104–7, 145–6,
198n70
Weber, Max, 5, 9, 80. *See also* social
order
Webster, Charles, 191n33

whig view of history, 5. *See also* histori-
ography
White, Allon, 202n55
White, James Boyd, 205n39
wife, as healer, 67–8. *See also* marriage
Wigham, Frank, 202n55
Williams, John, Bishop, 50, 184n13
Williams manuscript of *The Temple*,
136, 137, 138, 146, 147, 148, 149,
158, 165, 166, 167, 199n85,
205n38, 206n61
Williams, Raymond, 11, 195n32
Williamson, George C., 197n41
Wiltshire, 73, 76–7, 93–105, 137–8,
153–5
Winter, John, 35
Wither, Anthony, 155, 205n52
Witz, Anne, 192n42
Wolberg, Kristine, 179n2, 182n47
Wrightson, Keith, 180n5, 185n29,
192n63, 194n8, 197n54

Yates, Nigel, 187n75